An Emerging Approac
for Education and Care

An Emerging Approach for Education and Care provides a synthesis of the extensive research that has been conducted worldwide about the International Classification of Functioning, Disability and Health for Children and Youth (ICF-CY) in education and care. The main purpose of the ICF is to provide a classification of functioning for adults and children with difficulties, considering their everyday lives, all the activities they perform and the environments they are embedded in, in addition to their health condition, which has been the traditional focus of special education provision in many countries.

Each chapter presents an evidence-based study describing how the ICF has been used to improve the provision of services for children and young people with special educational needs around the world. Moreover, each chapter is written by an expert on the ICF from a different country, thus providing an overview of how the ICF can be applied in international educational contexts with different educational and health systems and cultural backgrounds. This synthesis of world-leading research focuses on the ICF as a framework to approach assessment, intervention and classification for children and young people with special educational needs (SEN), whilst also providing practical examples of how it can be implemented.

An Emerging Approach for Education and Care will be an essential reading for academics, researchers and practitioners working on SEN provision and rehabilitation. It should also be of great interest to those involved in the study of early childhood education and for postgraduate students aspiring to work in these settings.

Susana Castro is a psychologist and senior lecturer in Education Studies at the University of Roehampton, London. She has a background in early childhood intervention and has an extensive research background on research and professional applications of the ICF/ICF-CY in education and care. She has also conducted extensive training on the use of the ICF-CY for education and care.

Olympia Palikara is a senior lecturer in Educational Psychology at the University of Roehampton, London. She trained as an educational psychologist and her research interest concerns the educational and psychosocial outcomes of children and young people with SEN. She is an Associate Fellow of the British Psychological Society, a Fellow of Royal Society of Arts and a Fellow of the Higher Education Academy.

An Emerging Approach for Education and Care

Implementing a Worldwide Classification of Functioning and Disability

Edited by
Susana Castro and
Olympia Palikara

Routledge
Taylor & Francis Group

LONDON AND NEW YORK

First published 2018 by Routledge

2 Park Square, Milton Park, Abingdon, Oxfordshire OX14 4RN
52 Vanderbilt Avenue, New York, NY 10017

Routledge is an imprint of the Taylor & Francis Group, an informa business

First issued in paperback 2018

British Library Cataloguing-in-Publication Data
A catalogue record for this book is available from the British Library

Library of Congress Cataloging-in-Publication Data
A catalog record for this book has been requested

ISBN: 978-1-138-69817-8 (hbk)
ISBN: 978-0-367-19703-2 (pbk)

Typeset in Bembo
by Apex CoVantage, LLC

Contents

Preface

I am delighted to write this preface and welcome this edited book about the use of the International Classification of Functioning (ICF) in relation to children and young people's education, health and care services.

This book brings together leading researchers who have promoted and developed the use of the ICF in different countries in different service settings to illustrate the potential and prospects of this framework. Contributors come from Europe (Sweden, Portugal, Germany, Switzerland and the United Kingdom); the East Asia (Japan and Taiwan); from Africa, Middle East and Western Asia (Turkey, South Africa and Armenia); and the USA.

This is a timely bringing together of these diverse contributions about the ICF framework. It will be a unique source for anyone interested in seeing how the ICF can inform thinking, research, practice and policy and how it can be further used and developed. It will be relevant to those who are unfamiliar with ICF informed perspectives and approaches as well as those already with some knowledge, but wanting to finding out more about its scope and flexibility, on one hand, and its international use, on the other.

This scope and flexibility covers its use in the health and education services, for rehabilitation and individual education programme planning, at different phases in education and as a resource for interagency and inter-professional collaboration.

From my perspective, the ICF is a framework about functioning based on a particular set of causal assumptions about the interactions between social, psychological and biological factors. Its use needs to be informed by a values framework, such as the Convention on the Rights of Disabled People. Its use has also to take account of the purposes of assessment and the goals of the varied kind of programmes that set its context of use.

The potential of the ICF to bridge between different agencies, professional groups and between policy makers, practitioners, parents, children and young people is central to its continued use. But there are risks in its uncritical adoption and over-blown promotion in the current political and economic context of services for disabled children and young people. There are also technical problems to be solved in the development of quality assessment methods. The

ICF framework and language has also to be responsive to the changing demands that will be placed on it.

The editors of this book are to be commended for bringing together these contributions as well as for their own research work in the United Kingdom, which is the first UK use of the ICF in the special needs and inclusive education system. I hope this book contributes further to continuing international interest in the framework, encouraging researchers to share their approaches, insights and set up future collaborations.

Brahm Norwich
Professor of Educational Psychology and Special Education Needs
Graduate School of Education, University of Exeter

Contributors

Margareta Adolfsson, Jönköping University, Sweden

Sílvia Alves, School of Education, Porto Polytechnic, Portugal

Eva Björck-Åkesson, Jönköping University, Sweden

Maria Björk, Jönköping University, Sweden

Juan Bornman, University of Pretoria, South Africa

Susana Castro, University of Roehampton, United Kingdom

Meng-Ting Chen, University of North Carolina at Chapel Hill, USA

Vera Coelho, Porto University, Portugal

Laura Darcy, Jönköping University, Sweden

İbrahim H. Diken, Anadolu University, Turkey

Kirsten Ellingsen, Parent and Child Psychological Services, USA

Karin Enskär, Jönköping University, Sweden

Catarina Grande, Porto University, Portugal

Mats Granlund, Jönköping University, Sweden

Judith Hollenweger, Zurich University of Teacher Education, Switzerland

Ai-Wen Hwang, Chang Gung University, Taiwan

Lin-Ju Kang, Chang Gung University, Taiwan

Eda Karacul, University of North Carolina at Chapel Hill, USA

Andrea Lee, Licensed Clinical Psychologist, USA

Hua-Fang Liao, National Taiwan University, Taiwan

Ya-Tzu Liao, Chang Gung University, Taiwan

Olympia Palikara, University of Roehampton, United Kingdom

Ana Isabel Pinto, Porto University, Portugal

Manfred Pretis, Medical School of Hamburg, Germany

Yutaka Sakai, Teikyo University, Japan

Manuela Sanches-Ferreira, School of Education, Porto Polytechnic, Portugal

Mónica Silveira-Maia, School of Education, Porto Polytechnic, Portugal

Rune J. Simeonsson, University of North Carolina at Chapel Hill, USA

Koji Tanaka, Tokyo Seitoku College, Japan

Akio Tokunaga, Yokohama National University, Japan

Mehmet Yanardağ, Anadolu University, Turkey

A classification for functioning

The International Classification of Functioning, Disability and Health

Susana Castro and Olympia Palikara

The ICF – International Classification of Functioning, Disability and Health – was published in 2001 and 2007 (children and youth version) by the World Health Organization (WHO) and since then, a considerable body of research has been developed worldwide on its applications in a variety of fields (education, health, rehabilitation, early childhood, etc.). Its main purpose is to provide a classification of functioning for adults and children with disabilities, considering their everyday lives, all the activities they perform and the environments they are embedded in, in addition to their health condition, which has been the traditional approach to disability in many countries. In fact, if we think of any two children with the same diagnosis, often they present different functioning profiles/general behaviours; this individual functioning is what the ICF classification system aims to help documenting (WHO, 2007). The ICF provides a holistic approach to special educational needs (SEN), considering each individual child from the point of view of the activities they perform, their participation and the environments they grow up in, in addition to body functions and structures.

The book *An Emerging Approach for Education and Care: Implementing a World-Wide Classification of Functioning and Disability* provides a synthesis of the extensive research that has been conducted worldwide about the International Classification of Functioning, Disability and Health for Children and Youth (ICF-CY; WHO, 2007) in education and care of children and young people. This synthesis of world-leading research in the ICF is presented in a way that is suitable for professionals working in special educational needs provision, rehabilitation, early childhood and students aspiring to work in these settings. Each chapter presents an evidence-based study or project describing how the ICF has been used to improve the provision of services for children and/or young people with SEN in a given context. Moreover, each chapter/evidence-based study is written by an expert on the ICF from a different country, thus providing an overview of how the ICF can be applied in educational contexts with different policy systems and cultural backgrounds.

The book is divided into three sections: 1) the theoretical foundations of the ICF, 2) contributions of the ICF to policy and 3) contributions of the ICF to education and care – applications in professional practice. These three sections reflect three of the ways by which the ICF has been implemented: a theoretical model that helps to rethink disability and special needs, a model that can be applied to support policy decision making about service provision for disabilities and special needs and a tool to support the work of professionals who directly intervene with children with disabilities and special needs.

The chapters included in these three sections were written by colleagues, world-leading experts in the field of education and care that have either been involved in the development of the ICF (children and youth version) or have been consistently engaged in its application at any of the mentioned levels (theory, policy or practice). It is an honour to be able to reunite all this expertise in one single publication, which we hope will make a significant contribution to the field of education and care.

Reference

World Health Organization. (2007). *International classification of functioning, disability and health for children and youth*. Genève: WHO.

Part I

Theoretical foundations of the ICF

The International Classification of Functioning, Disability and Health-Children and Youth

A universal resource for education and care of children

Rune J. Simeonsson and Andrea Lee

The development of every nation state is paralleled by the nation's responsibility to promote the development of children and youth as healthy and educated citizens. These responsibilities are typically assumed by national agencies of public health and public education with shared mandates, to promote health and a knowledgeable and informed citizenry, and to prevent disease and illiteracy, respectively. Although the nature and level of implementation of these responsibilities varies in nations around the world, the underlying premise for promoting the health and education of citizens rests on universal human rights. Viewed within the perspective of the child as the developing citizen, these rights correspond to representative universal rights of all children to the highest attainable state of health (Article 24) and to education (Article 28) as defined by the UN Convention on the Rights of the Child (UNICEF, 1989).

The mandate for public health and public education to address these universal rights of children in a systematic manner rests on a common framework and language to define and implement policies and programs. In public health, this approach takes the form of an epidemiological framework of the causes and distribution of disease and the taxonomic language of the International Classification of Diseases, ICD-10 (WHO, 1992). These complementary resources serve to define policies and an array of public health prevention and promotion initiatives such as vaccination, eradicating vectors of disease, insuring a potable water supply and sanitation.

The mandate for public education to address the right to education and to prevent illiteracy is informed by policies and programs grounded on a framework of sequenced formal, graded instruction covering the first and second decade of children's lives. A universal framework of education has been codified in the International Standard Classification of Education (ISCED) (UNESCO, 2011), providing a universal basis for defining and classifying the form and sequence of instruction. The sequence typically begins with primary or basic schooling, followed by levels of secondary education and possibly post-secondary education. Increasingly countries are recognizing the importance of beginning the sequence with preschool education – that is, instructional programs provided prior to the age of entry for formal schooling. Attendance in school is mandatory in most countries, but the actual amount of schooling received by a child varies significantly as a function of the extent of schooling provided by a country and the enforcement of attendance laws in that country. As shown in Table 1.1, ISCED classifies education on the basis of two classification variables, one defining nine fields of education and the other defining nine levels of programmes as well as level of attainment.

Although the ISCED provides a formal system for describing the structure of public education in broad terms, it does not offer a comprehensive system for documentation of what defines population and environmental characteristics of education in a manner paralleling the etiological and population information available in the ICD-10 for public health. Other than the ISCED, there has been no classification unique to the field of education for systematically describing the physical and instructional environment, dimensions of teaching and learning, teacher-student characteristics or educational goals and their attainment. In short, up to the present time, education has lacked a common language for describing population and environmental characteristics as well as for evaluating the extent to which schools are fulfilling their responsibility in addressing the universal rights of children.

The historical lack of a classification for education however, may be addressed, at least in part, with the availability of the ICF, published by the World Health Organization (WHO, 2001), The ICF is a universal taxonomy of human

Table 1.1 International Standard Classification of Education: fields and programme levels

Fields	Programme / Attainment	Level	Duration
0-General programmes	Early childhood	0	2 hours/day/100 days
1-Education	Primary	1	4–7 years
2-Humanities and arts	Lower secondary	2	2–5 years
3-Social sciences, business and law	Upper secondary	3	2–5 years
4-Science	Post-secondary, non-tertiary	4	½-2–3 years
5-Engineering, manufacturing and construction	Short-cycle tertiary	5	2–3 years
6-Agriculture	Bachelor/ equivalent	6	3–4 years
7-Health and welfare	Master/ equivalent	7	1–4 years
8-Services	Doctoral	8	3 years
	Not elsewhere classified	9	

functioning and associated environmental factors that classifies "them in terms of health domains and health-related domains . . . Examples of health domains include seeing, hearing, walking, learning and remembering, while examples of health-related domains include transportation, education and social interactions" (WHO, 2001, p. 7). As a cross-disciplinary tool, the ICF is increasingly being applied by services and disciplines for the development of a range of measures to assess functioning, disability, environments and intervention outcomes (Mpofu & Oakland, 2010). As such, it covers domains relevant to education and offers a timely resource for systematic documentation of populations across educational settings. However, in that the population served by public education is inclusive of the age range of the child as defined by the UNCRC, this chapter and the other chapters in this book presents the ICF-CY (WHO, 2007), the ICF version for children and youth, as a classification with utility for education.

As the ICF-CY has a descriptive rather than a diagnostic focus, the ICF-CY offers a common language that can serve to document the characteristics of schools and functioning of students in the educational environment. The multifunctional framework and taxonomy of the ICF-CY is applicable to an array of activities which support the education and care of children. A range of applications of the ICF-CY for policy, practice and research in education and care of children have been identified in the literature (Moretti, Alves, & Maxwell, 2012; Bjorck-Akesson et al., 2010). This chapter introduces selected ways in which the common language of the ICF-CY can advance policy as well as practice in education. Specifically, the ICF-CY can inform policy in education by offering (a) a holistic framework, (b) a common language and (c) a standard reference for student rights. With reference to educational practice, the common language of the ICF-CY can serve to document (d) functioning and engagement of students, (e) the nature of their school environments and (f) the outcomes of their education.

Holistic framework

Children served by public education also often receive services from other supportive institutions and agencies. It is common for a nation state to establish separate agencies or departments to manage education and health/human services, even though the child experiences overlapping support from these fields. There is a growing appreciation that separation of these fields is a false dichotomy, but one challenge to their integration, in support of the child, has been the difficulty in identifying a common language and taxonomy to describe the child and the environment in a comprehensive and meaningfully.

The common language of the ICF-CY builds on a framework of dimensions or components encompassing body functions, body structures, activities and participation and environmental factors as shown in Figure 1.1. The number of two-level classification codes is provided for respective domains, however the total number of higher-level codes is much greater. The diagram illustrates the fact that a child' functioning is reflective of a dynamic relationship of child characteristics and the environment. As such, it provides a conceptual model for public agencies offering a holistic and interdisciplinary approach to services for children (Simeonsson, 2009). This approach is consistent with the mission of public health, education and other helping professions to promote the child's health, development, education and quality of life.

As noted earlier, a central contribution of the ICF-CY is a multidimensional framework defining characteristics and attributes of persons and their environmental contexts. In that the ICF offers a dimensional framework of components, it can integrate multidisciplinary efforts. The components of the ICF-CY model (Figure 1.1) can thus provide the framework for assessment, intervention and monitoring of child progress and outcomes. For assessment, the focus may often involve the components of body functions, body structures and activities. For intervention, the focus will likely be on documentation of the nature of activities and participation and their impact on outcomes. In interdisciplinary programs for young children, the ICF-CY framework has been applied to clarify of the role of biological and environmental factors (Hwang et al., 2014).

The ICF-CY responds to the call for a needed universal framework and shared language, and it has been proposed for use as a common language in education (Hollenweger, 2010), special education (Florian et al., 2006; Simeonsson, Simeonsson, & Hollenweger, 2008) and a variety of care-related and health fields. Using the ICF-CY, *any* agency, department or institution can use a common code to describe a child's functioning, document the characteristics of the environment serving or hindering a child, and qualify the focus, scope

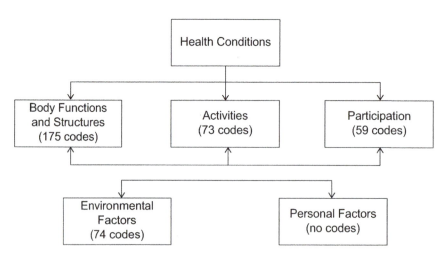

Figure 1.1 ICF, Disability and Health-Children and Youth (adapted from WHO, 2007)

and outcome of interventions designed to meet a child's needs. In removing the differences in institutional or disciplinary language, there is greater ability to perceive commonality across policies, which allows for greater alignment, and perhaps even streamlining of resources. As a result, the ICF-CY has been proposed and/or used to provide a common language for eligibility determination (D'Alessio, 2008; Simeonsson et al., 2008), discussions on how to modernise policy language (D'Alessio, 2008) and as a tool for policy analysis, evaluation and development (Hollenweger, 2008).

Care providers and other in-service settings are often faced with the frustration of trying to use data on just one aspect of a complex truth in order to "make the case" for improving a situation which in fact consists of interacting variables. The concept of assessment for the purpose of intervention development reflects this need to somehow capture features of an individual in order to inform interventions which involve environmental manipulation (including services). As a framework capable of documenting *all aspects* of individual functioning, activities/participation and the environment, the ICF-CY helps bridge this gap to allow for integration of factors in order to understand the complex whole.

For special education, the ICF-CY can provide a common language bridging between disability-focused determinants and education-related knowledge (Simeonsson, Simeonsson, & Hollenweger, 2008). In the school setting, school nurses, special educators, allied health professionals and psychologists can share the common language of the ICF-CY to document characteristics of the child and to identify needed interventions and environmental supports. This may reduce the problem of discipline-specific languages and promote a holistic and integrated view of the child. In the Swiss context, the ICF-CY has been advanced as a platform or map for a shared understanding of interactive effects providing "an information system to help negotiate between different views on reality and different areas of expertise" (Hollenweger, 2013, p. 1088). In practice, instead of restraining professionals to their field-specific classifications (Bowker & Star, 1999), policies and procedures applying the ICF-CY standardise the approach and language across professions to support sharing of knowledge and identification of supports to address student needs.

Common language

In the ICF-CY, body functions are defined as "physiological functions of body systems (including mental functions)" and body structures are defined as "anatomical parts of the body such as organs, limbs and their components" (WHO, 2007, p. 10) with each component consisting of eight chapters. In the component of activities and participation activities are defined as the "execution of a task or action" and participation as "involvement in a life situation" (WHO, 2007, p. 10), together constituting of nine chapters. The component of environmental factors is defined as "the physical, social and attitudinal environment in which people live and conduct their lives" (WHO, 2007, p. 10) is organised into five chapters. The chapters of the aforementioned four components are listed in Table 1.2; each chapter in turn represents a hierarchical listing of alphanumeric elements defining content specific to body functions, structures, activities, participation and environmental factors, respectively.

Given the comprehensive scope of education and other disciplines working with children in related settings, many of the chapters and codes of the ICF-CY are applicable to document the populations served and their environments. As the ICF-CY is cross-disciplinary in nature, it should be recognised that specific instructional and academic content is limited. However, focusing on the student's experience in the school, there are specific chapters and accompanying codes that may be particularly relevant. Applicable codes can be identified that correspond to the following questions. What characterises the student's physical and mental functioning (BF Chapters 1–8)? What characterises the students learning and response to instruction (BF 1; A& P 1–3)? How does the student respond to situational demands (A&P 2)? What characterises the student's independence (A&P 4–6)? What is the nature of the student's engagement and participation (A&P 7–9)? What barriers and facilitators impact the student's school functioning (EF 1–5)? Although there is potential utility in documenting these characteristics with all students, they have unique implications for education of children with special needs and disabilities. There is great variability in naming and classification of children with disabilities across countries (Florian & McLaughlin, 2008; Hollenweger, 2008). That variability significantly limits comparison not only of the proportion of children needing special services but also precluding exchange of information on student characteristics

Table 1.2 ICF-CY components and associated chapters

Body Functions	Body Structures	Activities and Participation	Environmental Factors
1 Mental	1 Nervous	1 Learning	1 Products/ technology
2 Sensory	2 Eye, ear	2 General tasks and demands	2 Natural environment
3 Voice/speech	3 Voice/speech	3 Communication	3 Support and relationships
4 Cardiovascular	4 Cardiovascular	4 Mobility	4 Attitudes
5 Digestive, metabolic	5 Digestive	5 Self-care	5 Services, systems, policies
6 Genitourinary	6 Genitourinary	6 Domestic life	
7 Neuromuscular	7 Movement	7 Interpersonal interactions	
8 Skin	8 Skin	8 Major life areas	
		9 Community, social and civic life	

and effective interventions. Using the ICF-CY in naming and classification of children with disabilities can provide information about the nature of their conditions in the diagnostic process. Such documentation can serve to influence perceptions of their needs and the design of programs to meet their needs (Florian et al., 2006).

Reference standard for student rights

Although the child's right to education may be recognised in most countries, the extent to which that right is realised varies widely. Realisation of that right requires evidence not only of the availability of public education for all children, but accessibility by the child to a structured learning experience that is appropriate for age without discrimination on the basis of gender, ethnicity or disability status. In this regard, populations for whom accessibility may be abridged in developed countries include children of poverty, children with disabilities, second-language learners, migrant and refugee children. In developing and low- and middle-income LAMI countries, the right to education is often curtailed for girls, for children with disabilities and for children on the basis of ethnic or racial identity. The reality of limitation of these rights for children in many countries of the developing world is evident in the education targets established in the Millennium Goals and the Sustainable Goals (UN, 2015, 2016).

At a universal level, the ICF may serve as standard reference for documenting the rights of children. The rights of children to equality of opportunity, participation and independence have been elaborated in the articles of the UN Convention on the Rights of the Child (UN, 1989). In practice, these rights involve access to education, care and support as well as protection from exploitation in developed and developing countries. Such access can be documented by equal opportunity to engage in activities and to participate in the instructional and social context of education as defined by a variety of codes in the ICF-CY. Specifically, evidence of restricted access to education by an individual child or of groups of children can be documented with ICF-CY codes related to a lack of learning opportunities, providing evidence of the deprivation of their rights. The common language of ICF-CY codes may thus be of particular value in documenting the limited access to education of children in developing countries due to discrimination on the basis of gender or disability (Simeonsson et al., 2003; Simeonsson, Björck-Åkesson, & Bairrao, 2006).

Documentation of student performance and school engagement

For teachers and school professionals providing instruction and care to children, the ICF-CY is a departure from other frequently referenced tools. As the classification of the ICF-CY is descriptive rather than diagnostic in nature, a key contribution is its use to document the nature of the children's functioning, their activities and engagement with the school environment. It is important to emphasise that the ICF-CY is not an assessment tool; it can be used to identify selected codes for the development of new assessment measures or to "back-code" existing measures to determine their coverage of relevant ICF-CY components. Thus, unlike a diagnostic manual, the use of the ICF-CY is not to derive diagnoses but rather to identify a profile of codes uniquely reflecting problems characterizing the child in the school environment. In fact, the ICF-CY is far more flexible in that it provides a universal taxonomy for documenting the characteristics or the child and the environment to guide assessment and to facilitate intervention planning and delivery. This is specifically different from information obtained from intelligence or achievement tests that do not capture broader aspects of the child's physical, mental and social adaptation to the school environment. For example, consider the value of objectively documenting differences among children in how they manage their behaviour (d250) in response to problem solving (d175) academic tasks. Coding of social skill development in this way, may identify important individual differences across children depending on environmental context (i.e. whether the home, school, community or other environment are being considered) and respondent perceptions (i.e. differences in expectations or conceptualisations across parent, teacher, care provider). In other words, "social skill development" is not a static concept, and it is a child's ability to engage in various social skills across different environments which is actually of interest. When reporting on findings, then, it is of great importance to provide adequate descriptions of the interactional effects in education when capturing data and reporting their implications, a dynamic framework congruent with the ICF-CY and inconsistent with reporting fixed numbers without further context

Compared to a diagnostic manual, the ICF-CY has further merit in its ability to support documentation of the realistic, dynamic interplay between a child and environmental factors that support or inhibit the child's functioning. In order to use ICF-CY codes to document problems that a child may have while engaging in school activities or by experiencing barriers in accessing the physical, instructional or social environment of the school, the concept of the universal qualifier must be applied. Since a major purpose for the ICF and the ICF-CY is to provide a formal classification of disability, the universal qualifier was designed as a metric to quantify the extent of impairment, limitations, restrictions or barriers representing the disability. Thus the universal qualifier provides a systematic basis for defining the level of problem or limitation that may apply to aspects of a child's functioning or the extent to which an environmental factor may be a barrier or facilitator for learning or participation. Within the taxonomic framework of the ICF-CY, the universal qualifier is defined by values of 0, 1, 2, 3 and 4 to reflect no problem or limitation, mild, moderate, severe and extreme limitation, respectively. It should be emphasised that the evidence for assignment of a qualifier value to codes relevant to a child should be based on observation, clinical judgement and/or assessment. Although disability determination has been a primary application of the universal qualifier in clinical fields, a more general application in the context of education can be to indicate the nature and the degree of difficulty or problem a child may have in an area of functioning without being identified as having a disability. For example, the code for a child with mild difficulty (qualifier level of 1) in the activity of "completing a simple task" would be d2104.1, whereas the designation for another child with a greater difficulty in "completing a simple task" could be d2104.3, with the qualifier of three indicating a severe limitation. In either case, the code and the qualifier provide meaningful information for differentiating intervention for the children.

Existing forms of evaluation in public education typically focus on child performance in the form of grades and tests of achievement. Such evaluation has a narrow focus on single measures and does not address the dynamic aspects of the child's engagement with the demand characteristics of the school. In this regard, it should be recognised that such forms of evaluation capture the academic *outcomes of instruction* rather than the characteristics of the child in interaction with the environment. The systematic documentation of child functioning using relevant codes from the ICF-CY could significantly expand such evaluation. A valuable contribution of the ICF-CY to educational practice is thus to develop approaches to document characteristics of the child and the school environment in a systematic manner using the universal qualifier with relevant codes. The focus in this regard would be the identification of a selected number of codes that best capture characteristics associated with required performance. As noted earlier, Chapter 1 body functions and Chapters 1, 2, 3 and 7 activities and participation would seem particularly relevant for identifying a set of codes capturing the school experience of children. Reviewing the characteristics of each child could yield a profile reflecting the nature and extent of the child's limitations of functioning in meeting the demands of the school environment. Further, documentation can also be made of environmental factors that represent barriers to child performance of activities and school participation. Profiles of individual children could be aggregated to reflect the problems of students in a class, school or a larger educational entity.

Although the documentation of functioning of students in general is proposed as a valuable application for public education, the use of the ICF-CY in documenting functioning of children with disabilities and in special education practice is well under way. Such applications have focused on documenting eligibility for special education by deriving profiles of impairments, limitations and restrictions of functioning (Sanches-Ferreira, Simeonsson, Silvereia-Maia & Alves, 2014). Parallel identification of significant environmental barriers can be incorporated into the development of individualised education programs.

A useful application of the ICF-CY can be in work with parents of children with disabilities in which they are asked to response to the question "tell me about your child". In this situation, very few parents will respond by giving a diagnostic label. Instead of saying, "He has autism," parents are likely to give descriptions of how their child functions and participates in daily life situations. This is important in that a diagnosis provides limited insight into the functioning of a particular child, especially in light of the variable ways in which children with similar (or even the same) diagnosis present in very different ways. Just as a parent is unlikely to define their child with a label, so should assessment be directed away from a single diagnosis towards a fuller description of a child's functioning and participation as products of the child-environment interaction. The ICF-CY framework is consistent with a narrative description of the child, creating a profile of functioning elucidating a picture of how the individual facets work together in different environments.

A review of the application of the ICF-CY for assessment practice is beyond the scope of this introduction. Elsewhere, we have described comprehensive approaches for applying the ICF-CY in psychological assessment (Simeonsson, Lee, Granlund, & Bjorck-Akesson, 2010; Simeonsson & Lee, 2013). These provide guides to practice, detailing approaches for developing and implementing assessment protocols and reporting findings in a manner consistent with the whole-child, interactional focus of the ICF-CY. Since publication of this earlier work, additional publications have responded to the need to offer evidence-based assessment tools consistent with classifying features of body functioning, activities/participation and environmental factors (Majnemer, 2012), expanding the discussion and ability to use a functioning-oriented approach to assessment that references environmental features which support or hinder a child's participation in education or other daily activities.

Documentation of the school environment

Every school, whether in a developed or developing country is a complex environment defined by physical, social and policy elements. To the extent that the nature of these elements constitute problems for children or limit their participation in school activities, they can be represented by codes from the domain of environmental factors. Although the codes of the environmental factors domain are not as detailed as codes in the other ICF-CY domains, elements of the school environment can be documented at some level with representative codes. For the physical environment, representative codes in chapters 1 and 2 include products and technology (e130), building design (e150) and geographical setting (210-e299). Problems encountered by children in the social environment can be documented with codes from Chapter 3 of environmental factors related to lack of supports from friends (e320), peers (e325) and persons in authority (e335) and from Chapter 4 for non-supportive attitudes of friends (e420) peers (e425) and persons in authority (e430). Broader aspects of the educational environment may well be documented with the codes under e585 (education and training services, systems and policies).

Documentation of the educational environment may be particularly relevant to education for children with special needs to assess the level of participation as a result of interaction between the student and the school (Ilum, Bonderup, & Gradel, 2016). The concept of the least restrictive environment, as defined in the special education law (IDEA) in the United States (IDEA, 2004), offers a useful example for considering the merit of systematically documenting the characteristics of the environment to match the needs of the child. The concept of the least restrictive environment is respectful of the child, but it can be difficult to establish parameters which consistently capture aspects of a child's functioning with characteristics of the learning environment that make it more or less supportive (and also more or less restrictive). According to IDEA, a child with an identified disability must be provided an education in the environment which is least restrictive when considering access to "typically developing" peers and the "typical" learning experience. School systems are tasked with developing a hierarchy of environments available to a child, from a "regular" or "expected placement" within the usual classroom, to increasing levels of support within the classroom, to increasing periods of time in a separate classroom, to a separate classroom full-time, to alternative schools or institutions. In order to determine the least restrictive environment, a compilation of data regarding the student is used to consider whether a child is meeting his/her educational goals within the current environment or a higher level of support (in a more restrictive environment) is necessary. The ICF-CY may offer a framework for coding the nature of environmental support, ranging from modifications within an activity, to those within a classroom, to those within a school, to those offered in an alternative environment altogether and the level to which those supports are facilitative. In applying a systematic language and framework across school systems, family-school partnerships may be enhanced, making the process transparent and consistently implemented.

Documentation of intervention and education outcomes

A current priority in education in many developed countries is evidence-based documentation of outcome. There is a growing literature on the utility of the ICF-CY for the activities of planning interventions (Maia & Lopes-dos-Santos, 2009; Simeonsson et al., 2003; Simeonsson et al., 2008) and setting goals (Campbell & Skarakis-Doyle, 2007; McLeod & Bleile, 2004). Particularly in an era of accountability and progress monitoring, the ICF-CY satisfies the important need for a consistent language to communicate the target of an intervention, describes its implementation and reports on its outcomes whether they reflect a change in body functioning, an alternative use of environmental resources, or a different degree of participation. In multidisciplinary settings, a great advantage of this common language is the ability for different professionals to communicate the focus of an intervention, the environmental resources leveraged in the process and the actual outcomes of the intervention itself across disciplines effectively (Hwang et al., 2013).

Maintaining a functional perspective on intervention selection and implementation is helpful to clinicians and educators. Selecting an intervention defined simply as good for "a reading learning disability" for a child with this label may or may not be effective. If the intervention focuses on enhancing letter-sound correspondence but the child has mastered this concept already, the intervention may not be appropriate for supporting the child's learning. Although this may be a simple example, it reflects the fact that helping professionals can be overburdened with the challenge of having to identify the actual focus and activities of an intervention and then determining if they are effective in enhancing the functioning and participation of identified students. In this case, it would be appropriate to classify interventions based on expected outcomes using the ICF-CY as a common language for clarity and understanding across disciplines. In doing so, intervention selection and implementation could be streamlined as well as removed from the danger of overlooking effective interventions because they appear to be designed only for children with specific diagnoses.

School-based interventions should be described in terms of aspects of child functioning and the environmental supports designed to enhance that functioning. For example, the child's school day may consist of periods of physical movement interspersed with direct instruction during which the child manifests disturbed activity level and/or difficulties in sensory perception and integration. By clearly defining the environmental supports provided to enhance engagement in learning and participation by the student, a school is better able to communicate its approach among teachers, other school professionals and the child's family.

In the context of special education, consistent language focusing on child functioning is important for families to understand whether an offered intervention is matched to the identified needs of the child. Consider a family looking for a school that "serves children with ADHD". There are 18 criteria available to document a possible attention deficit hyperactivity disorder (ADHD) diagnosis, and these criteria are not exclusively observed in children with ADHD but also observed in children with other diagnoses – or no diagnoses at all. In addition, a child with ADHD may experience associated problems, which are not captured by an ADHD diagnosis, such as difficulties in social communication. As a result, families often feel challenged in trying to find the correct resources to serve their child when they are simply relying on a diagnostic label for their child's condition.

The ICF-CY can address the problem of limited information of diagnoses for the development of individualised intervention plans by matching a child's e profile of functional characteristics based on the ICF-CY with needed environmental supports and services. The profile defines the nature and level of difficulties the child experiences in meeting the demands of the instructional and social environment. As such, the ICF-CY can serve as the framework for selecting measures not only for assessment of functioning but also for monitoring of educational outcomes (Sanches-Ferreira et al., 2014)). Current difficulties in child performance can be documented by assessment of activities and body functions and environmental barriers, whereas changes in mastery of skills, social integration and levels of engagement constitute outcomes in the domains of activities and participation. In that outcomes can be defined by activities and participation, indicators of progress may take the form of a shift of codes within a hierarchy from a lower code, completing a simple task (d2104.2) to a higher code, completing a complex task (d2105.2). In this case the qualifier level reflects the same level of difficulty of -2-(moderate) but the nature of the task reflects a higher hierarchical code, indicating functioning at a higher level. A child's progress may also be documented by a reduction in the severity level of the qualifier over time. In this case, a child may manifest a severe difficulty in learning to read (d140.3) but progress is noted in learning to read with the child only manifesting a mild level of difficulty (d140.1) on follow-up.

A broader application of the common language of the ICF-CY is related to progress monitoring and documentation of outcome at the population level in terms of aggregation of data on student performance and achievement. This policy application often takes the form of annual reports to departments and agencies. In practice, compliance with policies is often linked to receipt of fund to continue programming. In order to demonstrate compliance, schools and places of care are tasked with reporting measurable outcomes, a task that can be arduous if it appears to be an extra action or requirement beyond the daily activities of educating or care provision. The ICF-CY may offer a framework for alignment of all tasks, inclusive of annual reporting, thus streamlining processes and helping to reframe reporting expectations to be congruent with the actual expected outcomes of service delivery.

Implications of the ICF-CY for research in education

Research informs our understanding insofar as the captured data can be presented within a framework with relevance to the actual experience of the child in education. In education and care, the focus of policies and interventions is to promote the child's acquisition of skills and knowledge by enhancing the role of the environment. Good research begins with well-defined constructs, which are then operationalised so that suitable measures can be utilised to capture the intended concept. The multidimensional framework and associated taxonomic language of the ICF-CY can provide the language and codes needed to allow for intellectual discourse on frequently used concepts which have been inconsistently defined and applied in the research. To that end, contributions to the literature on, the ICF-CY framework has revealed the need for a standard definition of participation, given its varied use in outcome research (Maxwell, Alves, & Granlund, 2012). Operationalizing the concept of participation and applying it within research studies is needed in order to facilitate interpretation of findings across populations and settings (Granlund et al., 2012). Leveraging the ICF-CY framework as a platform for inquiry and discussion, Maxwell et al. (2012) have noted the need for continued development of a balanced approach to participation inclusive of both social and psychological/individual approaches (Gaidhane et al., 2008), that fully incorporates environmental dimensions of availability, accessibility, affordability, accommodation and acceptability (Badley, 2008; Tomasevski, 2001). Such applications of the ICF-CY foster an important opportunity to advance definitions of constructs leading to more rigorous research reflecting a more accurate description of reality and thus better informing our collective understanding of how to best support children.

With reference to challenges in reframing research within a multidimensional approach, the area of practice/direct service is perhaps the least developed in its clarity of how to incorporate the ICF-CY in the activities of assessment, intervention and interactions in the process of determining eligibility and developing individualised intervention plans. A reflection of this challenge is that even the concept of "disability" is not unanimously defined (Florian & McLaughlin, 2008; Richardson & Powell, 2011). The universal taxonomy of the ICF-CY can aid collaboration across disciplines, particularly when practices or tools traditionally considered part of one field have relevance for yet another. Being applicable across disciplines, the ICF-CY has already advanced the ability of different professionals to share expertise in selection and use of measures. For example, Majnemer (2012) has provided a summary of available tools and measures for capturing a wide array of body functions, activities, participation and environmental factors. By utilizing the organisation of the ICF-CY and relying on a common language, this resource allows professionals across disciplines to identify the intent, focus and scope of available tools. A common language is of particular relevance for education of children with disabilities in which the focus is to promote the child's acquisition of academic, social and life skills necessary for societal participation as a citizen. In this context, the ICF-CY reframes disability from a diagnostic label to manifestations of functional limitations of the child's interaction with the environment. Further, as the child develops, disability is not documented as a static condition but rather as the progressive mastery of activities and levels of participation.

The nature and impact of the environment as a contextual factor of child functioning is a key element of the multidimensional framework of the ICF-CY for which a research base in education is needed. Instead of reporting isolated outcomes of single variables, advances in data analyses have allowed researchers to make effective use of multi-factor approaches that can capture the unique contribution of multiple ICF-CY elements that define the child-environment interaction. The ICF-CY can facilitate this research by contributing to the conceptualisation of variables and confirmation of their relationships with advanced statistical modelling (Lee, 2011). A further focus for research is the development of code sets or a limited set of ICF-CY codes to define populations served in education, extending prior code sets that have been derived for age groups (Ellingsen & Simeonsson, 2010) as well as children with special needs (Castro, Pinto, & Simeonsson, 2012; Pan, Hwang, Simeonsson, Lu, & Liao, 2014). Codes sets relevant to education practice would offer useful ways of conceptualizing and reporting on the multifaceted interrelated variables defining children and their participation in school environments.

In conclusion

At the heart of all of the aforementioned applications of the ICF-CY is the very real fact that children, education and public health consist of multiple, complex and occasionally disorganised concepts and variables (Sowa, 2000). Given that the knowledge and language base in education, public health and other caring professions is diverse, the need for a common language defining children in their environments constitutes a priority for synergism of policy, practice and research. The ICF-CY is a universal tool and framework for synchronizing the language and efforts of professionals across disciplines in order to achieve a common goal: the education, care and well-being of children.

Highlights from this chapter

- The ICF-CY is a universal taxonomy, applicable for multidisciplinary use within education and care of children. As a holistic framework, the ICF-CY allows for documentation of *all aspects* of individual functioning, activities/participation and the environment.
- By standardising language and providing an organising framework, the ICF-CY can help document realisation of the student's right to education, the student's performance and the student's level of engagement within school.
- The ICF-CY provides codes for characterising different learning environments and levels of educational intervention as a function of the interplay between the student's functioning, ability to participate and availability of environmental supports.
- The ICF-CY has particular utility for the education of children with disabilities in which child functioning, (rather than diagnoses) serves as the basis for organising interventions, providing learning supports and documenting outcomes.
- Research can be enhanced by sharing a language and framework for conceptualising and qualifying a child's "participation" as an outcome. Multidisciplinary research could be fostered by organising findings and outcomes using the universal ICF-CY codes.

References

Badley, E. M. (2008). Enhancing the conceptual clarity of the activity and participation components of the International classification of functioning, disability, and health. *Social Science and Medicine 66*, 2335–2345.

Björck-Åkesson, E., Wilder, J., Granlund, M., Pless, M., Simeonsson, R., Adolfsson, M., Almqvist, L., Augustine, L., Klang, N., & Lillvist, A. (2010). The international classification of functioning, disability and health and the version for children and youth as a tool in child habilitation/early childhood intervention feasibility and usefulness as a common language and frame of reference for practice. *Disability Rehabilitation, 32* (Suppl 1), S125–S138. Epub September 15, 2010.

Bowker, G. C., & Star, S. L. (1999). *Sorting things out: Classification and its consequences.* Cambridge, MA: MIT Press.

Campbell, W. N., & Skarakis-Doyle, E. (2007). School-aged children with SLI: The ICF as a framework for collaborative service delivery. *Journal of Communication Disorders, 40*, 513–535.

Castro, S., Pinto, A., & Simeonsson, R. J. (2012). Content analysis of Portuguese individualized education programmes for young children with autism using the ICF-CY framework. *European Early Childhood Education Research Journal.* 22(1), 91–104.

D'Alessio, S. F. (2008). Made in Italy: Integrazione scolastica and the new vision of inclusive education. In L. Barton & F. Armstrong (Eds.), *Policy, experience and change: Cross-cultural reflections on inclusive education.* Dordrecht, The Netherlands: Springer.

Ellingsen, K. M., & Simeonsson, R. J. (2010). *WHO ICF-CY developmental code sets.* Retrieved from www.icf-cydevelopmentalcodesets

Florian, L., Hollenweger, J., Simeonsson, R. J., Wedell, K., Riddell, S., Terzi, L., & Holland, A. (2006). Cross-cultural perspectives on the classification of children with disabilities: Part I. Issues in the classification of children with disabilities. *Journal of Special Education, 40*, 36–45.

Florian, L., & McLaughlin, M. (2008). *Disability classification in education: Issues and perspectives.* Thousand Oaks, CA: Corwin Press.

Gaidhane, A. M., Zahiruddin, Q. S., Waghmare, L., Zodpey, S., Goyal, R. C., & Johrapurkar, S. R. (2008). Assessing self-care component of activities and participation domain of the International Classification of Functioning, Disability and Health (ICF) among people living with HIV/AIDS. *AIDS Care, 20*, 1098–1104.

Granlund, M., Arvidsson, P., Niia, A., Björck-Åkesson, E., Simeonsson, R., Maxwell, G., Adolfsson, M., Eriksson-Augustine, L. and Pless, M. (2012). Differentiating activity and participation of children and youth with disability in Sweden: a third qualifier in the International Classification of Functioning, Disability, and Health for Children and Youth? *American Journal of Physical Medicine & Rehabilitation*, 91(13), pp. S84–S96

Hollenweger, J. (2008). Cross-national comparisons of special education classification systems. In L. Florian & M. McLaughlin (Eds.), *Disability classification in education: Issues and perspectives* (pp. 11–30). Thousand Oaks, CA: Corwin Press.

Hollenweger, J. (2010). MHADIE's matrix to analyse the functioning f education systems. *Disability and Rehabilitation, 32*, S116–S124.

Hollenweger, J. (2013). Developing applications of the ICF in education systems: Addressing issues of knowledge creation, management and transfer. *Disability & Rehabilitation, 35*(13), 1087–1091.

Hwang, A. W., Liao, H. F., Chen, P. C., Hsieh, W. S., Simeonsson, R. J., Weng, L. J., & Su, Y. N. (2014). Applying the ICF-CY framework to examine biological and environmental factors in early childhood development. *Journal of the Formosan Medical Association, 113,* 303–312.

Hwang, A. W., Liao, H. F., Granlund, G., Simeonsson, R. J., Kan, L. J., & Pan, Y. L.(2013). Linkage of ICF-CY codes with environmental factors in studies of developmental outcomes of infants and toddlers with or at risk for motor delays. *Disability and Rehabilitation 36*(2), 89–104.

Illum, N. O., Bonderup, M., & Gradel, K. O. (2016). Environmental needs in childhood disability analyzed by the WHO ICF, child and youth version. *Danish Medical Bulletin, 63*(6), A5238.

Individuals with Disabilities Education Act. (2004). P.L. No. 108–446, 118 Stat. 2647. Retrieved from www2.ed.gov/policy/speced/guid/idea/idea2004.html

Lee, A. M. (2011). Using the ICF-CY to organize characteristics of children's functioning. *Disability & Rehabilitation, 33*(7), 605–616.

Maia, M., & Lopes-dos-Santos, P. (2009, May). The ICF-CY use to support disability documentation and to plan interventions on individualized education programs. *Proceedings of the International Turkish Educational Research Congress.* Çanakkale, Turkey.

Majnemer, A. (Ed.). (2012). Measures for children with developmental disabilities: An ICF-CY approach. *Clinics in Developmental Medicine,* CDM 194–195.

Maxwell, G., Alves, I., & Granlund, M. (2012). Participation and environmental aspects in education in the ICF and ICF-CY: Findings from a systematic literature review. *Developmental Neurorehabilitation, 15*(1), 63–78.

McLeod, S., & Bleile, K. (2004). The ICF: A framework for setting goals for children with speech impairment. *Child Language Teaching and Therapy, 20,* 199–219.

Moretti, M., Alves, I., & Maxwell, G. (2012). A systematic literature review of the situation of the international classification of functioning, disability, and health and the international classification of functioning, disability, and health–children and youth version in education: A useful tool or a flight of fancy? *American Journal of Physical Medicine & Rehabilitation, 91*(2, Supp.), S103–S117.

Mpofu, E., & Oakland, T. (Eds.). (2010). *Rehabilitation and health assessment: Applying ICF guidelines.* New York: Springer Publishing Co.

Pan, Y. L., Hwang, A. W., Simeonsson, R. J., Lu, L., & Liao, H. F. (2015). ICF-CY code sets for infants with early delays and disabilities (EDD Code Set) for interdisciplinary assessment: A global experts survey. *Disability and Rehabilitation 37*(12), 1044–1054.

Richardson, J. G., & Powell, J. J. W. (2011). *Comparing special education: Origins to contemporary paradoxes.* Stanford, CA: Stanford University Press.

Sanches-Ferreira, M., Simeonsson, R. J., Silvereia-Maia, M., & Alves, S. (2015). Evaluating Implementation of the ICF in Portugal's special education law. *International Journal of Inclusive Education 19*(5), 457–468.

Simeonsson, R. J. (2009). ICF-CY: A universal tool for documentation of disability. *Journal of Policy and Practice in Intellectual Disabilities, 6*(2), 70–72.

Simeonsson, R. J., Bjorck-Akesson, E., & Bairrao, J. (2006). Rights of children with disabilities. In G. Albrecht (Ed.), *Encyclopedia of disability* (pp. 257–259). Thousand Oaks, CA: Sage Publications.

Simeonsson, R. J., & Lee, A. (2013). The ICF-CY: A universal classification for psychological assessment. In D. B. Saklofske, C. R. Reynolds, & V. L. Schwean (Eds.), *The Oxford handbook of child psychological assessment* (pp. 202–221). Oxford: Oxford University Press.

Simeonsson, R. J., Lee, A., Granlund, M., & Bjorck-Akesson, E. (2010). Developmental and health assessment in rehabilitation with the ICF for children and youth. In E. Mpofu & T. Oakland (Eds.), *Rehabilitation and health assessment: Applying ICF guidelines.* (pp. 27–46). New York: Springer Publishing Co.

Simeonsson, R. J., Leonardi, M., Lollar, D., Bjorck-Akesson, E., Hollenweger, J., & Martinuzzi, A. (2003). Applying the International Classification of Functioning, Disability and Health (ICF) to measure childhood disability. *Disability and Rehabilitation, 25*(11-12), 602-610.

Simeonsson, R. J., Simeonsson, N., & Hollenweger, J. (2008). The international classification of functioning, disability and health for children and youth: A common language for special education. In L. Florian & M. McLaughlin (Eds.), *Disability classification in education: Issues and perspectives* (pp. 207–226). Thousand Oaks, CA: Corwin Press.

Sowa, J. F. (2000). *Knowledge representation: Logical, philosophical and computational foundations.* Pacific Grove, CA: Brooks/Cole.

Tomasevski, K. (2001). *Human rights obligations: Making education available, accessible, acceptable and adaptable.* Lund, Sweden: Raoul Wallenberg Institute of Human Rights and Humanitarian Law.

United Nations. Millennium development goals. (2015). Retrieved from www.un.org/millenniumgoals/2015_MDG_Report/pdf/MDG%202015%20rev%20(July%201).pdf

United Nations. Sustainable development goals. (2016). Retrieved from www.un.org/sustainabledevelopment/sustainable-development-goals/

United Nations Educational, Scientific and Cultural Organization. International Standard Classification of Education. (2011). Retrieved from www.uis.unesco.org/Education/Documents/isced-2011-en.pdf

United Nations Office of the High Commissioner for Human Rights (1989). Convention on the rights of the child. Retrieved from www.unhchr.ch/html/menu3/b/kcrc.htm

World Health Organization. (1992). *International statistical classification of diseases and related health problems-tenth revision.* Geneva: Author.

World Health Organization. (2001). *International classification of functioning, disability & health.* Geneva: Author.

World Health Organization. (2007). *International classification of functioning, disability & health-children and youth.* Geneva: Author.

Chapter 2

Applying ICF in education and care

Judith Hollenweger

Using the ICF beyond the contexts of health conditions

The International Classification of Functioning, Disability and Health (ICF, Version for Children and Youth, ICF-CY) was developed as a classification and common language to conceptualise and classify functioning and disability in the context of health. Can it be used just as well in the context of education? Is there a difference between using ICF in health and in education and if so, which considerations should guide the development of applications? In the ICF, education is an area of services, systems and policies shaping a child's environment, but unlike health, it is also a major life domain in which children participate. What are the consequences of this double representation for measuring functioning and disability in education? The ICF is able to describe health and health-related states associated with any health condition, allowing a better understanding of functional limitations across disorders or diseases. Contrary to its predecessor classification, the International Classification of Impairments, Disabilities and Handicaps (ICIDH; WHO, 1980), the ICF "does not model the 'process' of functioning and disability" (WHO, 2001, p. 18); participation restrictions and activity limitations are no longer seen as direct consequences of health problems. "A person's functioning and disability is conceived as a dynamic interaction between health conditions (. . .) and contextual factors" (ibid, 8). But education in general does not view "health condition" as a key concept around which knowledge is organised. So when using the ICF in education contexts, functioning and disability would not necessarily be considered in the context of a health condition, at least not exclusively. Would this create conceptual or practical problems and what happens if the health condition is not known or if the idea of using health conditions as guiding concepts is explicitly rejected?

If the ICF were only to be used in the context of a health condition, the application of the ICF in education would be very limited. In addition, a health-based conceptualisation of disability is not compatible with today's philosophy of inclusive education. The education of children with disabilities is no longer viewed as "special" or "remedial" aiming primarily at relieving the negative consequences of a health condition (for a critique of medical model in education, see Gabel, 2009). Such a medical approach to education is associated with special schools and segregated education systems, which have been discredited as a paradigmatic approach. Inclusive education is conceptualised as a life domain in which all children participate independent of the type of health condition they have (Florian & Black-Hawkins, 2011). The focus in education is not primarily to rehabilitate, but to educate. Education takes health conditions into account, but its main focus is on characteristics relevant for participation in education and for learning. Participation restrictions in education are not necessarily viewed as associated with a health condition, and these may or may not be contributing factors. Developmental delays and problems in biopsychosocial functioning may or may not be linked to biomedical problems. Social vulnerability due to poverty or neglect may or may not contribute to future functioning limitations and health problems. The value of the ICF in education setting would be to help analyse and understand the multiple interactions and interdependencies between educational provisions, participation, learning and the overall functioning of children, both at a specific moment in their lives as well as across time. But not using the concept of health condition as the organising principle to understand functioning will require some clarifications.

So what needs to be considered if the ICF is used in a broader context than to map functioning in the context of a health condition? In the context of a health condition, it is possible to differentiate between functional problems associated with the health condition and activity limitations that are believed to be non-health related (e.g. due to lack of opportunities to learn or socio-economic factors). For example, Down syndrome has generally an impact on the capacity to learn and is associated with difficulties in carrying out activities that are directly associated with learning (e.g. focusing attention, thinking). But if a child with Down syndrome is discouraged, sad and unmotivated in school, this would not be directly associated with the health condition. Consequently, reasons would be sought in the environment, for example in instructional strategies of the teacher that may not meet the child's needs. Depression or anorexia are not associated with a limitation of the capacity to learn, therefore problems in learning would be considered performance problems. Here, the emotional problems would be associated with functioning, not with the environment. Often, cerebral palsy does not necessarily affect the capacity to learn, but the child will experience difficulties in carrying out activities relevant for learning, such as speaking or fine hand use due to underlying impairments of neuro-musculoskeletal and movement-related functions. Frustration and discouragement here may be a direct consequence of an intelligent youngster not being able to express herself due to problems with articulation. Pre-established health conditions therefore provide the organising principle to distinguish between body functions, activity limitations and participation restrictions. It is against this background that the ICF excludes the classification of not health-related restrictions of participation "brought about by socioeconomic factors" (WHO, 2001, p. 7). Without a health condition as the guiding concept, the differentiation between activities and participation and between functioning and contextual factors is more complex and less specifiable.

From what has been said so far, two conclusions can be drawn. Firstly, breaking down a person's biopsychosocial functioning into the components and codes of the ICF is not necessarily straightforward, at least if used in education. It is the result of clinical reasoning and professional sense making, not a matter of objective observation and measurement. In the medical world, the primary outcome of this sense-making process is to first identify the disorder, which then provides the structure or organisational principle guiding the selection of the ICF codes. In education, professional sense making is broader and more diverse and the diagnostic criteria are less well described and more sensitive to the specific social context. In the past, education has borrowed from the health sciences to diagnose children, also to deflect from its own conceptual problems. But a purely functional and person-focussed approach to understanding complex life situations has been rightly criticised and to re-introduce it with the ICF would not be useful. Secondly, if a disorder is not presupposed and not used as the primary knowledge object to organise information, the differentiation between health-related and non-health-related information dissolves. The boundaries of what should be covered by the ICF and what not becomes less certain. Unlike health systems, education systems are environments and life domains in which children live and participate. Participation restrictions can have many reasons and the dynamics involved are complex. A transdisciplinary perspective bringing together the knowledge of different professionals is needed here, but the "methodological primacy of illness over health" (Keane, 2015, p. 70) cannot guide their sense-making process. The premise here is that the ICF is able to provide the necessary structure, but a different methodological approach needs to be developed. Before drafting such an approach, the consequences of abandoning "health condition" as the primary organising principle needs to be explored more, especially where the distinction between activities and participation is concerned.

Conceptualisations of activity and participation in education

The natural entry point for using the ICF in education settings is the concept of participation restriction, not a disorder. Participation restrictions can be observed and are experienced in the current environment. But how differentiate between activity and participation without presuming a specific health condition? And is such a differentiation even helpful in the context of education? The ICF introduces the capacity and performance constructs to help clarify the activity and participation component. The "capacity" construct strips away all contextual influences that are not directly necessary for the execution of a task. It is based on the premise that activities can be observed and measured in a "standard environment" (WHO, 2001, p. 11) to create a setting where people's innate abilities are revealed and objectively measured. When activity and participation domains are used together with the "capacity construct" (individual's ability to execute a task), they are considered as health domains. If used with the "performance construct" (what an individual does in his or her current environment), activity and participation domains are seen as health-related domains (WHO, 2001, p. 15; Cieza, Bickenbach, & Chatterji, 2008). Here as well, the differentiation is guided by the concept of disorders and the premise that clinical environments uncover a person's functional capacities a part from of their current life situation. This may be a valid method to assess basic functioning, but complex activities such as learning, communicating or creating and maintaining relationships are not as easily stripped off their social and cultural contexts. Education systems are directly involved in the acquisition and development of children's capacity to carry out such activities. Therefore the possibility that schools and teachers themselves have contributed or are contributing to functional problems cannot be excluded (e.g. negative effect of labelling and low expectations – see Clark, 1997). This raises three issues related to the differentiation between activity and participation and the use of the capacity and performance constructs. Firstly, is it adequate to use test performance as a proxy for capacity limitations or impairments, especially of mental functions? Secondly, how useful is the capacity construct when applied to complex activities like "respect and warmth in relationships" (d710)? Thirdly, is it adequate to use the same conceptualisation for simple life situations like "writing a message" and for comprehensive life situations like "learning to write?"

It is standard clinical practice to use low-test performance as a proxy for capacity limitations and impairments. The ICF cautions against simplistic differentiations between activities and participation and highlights the fact that different approaches of professionals and different theoretical frameworks may lead to different conclusions (WHO, 2001, p. 16). High-test performance is a good indicator for what a person is capable of, but there are many explanations for failure, especially where children are concerned. Many countries still today use low performance in intelligence tests as a proxy for intellectual disability (formerly mental retardation) (ICD-10; WHO, 1990). An IQ test score of around 70 or as high as 75 is used as an indicator of a limitation in intellectual functioning (Bergeron, Floyd, & Shands, 2008; AAIDD Definition online). Previously intellectual disability was conceptualised as a disorder, since the ICF was published, a redefinition is underway, but still debated (Harris & Greenspan, 2016). The World Health Organization suggests that "cognition" as a mental function should be captured with "b140, b144, b164 – Attention, memory and higher-level cognitive functions" (WHO, 2001, p. 253). Cognition as a broad mental function is inferred from test performance, not directly measured, as IQ tests require people to carry out activities rather than read brainwaves. The tested person needs to apply his/her knowledge (d160–d179), manage general tasks and demands (Chapter d2) and communicate (d3). They need to be moti-vated to carry out the tasks at hand; their education, upbringing and social background will have an impact as well. There is evidence that 30% to 50% of the variance in IQ tests is due to test motivation and other personal factors (Duckworth et al., 2011). If children are given one M&M candy for each cor-rect answer in an IQ test, then the "low–IQ children" improve their IQ scores from an average IQ of 79 to an IQ of 97 (Tough, 2012, 65). Clinical settings may be standard environments, but they do not affect all children in the same way depending on their cultural and social backgrounds (Reynolds & Suzuki, 2013). For example, children from minority groups are more frequently identi-fied as having an intellectual disability and have a higher risk of being referred to special schools or special classes (Artiles, 2003). Such evidence leaves little doubt: results of IQ tests are influenced by personal and environmental factors, reducing complex social dynamics to a permanent personal lack of capacity renders all information invisible that would be relevant for education.

Is the capacity construct of the ICF conceptualised as "functioning" and "health-related" at all useful in education? Once asked about the difference between activities and participation, the author of this book chapter responded: if everybody agrees, it is more about activity; if people disagree, then it is more about participation. In other words if the same limitation is observed consist-ently from different perspectives, by different people and across different social contexts, it is fair to assume the presence of a limitation of ability or "capacity". If all evidence on performance yields the same results, to infer from perfor-mance to capacity seems justified. But while it is easy to assess the capacity of using a pencil to produce symbols on a piece of paper (writing as an operation), it is more complex to assess the capacity of writing a letter (writing to commu-nicate) and even more difficult to assess the capacity of writing professionally for a newspaper (writing as remunerative employment). The more complex the activity, the less agreement there will be on operationalisation and the more difficult it will be to adequately assess such activities. This fact has led to endless debates in education around testing and its validity (Stein, 2016). In essence, the attempt to reduce complex social activities to simple actions that can be meas-ured in a standard environment has been abandoned in education in favour of more complex approaches to understanding "competence" (Elliot & Dweck, 2005).

One approach is to try to better understand the relationship between basic and complex activities. There are different theories in psychology exploring and describing the fact that human action is organised hierarchically; what people do can be broken down into smaller units or built up into larger units. Activity theory is one of the more prominent theories amongst these and of special importance to education. The theory distinguishes three levels (Leont'ev, 1959): "operations" are dependent on conditions in which they are carried out (walking straight on a line vs. walking uphill), "actions" are dependent on goals they seek to achieve (walking in the park with friends vs. walking to work) and "activities" or "occupations" are dependent on the motives that drive them (walking the Road to Santiago for recreation vs. as a spiritual journey). As illustrated earlier, "writing" can be understood as an operation, an action or an occupation (the term "activity" as defined by Leont'ev will not be used here to avoid confusion). The distinction between "operations", "actions" and "occupation" helps to clarify the relationship between basic and complex human activities. And differences in conditions, goals and motives can help explain the nature of the activity and the extent of experienced limitations. Actions are defined against what they seek to achieve; the "where" and "how" of actions depend on the purpose. In the ICF, the life domains provide orientation as to the broad function of the activities listed in a specific chapter. For example, in the ICF "writing" is represented as "d170 writing" (to convey information) and as "d345 writing messages" (to convey meaning through written language). What seems to be the same activity, is differentiated by the purpose the specific activity serves. The idea of capacity disregards these differences and the hierarchical nature of human action. It is therefore not a very useful construct to be applied to understand complex activities, especially not in education. Different operationalisations are needed that are able to create bridges between the ICF and concepts used in education. Participation as "involvement in life situations" is the starting point for such an endeavour, as mentioned in the beginning of this section. Therefore, some time will be spent now to lay the necessary foundations.

A situational approach to participation

The ultimate motivation to educate children is to affect their lives positively, promote growth and learning and help children become responsible adults. Learning to read and write, sitting quietly in class, showing respect to others on the playground and communicating are all means to this end. Similarly, using a pencil or a pen to write, walking into the classroom, hearing what the teacher says or seeing the blackboard are important because they help acquiring those means or tools relevant for participating and learning now and in the future. If functional problems restrict the use and development of these means, education needs to find other ways of promoting growth and learning. To focus on the broad vision of what education seeks to achieve is in line with Article 24 of the Convention on the Rights of Persons with Disabilities (CRPD; United Nations, 2006). For schools to find ways of overcoming barriers and provide learning opportunities accessible for all is the basic premise of inclusive education.

> Thus in the total flow of activity that forms human life, in its higher manifestations mediated by psychic reflection, analysis isolates separate (specific) activities in the first place according to the criterion of motives that elicit them. Then actions are isolated – processes that are subordinated to

conscious goals, finally, operations that directly depend on the conditions of attaining concrete goals.

(Leont'ev, 1978, 66f.)

In other words, education is about understanding the interplay between operations, actions and occupations (Leont'ev = activities) and finding ways to influence it positively. In this context, the ICF is useful to education to understand the impact of functional limitations on the overall life situation of children and how any negative impact on participation and learning can be minimised.

The ICF defines participation as "involvement in a life situation" and as the "lived experience" of people in the actual context in which they live (WHO, 2001, p. 123). Participation is at the same time social and personal; objective and subjective. Here, the social sciences provide the necessary theoretical background to understanding and analyse situations (Argyle, Furnham, & Graham, 1981; Magnusson, 1981; Lave & Wenger, 1991) and situational awareness (Endsley, 1995; Endsley & Jones, 2012). Situations do not exist as such, they are always framed by the expectations, motives, goals or intentions of the people involved (Hollenweger, 2016). While environmental factors pre-exist action, situations are created through them. Situational awareness brings outer and inner conditions together to inform action (Endsley, 2004). Following Leont'ev, life situations are defined by motives. People may be engaged in the same activity, but find themselves in different life situations. While teachers are teaching a subject, students may be engaged in learning, trying to establish relationships or attempting to avoid disappointments. Participation in class is more than presence or going through the necessary motions, it is about being engaged (behaviourally, emotionally, cognitively) in typical routines or sequences of actions, which are carried out in typical settings that are directed towards personally or socially meaningful goals (European Agency, 2011; see also UNICEF, 2015, 17f.). A situational definition of participation brings together information on "who" is acting (subject of the activity), "what" is acted upon (object of activity), on "what for" or "why" the actions are carried out (outcome of activity), as well as on "how" (method or tools used) and "where" (context of activity). A model to conceptualise participation in situations is introduced in the Train-the-Trainer Modules on Inclusive Education developed by UNICEF (2015, 21f.) as a simplified version of the model developed by Engeström (2001). This model can be used to map operations, actions and occupations (Leont'ev = activities), depending on the selected "horizon" of the situation (Husserl, 1929). Such a model can help to develop a better understanding of frictions and contradictions of specific situations and how they can be overcome.

The claim made here is that beyond the immediate context of a health condition, participation in life situations cannot be reduced legitimately to a merely functional concept. By definition, "involvement in life situations" brings in context and an operationalisation of participation should reflect this. But a person's "life situation" cannot be directly observed, but indirectly inferred by observing a person in different situations or incidences. For example, the same action (speaking) may be executed in various situations (e.g. oral exam vs. chat with a friend) and indicators for successful participation will vary across situations. To understand participation restrictions, the execution of activities and tasks therefore need to be evaluated against specific situations and compared across situations. Children who are able to adapt to different situations and use "speaking" to solve a broad variety of problems – convey messages to strangers, create and maintain relationships, appease a teacher, learn new things – show competence. The overall involvement in "speaking as a life situation" is best understood as a competence, a construct that cannot be disaggregated solely into functional components. Competence brings together skills, beliefs, motivation and a sense of self-efficacy. As a concept, it goes beyond the ICF but helps to establish links between psychological, sociological, educational and health perspectives on participation. Using the concept of competence to understand overall participation in a life domain also helps address the reservations that professionals working in education context have against the ICF. Many reject the premise that human actions can be broken down into functional components (e.g. medical model – see D'Alessio, 2011) and according to Reindal (2009), human action is social-relational, not individual-functional. Others complain about the fact that everything important to understand behaviour disorders seems to be subsumed under "personal factors" and thus not classifiable in the ICF (Stein, 2013). They rightly claim that especially for children, social background, education and upbringing describe life situations, not personal factors. If concerns of non-health professionals in education are to be taken seriously, assessment practices need to be reconsidered.

Assessment purposes in education

Assessment in education is about gaining information for shared problem solving, not about labelling children. The ICF can be used at each step of this process and thereby helps to develop a common understanding (Hollenweger, 2013). Problem solving in education follows a different logic from problem solving in health contexts. Its primary purpose is to ensure participation and learning, therefore assessment should primarily focus on identifying, assessing and understanding participation restrictions. The focus may be on operations, actions and occupations as explored earlier. Ideally, assessment is situational to help understand the interactions between micro and macro perspectives on participation restrictions. If performance restrictions are identified at the level of operations and can be observed in any situation, it is likely that underlying body functions will be impaired. If performance varies across situations, different conclusions need to be drawn. Assessment is always part of a sense-making process that guides data collection and analysis. Assessment as an activity is itself situational and assessment activities are framed by the motives of the assessor and guided by the expected outcomes. Unfortunately, most ICF-based assessment approaches developed for education purposes so far remain in the context of health conditions or pre-identified impairments and are guided by the positivistic belief that participation restrictions generally are health-related and therefore indicators of functional problems as documented in the ICF. The use of functional profile for educational planning reflects this thinking (e.g. in Italy, see Fusaro, Maspoli, & Vellar, 2009; in Portugal, see Sanches-Ferreira et al., 2013). The underlying premise is that all difficulties in participation can be conceptualised as functioning, thus belonging to or originating from the individual. Complex social and personal situations are dissected into functionality, atomised environments and isolated personal factors. Social problems are personalised and systemic influences or social dynamics slip out of focus. Such deficit-oriented thinking is still widespread despite being discredited as disempowering both for teachers and students (Garcia & Guerra, 2004). It would be counterproductive if the ICF was used in a way that reinforced such thinking. ICF-based information in education needs to guide professional activities, not to label children.

Unlike in health contexts, the ICF codes capturing functional problems are not necessarily the relevant codes to guide problem solving in education. In health settings, the codes describing nature and extent of impairments or activity limitations are generally indicative of key problems and able to direct or inform action or treatment. For example, a limitation in carrying out daily activities as assessed by the Functional Independence Measure for Children (WeeFIM) and coded with the ICF, describes the disability and sufficiently guides the interventions of the occupational therapist. But in education contexts, assessing functional limitations may be necessary but not sufficient to understand the life situation of a child and guide interventions. Functional profiles document functional problems by using stable sets of ICF codes (e.g. core sets). Situational analyses instead focus on life situations and explore the dynamics or interactions between functional limitations and other factors relevant for participation and learning. Planning processes are projections of present situations into the future and therefore require considerations about goals to be achieved and future situations to be created. Assessment in education serves three overall purposes: to understand where children are in their learning (summative, assessment of learning), to plan learning processes (prognostic, assessment for learning) or to promote learning (formative, assessment as learning). Functional profiles are not adequate or at least not sufficient to serve any of these purposes.

When using the ICF in education settings, it is therefore important to be aware of and reflect on the specific purpose of using specific codes. Should assessment practices lead to a description of functional limitations, should they describe participation restrictions experienced in a life situation or should they guide professional actions to achieve certain goals? For example, a functional profile can be developed for a boy with severe impairment of hearing functions as assessed in a clinical setting. Yet such a functional profile will not contain all relevant information about his social situation to decide about eligibility for social benefits within a national disability insurance system. For the education sector, the delay in acquiring social skills and the boy's impulsivity in the classroom might be more critical for decision making although these problems are not directly related to the health problem. ICF codes may be included because they describe functional problems in the context of a health condition, because they describe participation restrictions in the context of the current life situation, because they are relevant for decision making or because they inform teaching and learning. To avoid misunderstandings across professions and contexts, it would therefore be helpful to always provide the rationale for including codes.

Whether participation restrictions are best explained against expected health states, developmental trajectories, social relationships or competencies, is not always a clear-cut decision. Different professionals focus on different domains and components of the ICF depending on expertise and training. Participation restrictions may result from a mismatch between beliefs, expectations, skills or competencies of teachers and their students' characteristics or social and cultural background (Artiles & Zamora-Durán, 1997). Financing mechanism, interests of professional organisations and cultural differences may have an impact on identification and service provision (for dyslexia see Bühler-Niederberger, 1991). Different thresholds and diagnostic criteria used by different professionals to identify disorders or impairments result in different identification rates (OECD, 2007). Often faced with a dilemma, parents may avoid identification to prevent discrimination or force identification to benefit from disability compensations (Norwich, 2013). A child may draw the attention of the education system but go unnoticed by the health system and vice versa. Ultimately, assessment is a social practice and a social product (Filer, 2000), not something carried out in a vacuum and certainly not an infallible practice. When using the ICF beyond health contexts it is impossible to avoid these complexities. But rather than despair in the face of such complexities, procedures should be developed making use of the ICF to facilitate collaborative sense-making and problem-solving processes.

Conclusions for applying the ICF in education

The logic and primary objective of education is to make children competent citizens and to expand the scope of activities they are able to carry out, not to repair or amend functional limitations. Therefore, applying the ICF in education needs to appreciate the full complexity of participation restrictions as they present themselves in schools and other settings where children learn and acquire knowledge. Functional profiles organised around health conditions or pre-established impairments are of limited use and run the risk of misguiding educational decision making due to a deficit-oriented, person-centred, purely functional view of participation restrictions. Functional profiles do not provide a useful representation of the child's life situation and they fail to inform educational planning. Research evidence shows that the very beliefs and attitudes guiding such an assessment approach contribute to low achievement of vulnerable children and processes of social exclusion (Stanovich & Jordan, 1998, 2001). Representations and tools using ICF-based information need to be fit-for-purpose. Switzerland, for example, uses two different tools based on the ICF: one to facilitate the development of a common understanding of the school situation of a child by facilitating collaborative sense-making processes and the other to establish eligibility in educational settings by comparing the current situation (functioning, home and school contexts) with an envisaged future situation (goals, provision, settings) (Hollenweger, 2011, 2013; Hollenweger & Moretti, 2012). More efforts are needed to understand which ICF-based information is needed and how it should be represented to facilitate problem solving.

The argument was made here that in education, ICF as a common language and as a classification, needs to focus on participation restrictions, not health conditions. The conceptual challenges and uncertainties arising from such an approach have been highlighted. If participation restrictions are selected as the entry point, the concept of "life situations" needs to be better defined and specified. An attempt was made to provide such a definition to understand contexts in which "activities" are carried out rather than use the concept of a decontextualised, objectified "capacity" which is always hypothetical in non-clinical settings. An attempt was made to clarify the different scopes of "activities", their coverage or expansion in time and space to develop a better foundation for the analysis of participation restrictions. While operations depend on conditions, task or actions are characterised and identified by the goals or purposes they seek to achieve. The concept of competence was mentioned to define complex sequences of activities needed to participate in a life domain. Here, the overall motive or motivation that drives activities becomes important. Personal and social aspects of situations come together to create a specific life situation that may be viewed differently from different perspectives. The objective at hand is to understand how functional limitations impact on participation in life situations, not to reduce participation to a mere issue of functioning. Such an approach also opens up new ways to think about personal and environmental factors and the role they play together in creating life situations.

Participation in education and education as an environment are intricately interwoven, therefore an approach that analyses the respective life situations of participants from subjective or intersubjective perspectives is more adequate than assuming the positivistic position that one person can objectively and adequately assess another person's life situation to which they themselves substantially contribute (e.g. as teachers). A situational approach to define participation in the broadest sense as involvement in life situations was introduced – as used by the European Agency for Special Needs and Inclusive Education (2011) to develop a framework for indicators on participation in inclusive education. The idea was subsequently further developed to create the conceptual foundations for the UNICEF Train-the-Trainer Modules on Inclusive Education (UNICEF, 2015) which introduces the ICF as a common language for multidisciplinary teams, parents and students to be used when participation restrictions are experienced in the context of functional problems. This attempt was made on the premise, that professionals, parents and students need a clear understanding of what they seek to achieve by using ICF as a common language or as a classification and reflect on their own role as participants in the life situations of children with functional limitations and as potential barriers or facilitators for participation and learning.

Highlights from this chapter

- Beyond clinical settings, the distinction between capacity and performance is hypothetical and therefore not useful to guide educational planning.
- The notion of the interaction between functioning and environment in the ICF needs to be linked to the interaction of persons and systems as conceptualised in the social sciences.
- ICF-based functional profiles draw too much attention on the individual and deficits, while education needs to understand interactions and human potential.
- If the ICF is to help guide educational processes, conceptual bridges need to be built between participation as defined in the ICF and the concept of competence. For this purpose, more attention needs to be given to the notion of "life situation".

References

Argyle, M., Furnham, A., & Graham, J. A. (1981). *Social situations*. Cambridge: Cambridge University Press.

Artiles, A. J. (2003). Special education's changing identity: Paradoxes and dilemmas in views of culture and space. *Harvard Educational Review, 73*, 164–202.

Artiles, A. J., & Zamora-Durán, G. (Eds.). (1997). *Reducing disproportionate representation of culturally diverse students in special and gifted education*. Reston, VA: Council for Exceptional Children.

Bergeron, R., Floyd, R. G., & Shands, E. I. (2008). States' eligibility guidelines for mental retardation: An update and consideration of part scores and unreliability of IQs. *Education and Training in Developmental Disabilities, 43*(1), 123–131.

Bühler-Niederberger, D. (1991). *Legasthenie: Geschiche und Folgen einer Pathologisierung* [Dyslexia: History and Consequences of a Pathologisation]. Opladen: Leske + Budrich.

Cieza, A., Bickenbach, J., & Chatterji, S. (2008). The ICF as a conceptual platform to specify and discuss health and health-related concepts. *Gesundheitswesen, 70*(10), e47–e56.

Clark, M. D. (1997). Teacher response to learning disability: A test of attributional principles. *Journal of Learning Disabilities, 30*(1), 69–79.

D'Alessio, S. (2011). *Inclusive education in Italy: A critical analysis of the policy of integrazione scolastica.* Rotterdam: Sense Publishers

Duckworth, A. L., Quinn, P. D., Lynam, D. R., Loeber, R., & Stouthamer-Loeber, M. (2011). Role of test motivation in intelligence testing. *Proceedings of the National Academy of Sciences, 108*(19), 7716–7720.

Elliot, A. J., & Dweck, C. S. (2005). *Handbook of competence and motivation.* New York: Guilford.

Endsley, M. R. (1995). Toward a theory of situation awareness in dynamic systems. *Human Factors: The Journal of the Human Factors and Ergonomics Society, 37*(1), 32–64.

Endsley, M.R. (2004). Situation awareness: progress and directions. In: Banbury S, Tremblay S (eds) *A cognitive approach to situation awareness: theory, measurement and application.* (pp. 317–341). Aldershot, UK: Ashgate publishing.

Endsley, M.R., & Jones, D.G. (2012). *Designing for situation awareness: An approach to human-centered design,* 2nd edn. London: Taylor and Francis.

Engeström, Y. (2001): Expansive learning at work: Toward an activity theoretical reconceptualization. *Journal of Education and Work, 14*(1), 133–156.

European Agency for Development in Special Needs Education. (2011). *Participation in inclusive education: A framework for developing indicators.* Report prepared by J. Hollenweger, M. Rouse, M. Kyriazopoulou and H. Weber. Brussels and Odense: European Agency.

Filer, A. (Ed.). (2000). *Assessment: Social practice and social product.* London: Routledge.

Florian, L., & Black-Hawkins, K. (2011). Exploring inclusive pedagogy. *British Journal of Educational Research, 37*(5), 813–828.

Fusaro, G., Maspoli, M., & Vellar, G. (2009). The ICF-based functioning profiles of school children in care with the neuropsychiatric community services in the Piedmont region: Evidences for better caring and programming. *Disability & Rehabilitation, 31*(S1), S61–S66.

Gabel, S. L. (Ed.). (2009). *Disability studies in education: Readings in theory and method.* New York: Peter Land.

Garcia, S. B., & Guerra, P. L. (2004). Deconstructing deficit thinking: Working with educators to create more equitable learning environments. *Education and Urban Society, 36*(2), 150–168.

Harris, J. C., & Greenspan, S. (2016). Definition and nature of intellectual disability. In N. N. Singh (Ed.), *Handbook of evidence-based practices in intellectual and developmental disabilities* (pp. 11–39). Switzerland: Springer International Publishing.

Hollenweger, J. (2011). Development of an ICF-based eligibility procedure for education in Switzerland. *BMC Public Health, 11*(S4), S7.

Hollenweger, J. (2013). Developing applications of the ICF in education systems: Addressing issues of knowledge creation, management and transfer. *Disability & Rehabilitation, 35*(13), 1087–1091.

Hollenweger, J., & Moretti, M. (2012). Using the international classification of functioning, disability and health children and youth version in education systems: A new approach to eligibility. *American Journal of Physical Medicine and Rehabilitation, 91*(13 Suppl 1), S97–S102.

Hollenweger, J. (2016). Situation Analysis. In I. Hedderich, G. Biewer, J. Hollenweger, R. Markowetz (eds). *Manual Inclusion and Special Education.* Bad Heilbrunn: Julius Klinkhardt, 674–679.

Husserl, E. (1929). Formale und transzendental Logik. Versuch einer Kritik der logischen Vernunft- [Formal and transcendental logic: An attempt at a critique of logical reason.] In *Jahrbuch für Philosophie und phänomenologische Forschung,* 10 (pp. 1–298). Halle: Max Niemeyer.

Jordan, A., & Stanovich, P. (2001). Patterns of teacher-student interaction in inclusive elementary classroom and correlates with student self-concept. *International Journal of Disability, Development and Education, 48*, 43–62.

Keane, N. (2015). On the origins of illness and the hiddenness of health: A hermeneutic approach to the history of the problem. In D. Meacham (Ed.), *Medicine and society: New perspectives in continental philosophy.* (pp. 57–72). Dortrecht: Springer.

Lave, J., & Wenger, E. (1991). *Situated learning: Legitimate peripheral participation.* New York: Cambridge University Press.

Leont'ev, A. N. (1978). *Activity, consciousness, and personality.* Englewood Cliffs, NJ: Prentice Hall.

Leont'ev, A. N. (1959). *Probleme der entwicklung des psychischen [Problems of the development of the mind].* Berlin: Volk und Wissen Verlag.

Magnusson, D. (1981). Wanted: A psychology of situations. In D. Magnusson (Ed.), *Toward a psychology of situations: An international perspective* (pp. 9–32). Hillsdale, NY.

Norwich, B. (2013). *Addressing tensions and dilemmas in inclusive education: Living with uncertainty.* London and New York: Routledge.

OECD. (2007). *Students with disabilities, learning difficulties and disadvantages: Policies, statistics and indicators.* Paris: OECD.

Reindal, S. M. (2009). Disability, capability, and special education: Towards a capability based theory. *European Journal of Special Needs Education, 24*(2), 155–168.

Reynolds, C. R., & Suzuki, L. (2013). *Bias in psychological assessment: An empirical review and recommendations.* Hoboken, NJ: Wiley.

Sanches-Ferreira, M., Simeonsson, R. J., Silveira-Maia, M., Alves S, Tavares, A., & Pinheiro, S. (2013). Portugal's special education law: Implementing the International Classification of Functioning, Disability and Health in policy and practice. *Disability & Rehabilitation, 35*(10), 868–873.

Stanovich, P., & Jordan, A. (1998). Canadian teachers' and principals' beliefs about inclusive education as predictors of effective teaching in heterogeneous classrooms. *Elementary School Journal, 98*, 221–238.

Stein, R. (2013). Kritik der ICF – eine Analyse im Hinblick auf die Klassifikation von Verhaltensstörungen [Critique of the ICF – an analysis with regard to the classification of behavioural disorders]. *Zeitschrift für Heilpädagogik, 64*(3), 106–115.

Stein, Z. (2016). *Social justice and educational measurement: John Rawls, the history of testing and the future of education.* London and New York: Routledge.

Tough, P. (2012). *How children succeed: Grit curiosity and the hidden power of character.* Boston, New York: Houghton Mifflin Harcourt.

UNICEF. (2015). *Trainer-of-trainer modules on inclusive education: Introductory module.* Author: Judith Hollenweger with contributions from Paula F. Hunt and Nora Sabani. New York: UNICEF.

United Nations (2006). Convention on the Rights of Persons with Disabilities. Retrieved from: https://www.un.org/development/desa/disabilities/convention-on-the-rights-of-persons-with-disabilities/convention-on-the-rights-of-persons-with-disabilities-2.html

World Health Organization (WHO). (1980). *International Classification of Impairments, Disabilities, and Handicaps (ICIDH).* Geneva: WHO.

World Health Organization (WHO). (1990). *International Classification of Diseases and Related Health Problems (ICD-10).* Geneva: WHO.

World Health Organization (WHO). (2001). *International Classification of Functioning, Disability and Health (ICF).* Geneva: WHO.

Part II

Contributions of the ICF to policy on education and care

Chapter 3

The education health and care planning process in England

Susana Castro and Olympia Palikara

Introduction

The definition of special educational needs and disabilities has changed considerably over time. These changes were often accompanied by modifications in the classification of special educational needs and disability (SEND) and in policy regulating its provision. In this context of change, classifications of disability are relevant because they reflect society's conceptions of disability and consequently the structure and organisation of services to address the observed needs of disabled people (Florian & McLaughlin, 2008).

In England, recent policy measures have introduced substantial change in the support services for children with SEND. These changes have been considered radically new (DfE, 2011) and reflect a willingness to shift the way that SEND are conceived. However, some controversy regarding the definition of SEND adopted in England seems to prevail; according to Norwich (2014), some of the changes introduced are not entirely new, but extend or expand previously introduced regulations.

Given the current picture of the political context in SEND provision in England, this chapter will provide: 1) a critical overview of the situation regarding support and provision for children with SEND in England; 2) an account of how the International Classification of Functioning, Disability and Health (ICF; WHO, 2001, 2007) could be regarded as the theoretical framework and taxonomy to support the implementation of the new SEND policy in England, with a specific focus on the practical contributions of the ICF for the education health and care (EHC) planning process; and 3) an illustrative case study providing a critical analysis of one EHC plan.

A critical overview of the situation regarding support and provision for children with special educational needs and disabilities in England

As in many other countries, the definition of SEND in England has observed substantial change throughout the twentieth century, from a medical conceptualisation of disability to a much more holistic approach, largely favoured by the human rights movements and social models of disabilities of the '60s and '70s (Simeonsson, 2006). Since the early twentieth century, a number of regulations for provision of care for children and young people with disabilities have been introduced in England. The 1944 Education Act (UK Parliament, 1944) categorised disability in medical terms with children considered *educationally subnormal* being segregated from mainstream educational institutions (Hodkinson, 2015). However, in 1979, the Warnock report, along with the 1981 Education Act introduced a radical change in the way services were provided for children with SEND, reflecting a revolutionary shift in the conception of special educational needs. According to these policy documents, children with SEND should have individual *statements*[1] reflecting an integrative provision, specifying educational goals for children of different abilities and promoting *inclusion* (Central Council for Education and Training in Social Work Great Britain & Warnock, 1979). Throughout the 1980s and 1990s, the Warnock report remained the key policy document regulating SEND provision, with consequent reduction in the number of special schools and a gradual increase in the number of children identified as having a *statement* of SEND. In 1997, the Green Paper *Excellence for all Children Meeting Special Educational Needs* was released by the new Labour Government in support of the United Nations statements which called for increased inclusion in mainstream settings. This was followed by the Special Educational Needs and Disabilities Act (SENDA; British Parliament, 2001), which provided an amendment to the Disability Discrimination Act (1995), by highlighting the rights of people with disability regarding education provision. In 2004 the Department for Education released the *Removing Barriers to Achievement: The Government's Strategy for SEN* document, aiming to increase access to education by children with SEN, raising standards of teaching and learning and strengthening partnerships between parents professionals and children. Despite these efforts the proportion of children in mainstream schools seemed to have remained stable since 2002; according to the Ofsted report *Special Education Needs and Disability: Towards Inclusive Schools* (2004), this has to do with staff attitudes, the facilities available and lack of appropriate teacher training. In 2005, a new report by Warnock called for the need to review the concept of special educational needs (SEN) and the actual concept of inclusion as well. The Baroness has stated that the statements should be considered only to children going to special schools and mainstream schools should only cater for SEN children when resources can be allocated by the school itself. In 2010, the Equality Act (which still regulates the definition of SEND today) was published, calling for the need to develop a specialised, often differentiated provision for people with disabilities, in order to ensure that these people have access to the same opportunities as those without1 disabilities (UK Parliament, 2010). In 2011, the Conservative/Liberal Democrat Coalition Government launched the *Support and Aspiration: A New Approach to Special Educational Needs and Disability* proposing a radically different system to support children with SEND, their parents and professionals. Recently, in 2014, the Children and Families Act along with the new SEND Code of Practice aimed to regulate the implementation of some of these radical reforms previously proposed in 2011. Castro and Palikara (2016) discussed the challenges and potential contradictions introduced by this new policy – namely, the definition of SEND focusing primary on *participation* outcomes, but conflicting with the Equality Act 2010 and its "types" of SEND, still in use; the emphasis on multi-agency working, without a clear framework to support communication and articulation between services; and the implementation of EHC plans, again, without a clear system to integrate the three sources of provision. Even though some of the introduced changes are aligned with international recommended practices, such as the integration of services, there is a lack of a common framework and system to enable professionals from different disciplines to work together in a collaborative, integrative and efficient manner. Castro and Palikara (2016) have described extensively how the ICF could contribute to establish this cross-discipline partnership using the ICF framework. In the following section, we will present the key points made by the authors.

The potential of the International Classification of Functioning Disability and Health as the theoretical framework and taxonomy to support the implementation of the new SEND policy in England

The International Classification of Functioning, Disability and Health (ICF) is the classification for disability endorsed by the WHO since 2001. In 2007, a children and youth version was also published (WHO, 2007). The ICF is based on a biopsychosocial model of disability, according to which within a specific health condition or status, each individual presents a unique functioning profile. This profile is characterised by a combination of *body functions and structures*, *activities and participation* and *environmental factors*, which altogether characterise the individual's behaviour and main life areas. The classification system comprises a set of codes for each of these three components. In order to describe an individual's functioning profile a selection of codes may be used, resulting in an individual holistic and detailed picture of the person or child. In addition to the code describing an individual or social feature of the child, a universal qualifier digit is added to describe the magnitude of the problem observed (from 0 – absence of problem – to 4 – complete problem) (WHO, 2001, 2007). Although the ICF is a classification system, and not an assessment instrument, this structural organisation in codes and qualifiers provides an excellent framework for the development of assessment measures of different aspects of an individual's life, overcoming the problem often faced when using diagnosis-based measures: two or more children with the same condition, actually have very distinct functioning profiles (e.g. Lollar & Simeonsson, 2005); this has been empirically observed by Castro and Pinto (2015) who developed an ICF-based observation tool for young children with SEND – the *Matrix for Assessment of Activities and Participation*; this tool was administered to a group of children with autism spectrum disorders, a group of children with various other types of SEND and a group of typically developing children; when performing a cluster analysis of the scores regarding these children's functioning characteristics, the authors observed that children with the same diagnosis would not group in one cluster, but rather they would group with other children of similar functioning severity regardless of the diagnosis; functioning predicted scoring more than the diagnosis. This shows that the use of a classification system such as the ICF has the potential to provide much more detailed and informative data for the purpose of conducting interventions, especially in educational settings. Diagnosis-based data provides very general information that often does not differentiate needs in natural daily life contexts. Therefore, and as extensively argued by Castro and Palikara (2016), there seems to be a theoretical overlap between the ideology portrayed in the new SEND policy in England and the ideology of the ICF. For example, the recommendation for holistic assessment of the child with SEND with a focus on participation outcomes according to the new law, can be facilitated by using a holistic framework and system, such as the ICF; the holistic assessment proposed aims to integrate health–related issues (potentially covered by the body functions and Structures component of the ICF), education-related issues (potentially covered by the activities and participation component of the ICF) and with a social context of care (potentially covered by the environmental factors component of the ICF). However, for a true holistic assessment, a clear separation between health, education and social care is artificial and ways of articulating information resulting from all three areas are needed. Adapting the ICF model to be used for this purpose has been considered promising (Norwich, 2016). In the following sections of this chapter, we will present an illustration of some of the problems currently observed in the newly developed EHC plans and ways by which the ICF could support the EHC planning process in England.

An illustrative case study providing a critical analysis of EHC plans in England

In the scope of a research project funded by the British Academy and the Leverhulme Trust (reference SG142214), the authors of this chapter are analysing EHC plans from a variety of different London Local Authorities, developed between 2015 and 2017. This analysis is being conducted at two overarching levels: the first addresses the level of consistency across plans in each section and according to the new policy's recommendations (the "HOW it's been done"); the second addresses the issue of the extent to which these plans are indeed biopsychosocial and holistic – are they efficiently integrating health, education and social care? (the "WHAT is being covered"). To address the first overarching level of analysis, inductive thematic analysis is being performed across plans, to identify the main themes covered in each section of the EHC plan and their frequency across plans; to address the second overarching level of analysis, deductive content analysis using the ICF codes as a pre-defined matrix of categories is being conducted, following ICF-based content analysis methods described in the literature (Castro, Pinto, & Simeonsson, 2014; Cieza, Fayed, Bickenbach, & Prodinger, 2016). Table 3.1 illustrates the usual structure of the EHC plans currently developed in England and the focus of analysis considered in the scope of this research project, per section of the plan.

In order to illustrate some of the preliminary results of this study, a case study will be presented, which reflects some of the issues that have been observed across the majority of EHC plans analysed.

The case under analysis is the EHC plan of a 5-year-old child (B).

First level of analysis – consistency across plans according the new policy's recommendation: the HOW it is done

The first section of the plan, as illustrated in Table 3.1, concerns the views, interests and aspirations of the child and their parents. In this section of B's plan, it was stated, "*I constantly progress in all areas. My speech is slowly but surely developing in three languages and I am loving school and starting to develop relationship with peers*". The main issue observed in this section (as an illustration of what happens across many EHC plans) is that there is no mention to whether this was the actual child's statement or the parents' understanding of the child's point of view. It is unlikely that such statement has been voiced by the child herself; however, the quote makes use of the first person in direct discourse. If this is the child's own statement it is necessary to document how the child's point of view was obtained, what were the strategies used and how the child has expressed her views. On the other hand, if this is the parents' perspective, the use of direct discourse from the point of view of the child is inaccurate and raises ethical concerns regarding its authenticity. Therefore, if we consider the points of analysis that we aim to address in this section of the EHC plan (see Table 3.1, section A), it is unclear how the voice of the child is portrayed, or whether it is the perspective of the child herself or the parents' at stake; however, it's interesting to observe that there is a focus on abilities and capacities of the child, rather than a discourse based on needs and deficits. This is highly informative for intervention purposes, as it gives the professionals a good picture of the child's current functioning level and main interests/motivations.

Sections B, C and D of the EHC plans refer to the education, health and social care needs of the child, respectively (see Table 3.1). In B's EHC plan, although information from all three domains is included, these are split, following the actual pre-defined structure of the EHC plan. This might justify why some of the information included in this section – namely, health-related information – seems detached from the rest of the child's needs: "*She has bilateral retinal Columbus, absent bilateral 6th cranial nerves, bilateral labyrinthine dysplasia with*

Table 3.1 Plan for the analysis of EHC plans in the scope of the funded British Academy Project "A Quality Evaluation Study of EHC Plans" (SG142214)

Section of the EHC Plan	Focus of the Analysis	Type of Analysis	
		Inductive (themes across plans)	Deductive Using ICF Codes
SECTION A (The views, interests and aspirations of the child and their parents, or of the young person)	• How is the voice of the child portrayed? • Is it clear that the content provided is the child's own view, or is it just the use of the first person? • If it's the parents' view, is it explicit? • How were the views of the children obtained? • How is the quality of the discourse in terms of a focus on abilities or disabilities? • What is the prevalence of needs and abilities related to body functions and structures, to activities and participation and to environmental factors? (What are the priorities for the child or parents?)	✓	✓
SECTION B (Strengths and SENs)	• How is the quality of the discourse in terms of a focus on abilities or disabilities?	✓	
SECTION C (Health Needs related to SEN)	• How is the quality of the information in terms of the severity of needs described? • How is the quality of the discourse in terms of using a lay language?		
SECTION D (Social Care needs related to SEN)	• How are health education and social care articulated? What is the prevalence of needs related to body functions and structures, to activities and participation and to environmental factors?		✓
SECTION E (Outcomes)	• Are the main needs defined in sections B C and D being targeted in the outcomes (is there a match between the ICF components observed in these sections and the ones observed in the outcomes)?		✓

- How specific are the outcomes in terms of the behaviours that will be achieved and the expected timeframe for achievement? ✓

SECTIONS F, G
(Provision)

- What characterises the resources put in place in terms of type of environmental factors? Is there a range of social, educational and health related resources?
- How does the support put in place match the outcomes and needs previously defined? ✓
- How specific are the strategies defined?
- How are health, education and social care provisions articulated?

SECTION I
(Placement)
SECTION J
(Personal Budget)

Frequency of type of provision

SECTION K
(Contributors)

Who are the contributors and how have they contributed to the plan (report, meeting, etc.)?

rudimentary posterior semi-circular canals, microcephaly and intention tremors". Information regarding the needs of the child that uses such technical terminology is not integrative, useful for all professionals from different fields supposedly working together to address the child's needs and certainly not clear for most parents. B's educational needs are described as *"needs frequent adult models to show her how to use spoken language for communicative purposes in different contexts before she spontaneously demonstrates and generalises the use of spoken language, gestures and body language in different contexts"*. Even though this describes communication needs of the child, it is unclear for those who read this section what is the level of support that is actually needed and which contexts of her daily life are being considered. We also do not have any potential reasons as to why these are particular needs of the child; pointing out potential reasons would provide a rationale for the development of intervention outcomes matching the needs observed. In sum, and addressing the points of analysis presented in Table 3.1, the quality of the discourse used to describe the needs of the child over-emphasises deficits without providing a picture of the current level of ability; there is no indication regarding the level of severity of the needs expressed, and the content of this section is not integrated; rather, it is split between health-only and education-only issues, often written in too technical terms.

Section E of the EHC plan describes the outcomes designed to address the child's needs. In B's EHC plan, we can read,

> B. will develop her play, cognition and learning skills, to a level where she can: Access a range of social and learning opportunities; Access learning opportunities within the context of her abilities, so that she can reach her potential as a learner.

This quote illustrates a common problem of many EHC plans analysed: outcomes are quite broad and could apply to all children; in the example provided, it would be necessary to further explain what kind of learning opportunities are to be provided; the outcome is not individualised, as all provision aims to help children reach their potential as learners; the question here is, for this child, what are the specific characteristics of the her learning profile, and what specific opportunities should be provided to match those characteristics.

In sections F, G and H, different forms of provision should be presented to match the outcomes included in section E. Considering the example provided earlier of an outcome developed for child B., section F of A's EHC plan indicates that this outcome should be targeted by the education sector, but not by the health or social care sectors. This does not match the multi-agency work model, as one cannot consider that health and social care professionals will not work towards promoting *play, cognition and learning skills to a level where the child can (. . .) reach her potential as a learner*. This artificial separation of provision measures is probably the result of the artificial separation in terms of description of needs and outcomes across EHC. A common system is required to describe needs and develop outcomes that can be targeted in an integrated way, as proposed by the new policy for SEND. This is a common problem observed in many of the EHC plans developed to this date.

The last section of the EHC plan under analysis refers to the contributors to the plan; although there are a good number of contributors across sectors, their role seems to be limited to having provided a written report; there is no mention to any form of integrated assessment and the parents' contribution is also not described.

Second level of analysis – deductive content analysis using the ICF codes: the WHAT is being covered

The EHC plans under analysis in the scope of the British Academy funded project were deductively linked with the ICF, following the recommended procedure for linking content with the ICF as well as the methodology adopted in previous studies of similar nature (Castro, Pinto & Simeonsson, 2014; Cieza, Fayed, Bickenbach, & Prodinger, 2016). This procedure was conducted section by section across plans. Frequencies of ICF components (body functions and structures, activities and participation and environmental factors) were computed.

Figure 3.1 illustrates the frequency of these components across sections of B's EHC plan. In this case, there seems to be a focus on activities and participation,

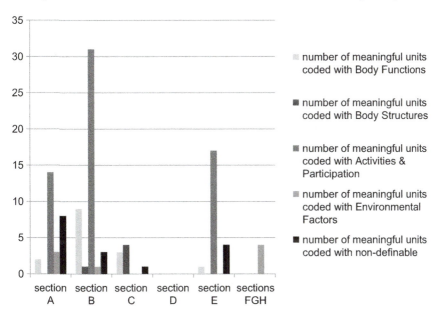

Figure 3.1 Number of ICF components found to match the different sections of B's EHC plan

which makes sense if we consider previously presented results: that the main contribution and direct involvement in the development of this plan was from the education sector and that there is a lack of health and social care integration. The increased number of body functions and structures in section C is illustrative of the over-emphasis on health-related issues in this section, without a clear link to participation outcomes. It is equally striking to see that section D was not coded with any ICF categories, reflecting the fact that this plan does not describe any social care needs. Considering that any participation outcome would necessarily involve a social dimension, this absence seems to be again the result of an artificial separation between intervention sectors. The majority of the outcomes included (section E) is linked to activities and participation, thus matching the needs described in section B, although the way this is done leaves room for considerable improvement in terms of individualisation and specification. Sections FGH document strategies adopted and resources needed. Resources were coded as environmental factors, but strategies were too broad and vague to be coded, thus demonstrating once again the need for a more specialised individualisation of these plans.

In sum, the example provided illustrates some of the issues that have been consistently observed across EHC plans. The analysis of the plans highlights the theoretical gap previously discussed (Castro & Palikara, 2016) between ideology and implementation regarding the new policy for SEND provision in England. Specifically, the voices of children are not being accurately documented, with the parents' views being taken as the children's in a direct discourse form that raises ethical issues; the is not a focus on participation (as proposed by the new policy), with entire sections focusing exclusively on health issues, which are not easily understandable by lay people; multi-agency working seems to be quite challenging still, with the three sectors (education, health and social care) working independently and with a disproportionate contribution of education on its own.

Concluding remarks

In recent times, much has been researched and written on applications of the ICF to educational settings (e.g. Sanches-Ferreira et al., 2013; Hollenweger, 2011; Norwich, 2016). Reports on the implementation of the ICF as a tool to support eligibility of children for the support services have been obtained from Portugal, one of the countries where the ICF was implemented by law. Sanches-Ferreira and colleagues (2013) analysed the individualised education programs and respective goals written for the pupils before and after the introduction of the ICF by law, having concluded that the use of the ICF favoured: more detailed and individualised portrayals of pupils' functioning, more emphasis on the role of the environment in influencing participation outcomes and a better match between goals and strategies planned. In Switzerland, a team lead by Hollenweger (2011, 2014) has developed a set of materials and models supporting the adoption of the ICF in the education system, particularly focusing on eligibility in accordance with the UN Convention on the Rights of Persons with Disability; according to Norwich (2016), the ICF is of particular relevance for the English context as it has the potential to address key issues in the recent history of identifying SEND in England; these issues are to ensure parent and child assessment rights to an adequate and relevant assessment and to participate in accessible and user-friendly assessment; adopt an interactive causal model of disability; be holistic; relevant to a range of areas of functioning; cover personal strengths not just difficulties; and support inter-professional collaboration (Norwich, 2016).

In this chapter, we make the case for the adoption of the ICF system in England, in particular to support the development of holistic and accurate EHC plans. There are three ways by which the ICF could support the new SEND policy and practice: as a tool for eligibility, as a tool for problem solving and as a tool to facilitate multi-agency working.

As a tool for eligibility, the ICF has the potential to overcome the previously mentioned contradiction between the willingness to focus on participation outcomes for children with SEND, but still relying on the definition of SEND presented in the Equality Act 2010, which is closer to a medical model of disability than to a participation/functioning based one (Castro & Palikara, 2016; Norwich, 2014). The ICF can provide a participation-focused framework for eligibility. The Swiss and the Portuguese models are good examples of how to do this, and they are of relevance for the English context. Both models included training for professionals, expert consultation and research trials.

The ICF has been proved to support rehabilitation and special needs provision in multi-agency teams (Adolfsson, Granlund, Björck-Åkesson, Ibragimova, & Pless, 2010). Its multidisciplinary structure provides a good basis for different services to develop hypothesis-oriented plans, which involve education, health and social care. Multi-agency working is a recognised principle in special education provision (e.g. Mitchell, 2013; Wilkinson, 2012; David, 2013); however, there are still considerable concerns about how to implement multidisciplinary actions in assessment and intervention, particularly in the context of the new policy for special education needs provision in England (Norwich, 2014). A problem-solving framework is very helpful in situations where decision making is necessary from a variety of individuals with different roles. In the general education and specifically in the special education context, problem-solving models for decision making have long been recognised has helpful means of achieving consensual solutions (Marston, Muyskens, Lau, & Canter, 2003; Tilly, 2002; Abbott, Townsley, & Watson, 2005). We posit that the deductive nature of problem-solving procedures provides a safe stage for action in the rather subjective field of special education provision, particularly in the current English SEND system and the ICF system provides the content for establishing hypothesis oriented goals (Adolfsson, Granlund, Björck-Åkesson, Ibragimova, & Pless, 2010).

Regardless of the potential of the ICF to be included in the English special education system as a tool for eligibility or problem solving in multi-agency teams, it can certainly be regarded as a tool to support research on the quality of provision. The British Academy funded project "A Quality Evaluation Study of EHC Plans" has provided data to support the adoption of the ICF system as tool to monitor the quality of the newly developed EHC plans, the quality of multi-agency working, the level and quality of parental and child involvement in the EHC plan development and the quality of the match between individual provision and individual needs assessed.

Highlights from this chapter

- Recent changes in special education provision legislation in England reflect a change in conceptualising assessment and intervention for children in need of special support; these changes require coordinated efforts from the education, health and social care sectors to provide a holistic provision to each child with special needs. The EHC plans should reflect this integration of services.
- There have been some critical analyses of this new SEND policy in England, particularly because the changes were introduced without a clear theoretical framework or classification system to support its implementation. It has been argued that the ICF can provide a relevant theoretical framework to support the implementation of the new SEND policy.
- This chapter presented an ICF-based analysis of an EHC plan, as an example of the data currently being analysed in the scope of the British Funded project "A Quality Evaluation Study of EHC Plans". This data suggests that there are some problems with the current EHC plans being developed: lack of detailed and individualised information that integrates education, health and social issues effectively; lack of accuracy in giving voice to the children's and the parents' perspectives; and poor match between outcomes and provision.
- This analysis has been enabled by the use of the ICF as a multidisciplinary, evidence-based classification system to describe functioning and disability.

Note

1 Statements are the documents that, according to this legislation mentioned earlier, formalised the special educational needs of the children.

References

Abbott, D., Townsley, R., & Watson, D. (2005). Multi-agency working in services for disabled children: what impact does it have on professionals?. *Health & Social Care in the Community, 13*(2), 155–163.

Adolfsson, M., Granlund, M., Björck-Åkesson, E., Ibragimova, N., & Pless, M. (2010). Exploring changes over time in habilitation professionals' perceptions and applications of the International Classification of Functioning, Disability and Health, Version for Children and Youth (ICF-CY). *Journal of Rehabilitation Medicine, 42*(7), 670–678.

Castro, S., & Palikara, O. (2016). Mind the gap: The new special educational needs and disability legislation in England. *Frontiers in Education* (Vol. 1, p. 4). Frontiers.

Castro, S., & Pinto, A. (2015). Matrix for assessment of activities and participation: Measuring functioning beyond diagnosis in young children with disabilities. *Developmental Neurorehabilitation, 18*(3), 177–189. doi:10.3109/17518423.2013.806963

Castro, S., Pinto, A., & Simeonsson, R. J. (2014). Content analysis of Portuguese individualized education programmes for young children with autism using the ICF-CY framework. *Europen Early Childhood Education Research Journal, 22*, 91–104. doi:10.1080/1350293X.2012.704303

Central Council for Education and Training in Social Work (Great Britain), & Warnock, M. (1979). *Report of the committee of inquiry into the education of handicapped children and young people.* Warnock Report.

Cieza, A., Fayed, N., Bickenbach, J., & Prodinger, B. (2016). Refinements of the ICF linking rules to strengthen their potential for establishing comparability of health information. *Disability and Rehabilitation, 17* 1–10.

David, T. (Ed) (2013). *Working together for young children: Multi-professionalism in action.* New York: Routledge.

Department for Education. (2011). *Support and aspiration: A new approach to special educational needs and disability: A consultation,* Vol. 8027. London: Stationery Office.

Florian, L., & McLaughlin, M. J. (2008). *Disability classification in education: Issues and perspectives.* Corwin Press.

HMSO. (1995). The Disability Discrimination Act 1995 explanatory notes. Retrieved from www.drc.org.uk/uploaded_files/documents/2008_227_copemployment.rtf

HMSO. (2001). *Special educational needs and disability act 2001, explanatory notes.* London: The Stationery Office.

Hodkinson, A. (2015). *Key issues in special educational needs and inclusion.* London: Sage.

Hollenweger, J. (2011). Development of an ICF-based eligibility procedure for education in Switzerland. *BMC Public Health, 11*(Suppl 4), S7.

Hollenweger, J. (2014). *Special education today in Switzerland. Special education international perspectives: Practices across the globe* (Advances in Special Education, Vol. 28, pp. 243–269). Bingley, UK: Emerald Group Publishing Limited.

Lollar, D. J., and Simeonsson, R. J. (2005). Diagnosis to function: Classification for children and youths. *Journla of Developmental & Behavioral Pediatrics, 26*, 323–330. doi:10.1097/0000 4703-200508000-00012

Marston, D., Muyskens, P., Lau, M., & Canter, A. (2003). Problem-solving model for decision making with high-incidence disabilities: The Minneapolis experience. *Learning Disabilities Research & Practice, 18*(3), 187–200.

Mitchell, H. (2013). Multi-professional working in the early years. In M. Wild & A. Street (Eds.) *Themes and debates in early childhood,* (pp. 141–155). London: Sage

Norwich, B. (2014). Changing policy and legislation and its effects on inclusive and special education: A perspective from England. *British Journal of Special Education, 41*, 403–425. doi:10.1111/1467-8578.12079

Norwich, B. (2016). Conceptualising special educational needs using a bio-psycho-social model in England: The prospects and challenges of using the International Classification of Functioning framework. *Frontiers in education* (Vol. 1, p. 4). Frontiers.

Office for Disability Issues. (2011). Equality Act 2010: Guidance. HM Government. Retrieved from http://odi.dwp.gov.uk/docs/law/ea/ea-guide-2.pdf

Ofsted. (2004). *Special education needs and disability: Towards inclusive schools* (HMI 2353). Department for Education.

Parliament of the United Kingdom (2010). The Equality Act. The National Archives. Retrieved from: http://www.legislation.gov.uk/ukpga/2010/15/contents

Sanches-Ferreira, M., Simeonsson, R. J., Silveira-Maia, M., Alves, S., Tavares, A., & Pinheiro, S. (2013). Portugal's special education law: Implementing the International Classification of Functioning, Disability and Health in policy and practice. *Disability and Rehabilitation, 35*(10), 868–873.

Simeonsson, R. J. (2006). Appendix C: Defining and classifying disability in children. In M. J. Field, A. Jette, & L. Martin (Eds.), *Workshop on disability in America: A new look* (pp. 67–87). Washington, DC: National Academy Press.

Tilly, W. D. III (2002). Best practices in school psychology as a problem-solving enterprise. In Thomas, A. & Grimes, J. (Eds.) *Best practices in school psychology IV* (pp. 21–36). Bethesda MD: National Association of School Psychologists.

WHO. (2001). *International classification of functioning, disability and health.* Genève: WHO.

WHO. (2007). *International classification of functioning, disability and health for children and youth.* Genève: WHO.

Wilkinson, J. (2012). *Addressing the needs of young people identified to be experiencing behavioural, emotional and social difficulties: A study of 'in-city' support and multi-agency working.* University of Exeter.

Chapter 4

The use of the ICF-CY for supporting inclusive practices in education

Portuguese and Armenian experiences

Manuela Sanches-Ferreira, Mónica Silveira-Maia, Sílvia Alves and Rune J. Simeonsson

The way disability is conceptualised in education says a great deal about how it will be approached in policy and practice. This assertion is evident in changes in the way that assessment and eligibility systems are conceived in education for children with disabilities. Within the context of the inclusive education zeitgeist, an increasing number of countries have been developing efforts to shift special education needs assessment and eligibility processes from deficit-based models of disability (centred on identifying students' impairments) to the biopsychosocial and person-environment fit perspectives of the ICF-CY. Although they are at different levels of implementation, Portugal and Armenia represent countries where the ICF-CY has been used to support the description of disability in childhood.

The aim of this chapter is to (a) review the role of disability classifications in education (b) describe ICF-CY as a framework and taxonomy for educational practice, (c) illustrate applications of the ICF-CY in two countries for disability classification and (d) propose guidelines for applying the ICF-CY in inclusive education

Disability classifications and their impact on educational and eligibility systems

Similar to any other domain of knowledge, the understanding of disability has been subject to several endeavours to organise and explain the phenomenon. Such organizing efforts undergo continuous reformulations according to the up-to-date knowledge on the origin, nature and consequences of disability (Simeonsson, 2006). In fact, as stressed by Sanches-Ferreira (2007), the assumed key concepts and their relation describing the disability phenomenon, reveal a given zeitgeist grounded on the epoch knowledge and set of values, which resulted – over time – in different disability classifications and taxonomies. Accordingly, influenced by medicine and biology domains of knowledge, the first attempts to explain disability phenomenon, were characterised by a linear relationship with the concept of impairment – meaning an injury/deficiency on person's body or mental functions. Indeed, first classifications were defined by the nature and severity of individuals' impairments. Triggered by developments on knowledge that recognised the same importance – as the one assigned to biologic factors – to environmental variables, and by human rights movements, further classifications and taxonomies on disability included also a social and psychological dimension (Hollenweger, 2008).

As such, with the evolving conceptualisation of disability, two main perspectives can be outlined: an unidimensional and biological one, conceiving disability as a state according to the presence or absence of a health condition or impairment, and a multidimensional and socio-ecological one, conceiving disability as a continuum determined by the interaction of multiple factors (Altman, 2001). The prevalence of one of these perspectives, through the adoption of a given disability classification, has had over the years different consequences for the provision of special education services due to its predictive role on how children should be assessed to determine eligibility and on the way of planning educational interventions (Florian et al., 2006). So far, the need for adopting an eligibility criterion to define *who* should receive additional supports has been an unquestionable requirement to accomplish children's rights. Such a requirement demands the implementation of assessment processes capable of defining if the nature and severity of a child disability fits eligibility criteria, which means the use of a certain classification system to ensure a common understanding of the target group (Simeonsson, Simeonsson, & Hollenweger, 2008). Historically, the identification of special education needs made use of categorical systems prominently influenced by a biological perspective of disability (Polo, Pradal, Bortolot, Buffoni, & Martinuzzi, 2009). A paradigmatic example of that was the classification system proposed by Horn in 1924 to support the educational decision making (Sanches-Ferreira, 2007). He suggested that differentiated education should be provided based on differences in students: children who are exceptional for reasons primarily mental, temperamental or physical. As such, the activation of additional supports was informed by a clinical diagnosis or the description of children's impairments corresponding to a "within-child" conceptualisation of disability (Florian et al., 2006).

However, several criticisms have been identified in the use of unidimensional classifications for eligibility purposes. An important limitation has been the paucity of correspondence between diagnoses and learning and social problems faced by children. In this sense, categorical and impairment-centred approaches have been considered to have limited use in identifying students' needs for intervention and, consequently planning teaching. Further, the field of education has lacked a coherent and universal approach for assigning diagnoses and categories to children with disabilities. This has resulted not only in inconsistencies in determining eligibility of children with disabilities but also in comparing prevalence within and across countries (Florian & McLaughlin, 2008). Beyond that, determining eligibility and classifying students' needs on the basis of a disability category has been identified as responsible for placing students in segregated schools or classrooms – in keeping with their identified category – with consequences in terms of prejudice and discrimination for children with disabilities.

Systemic perspectives of human development – advanced by Bronfenbrenner (1979) – called for an alternative view of disability, situating it in the context of the person's interaction with the environment. Bijou and Baer highlighted this interactional perspective, stating,

> We cannot analyse a child without reference to an environment, nor is it possible to analyse an environment without reference to a child. The two form an inseparable unit consisting of an interrelated set of variables, or an interactional field.
>
> (1978, p. 29)

Within this perspective, understanding the disability process depends on a comprehensive approach, in which individuals' characteristics are no longer perceived as independent factors but recognised as a consequence of the interaction between individuals and the environment where they have to function (Hollenweger, 2008). This view is compliant with the biopsychosocial and person-environment fit perspective of disability.

The recognition of disability as a multidimensional process, in which environmental factors play a nuclear role, was considered as a guiding reference in education for a greater coherence of practices with inclusive purposes (Norwich, 2008). This recognition demands moving the focus from children's deficits and types of disability widely accepted as a dead end to providing appropriate clues in planning contextual opportunities for all individuals' participation (Hollenweger, 2011). Further, the focus should be on functional difficulties children have in meeting academic and adaptive demands within the school environment, constituting the departure point to comprehensively adjust environmental demands and supports for successful engagement of all students (Sanches-Ferreira, Lopes-dos-Santos, Alves, Santos, & Silveira-Maia, 2013; Thompson, Wehmeyer, & Hughes, 2010). Central to this perspective is the need for a functional approach to assess and classify disability in childhood on the basis of a non-categorial system (Simeonsson, Simeonsson, & Hollenweger, 2008).

International Classification of Functioning, Disability and Health for Children and Youth as a conceptual framework and classification system compatible with current biopsychosocial and person-environment fit perspectives

Values and principles proclaimed by inclusive education have shown to be incompatible with labelling of children – which per se tends to work in service of prejudice and discrimination (Ebersold & Evans, 2008; Florian et al.,

2006; Simeonsson, Simeonsson, & Hollenweger, 2008). The need was, then, to develop alternative systems to provide services that were not exclusively focused on categories of disability, diagnoses and labels, but rather on the role of the environment on functioning of the child (Farrell, 2010).

Consolidating an evolutionary process from impairment-centred approaches towards a biopsychosocial and person-environment fit perspective, the ICF-CY (WHO, 2007) emerged as an interesting framework with applications, not only on eligibility and assessment processes but also on planning educational responses (Norwich, 2008). Disability and functioning are presented as umbrella terms in the ICF-CY, respectively defined as the negative and positive "aspects of the interaction between an individual (with a health condition) and that individual's contextual factors (environmental and personal factors)" (WHO, 2001, p. 213).

In its interactional model the ICF-CY provides a comprehensive framework and taxonomy to describe disability in childhood enabling to separately document impairments of body functions and Structures, limitations/restrictions of activities and participation and the role of environmental factors (Ustun, Chatterji, Bickenbach, Kostanjsek, & Schneider, 2003). As defined in the ICF-CY manual (WHO, 2007, p. 10), the body functions component encompasses the "physiological functions of body systems", and the body structures the "anatomical parts of the body such as organs, limbs and their components". activities refer to the "execution of a task or action" and participation to the "involvement in a life situation". The environmental factors component incorporates "physical, social and attitudinal environment in which people live and conduct their lives". These components are presented with a list of alphanumeric codes. Within each component, codes are organised hierarchically from broad to specific categories. By assigning a qualifier (0 = no problem to 4 = complete problem), the magnitude of functioning or disability of body functions and structures and activities and participation components is specified. In turn, environmental factors can be qualified as barriers or facilitators, according to their impact in supporting or hindering the individuals' functioning.

Through these structural and conceptual characteristics, the ICF-CY provides a spectrum of information that allows the description of holistic functioning profiles (Simeonsson, 2006). The description of functioning profiles as a person – environment dynamic relationship can support individualised practices, prompting the connection between assessment and intervention planning (Hollenweger, 2008, 2011; Norwich, 2008; Silveira-Maia et al., 2012). Therefore, the use of the ICF-CY has been considered a promising way to support more individualised practices as well as to determine the most appropriate educational responses to meet students' needs (Hollenweger, 2008; Sanches-Ferreira, Simeonsson, Silveira-Maia, & Alves, 2015; Simeonsson et al., 2008).

The functional basis for disability defined in the ICF-CY is consistent with the mandate for inclusive education in special education policies and legislation of the last decades (Florian et al., 2006; Sanches-Ferreira et al., 2013; Simeonsson, 2006; Simeonsson et al., 2008), since it offers a common language for determining special education eligibility based on limitations of functioning rather than on clinical diagnosis. The decision making about eligibility for special education should focus, then, on characteristics that define the nature and extent of a student's limitations in meeting the physical, social and psychological demands relevant to learning in the school environment.

From the literature and reported experiences, there is consensus that the ICF-CY is a framework that supports a more comprehensive and holistic view of students' needs and, therefore, offers useful descriptions for educational planning (Florian et al., 2006; Hollenweger, 2011; Sanches-Ferreira et al., 2015). These recognised potentialities motivated several international pilot experiences related to the ICF-CY application on special education assessment and eligibility processes – e.g. in Switzerland (Hollenweger, 2011); in Italy (Polo et al., 2009; Fusaro, Maspoli, & Vellar, 2009); in Japan (Tokunaga, 2008); and in Tawain (Chiu et al., 2013). In particular, Portugal was the first country decreeing – on special education legislation (i.e. Law No. 3/2008) the compulsory use of the ICF-CY as a reference framework on assessment and eligibility processes.

The usage of the ICF-CY supporting assessment and eligibility processes in special education services: the experience of two countries

In a time that the inclusive education is internationally claimed and that the ICF-CY has been consensually recognised as a framework that can support its accomplishment through research, political and practical spheres, the sharing of experiences that document its usage to support a successful engagement of students with disabilities in common educational settings is imperious. Portugal and Armenia are two countries connected by a solid experience in the usage of the ICF-CY as reference framework in SENs assessment and eligibility processes. Portugal was a pioneering country by decreeing, in 2008 (Law No. 3/2008), the mandatory use of the ICF-CY framework for guiding special needs assessment and to base eligibility decision making on students' functioning profiles, and Armenia initiated, in 2013, a systematic path to revise the methodology for SENs assessment and for developing individualised education programs (IEPs) in alignment with the ICF-CY framework and the CRPD (Unit Nations, 2006). The insights on both experiences are strongly based on authors' involvement as external evaluators of the implementation of Law No. 3/2008 in Portugal and as consultants of the revision of assessment and eligibility procedures in Armenia through a consultancy project commissioned by UNICEF.

Portugal: a pioneering country introducing the use of the ICF-CY in special education law

Over the last three decades, the SENs field has been subject to substantial changes from conceptual and practical perspectives. The human rights movement and the development of conceptual models of disability have placed inclusive education on the agenda of many countries and, in parallel, inspired advances regarding special education legislation – as it was preconised in the United Kingdom, establishing – with the Warnock Report – a non-categorical system based in students' needs (Department of Education and Science, 1978 as cited in Wedell, 2008). The adoption of systems based on students' additional support needs as well as multidimensional and socio-ecological classifications of disability entailed a set of efforts to shift the special education needs assessment and eligibility processes from impairment-centred approaches towards a biopsychosocial and person-environment fit perspective of disability (Gargiulo, 2012). Such challenge is clearly reflected in the current Portuguese special education law (Law No. 3/2008), which preamble states, "Inclusive education aims for educational equity ... whether in access or in outcomes ... conducive to the mobilization of specialized services to promote the biopsychosocial functioning potential" (Law No. 3/2008, Preamble).

Framed by this purpose, one of the major changes introduced by this law was the replacement of a clinical diagnosis with a description of the child's functioning profile as the basis for eligibility decision making and to outline appropriate educational supports. Accordingly, the target group for special education services was defined as students with "significant limitations in terms of activity and participation in one or more areas in life due to permanent functional and structural issues, which result in continued difficulty in terms of communication, learning, mobility, autonomy, interpersonal relationships and social involvement" (Paragraph 1 of Article 1, Chapter I). Within this definition, the Law No. 3/2008 requires the conduction of an assessment process centred on students' functioning – considering environmental influences as the base not only for eligibility decision making but also for planning of educational interventions and design of the IEP. Taking advantage of its multidimensional and context-sensitive approach, the ICF-CY was the framework selected to support that functioning-oriented assessment and the description of profiles of functioning of students referred for special education services and supports. In this profile the interdisciplinary team documents, in a comprehensive way, functional limitations of students across different activities and participation domains reflecting disability as the product of child-environment interactions.

The path taken by students within special education services starts with a referral form in which concerns about students' difficulties which may require special support are described. When a student is referred for assessment, the school interdisciplinary team has to decide, based on available reports and information, if the student needs a specialised assessment. In that event, the school principal may request the involvement of other disciplines or services (health services, specialised resource centres) to form an interdisciplinary team together with parents and regular and special education teachers to assess students' needs. The assessment process is then planned to identify problems of functioning of the student in need of assessment and how required information is to be gathered. This specialised assessment yields a profile of functioning of the student based on the ICF-CY taxonomy and based on which eligibility for special education is determined. If the student's profile of functioning meets the eligibility criteria, then an IEP is designed, specifying accommodations and modifications for the student's learning program. If the student is not eligible for special education services, the educational team recommends the student for other educational resources and services. These procedures are displayed in Figure 4.1.

A year after the enactment of the Law No. 3/2008, the Ministry of Education requested an external evaluation of its implementation, in order to examine the impact and supporting conditions for the use of the ICF-CY in educational contexts. This study, carried out during 2009–2010, included the evaluation of decisions taken by schools in the students' processes of assessment and eligibility, based on a nationally representative sample of 214 students for whom specialised assessments were available. Results showed support for the use of

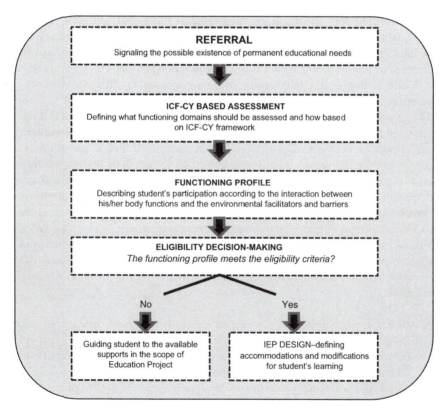

Figure 4.1 Process flow for special needs education assessment and intervention in Portugal

the ICF-CY in promoting a holistic view of students' functioning based on documentation of students' characteristics within a biopsychosocial perspective. The students' profiles of functioning included descriptions of body functions, activities and participation and environmental factors. Moreover, educational professionals captured the students' functioning emphasizing the activities and participation component in their profiles. However, the environmental factors component was not widely implemented suggesting a limited view of the environment's influence on functioning and participation of the student. This finding motivated the recommendation for the development of assessment tools considering the environmental influence on students' functioning as an essential priority to improve the use of the ICF-CY in educational contexts (Sanches-Ferreira et al., 2010). In addition to providing a systematic basis for documenting profiles of student functioning, the use of the ICF-CY framework also allowed a basis for differentiating eligible and non-eligible students for special education services. The comparison of functioning profiles of eligible and non-eligible students showed that the difference between groups was not the number of categories in the profiles, but rather associated severity levels. In keeping with the eligibility requirements for special education services, the qualitative difference defining eligible students pertained to the severity of limitations/restrictions experienced in activities and participation and the permanent nature of impairments in body functions.

Along with the implementation of an innovation in daily reasoning and practices a set of needs and challenges emerged related to the ICF-CY use. The evaluation of the Law No. 3/2008 implementation also included listening to professionals' opinions about the ICF-CY use in educational contexts. An important opinion of professionals was that the ICF-CY use allowed a deeper understanding of students' characteristics and needs by placing the focus of assessment on what students actually do (i.e. students' activities and participation) rather than on their impairments or deficits. Further, professionals expressed that the ICF-CY use prompted the inclusion of environmental factors as assessment targets – analysing how the environment can be a barrier or a facilitator for the student's functioning, providing information for the intervention planning, specifically the design of IEPs. However, professionals also associated difficulties and challenges related to the use of the ICF-CY with reference to

1   Professionals emphasised the lack of assessment measures congruent with the ICF-CY framework and identified the need for tools that could provide information about the impact of the environment on students functioning;
2   The establishment of better collaboration mechanisms between school-based and external professionals underlying the ICF-CY property of allowing a holistic view of students' functioning. The mention of difficulties in body functions classification are symptomatic of the need of making stronger the connection between schools and health services; and

3   The training of professionals on conceptual foundations and application of the ICF-CY reaching all persons involved in special education assessment and intervention (including physicians, parents and other educational professionals).

The results of this evaluation study provided support for the intent of the Law No. 3/2008 to incorporate a functional basis for determining eligibility for special education services. The Portuguese experience demonstrated that profiles of functioning based on the ICF-CY can yield a gradation of students' functioning to support eligibility decisions for special education services and the selection of appropriate targets for educational intervention for students. The identified challenges in using the ICF-CY within educational contexts need to be attended in future applications of this framework.

Armenia: a consultancy project for the revision of assessment and intervention planning aligned with the ICF-CY

Following the worldwide trend for inclusive education, Armenia is one of the countries that has made substantial progress in this domain in the last ten years. With a central role in this process, UNICEF-Armenia identified needs and key strategies to realise the right of children with disabilities to inclusive education (Poghosyan, 2012). One of the key challenges consisted of the need to restructure special needs assessment procedures and additional supports provision for children with disabilities. Prior to 2013, the approach to assessment was focused on medical diagnoses and on the use of developmental tests designed for children between the ages of 3–14 years (Poghosyan, 2012). Such approach was implemented through an assessment toolkit composed of a package of assessment measures and tasks covering five major areas of students' functioning: cognitive (e.g. attention, memory, reading and writing, math skills), socio-emotional (expressive, impressive, self-appraisal), speech (vocabulary, reproduction, comprehension), mobility and self-care (eating/drinking, hygiene/toilet, safety skills, health and reproduction skills). As documented in the protocol from the Medical-Psychological-Pedagogical Assessment Centre (MPPC) – responsible for the assessment of children's special education needs in Armenia – each area entailed a set of items, embodying structured tasks and questions to students. The assessment specialists had to identify items of high, middle and low levels of difficulty with reference to normative indicators. This assessment process resulted in a final report comprising a description of the child's difficulty level in each area.

The summative nature of the assessment findings were used to support the determination of eligibility for services, and with a final agreement by parents – would result in recommendations for the provision of inclusive education support (through increased per capita funding to "inclusive" schools) or the enrollment in a special school. As such, the identification of children in need of additional services and supports, and the allocation of additional funding, had been made according to seven categories (Hunt, 2009): (i) speech impairments, (ii) hearing impairments, (iii) sight impairments, (iv) mental underdevelopment, (v) impairments of movement system, (vi) psychological development problems and (vii) behaviour and emotional impairments.

The categorical approach to assessment and eligibility determination however, was of limited use to guide teacher decisions in intervention planning and facilitation of school environments for inclusion. This was the steering reason for UNICEF-Armenia to commission a consultancy project aimed at supporting the revision of procedures related to special education needs assessment and individual planning based on the best international practice and aligned with the ICF-CY framework.

The consultancy project entailed a partnership between consultants and the local team of experts from the MPPC, as well as key educational stakeholders, including representatives of the Bridge of Hope (a non-governmental organisation for children), the Ministry of Education and Science, the Pedagogical Department of Yerevan State University and the National Institute of Education.

The primary aim of the consultancy project was to support the MPPC team – the consultees – to achieve two outcomes: a revised package of tools and methodology for special education needs assessment and an effective methodology for developing IEPs based on assessment results. For this mission two guiding principles were adopted: i) students' assessment and documentation of their functioning profiles reflecting a holistic approach and ii) the gap between students' repertoire of capacities and environmental demands – or between students' needs and available environmental supports – should be the central feature for defining IEPs' goals and strategies.

The approach used for revising the assessment toolkit in Armenia mainly involved the exploration and selection of assessment measures/ tools that meet requirements for holistic and dynamic assessments. In this regard, the selection of measures was focused on comprehensive assessment tools of students' participation, considering the role of the environment on the nature and extent of students' performance (specifically, taking into account the student's performance with and without assistance). The strategy adopted in the revision of the age-based toolkit took advantage of the universal language and functioning centred approach embodied in the ICF-CY through the broad spectrum of indicators of functioning and environmental factors. In particular, the target contents from the age-based toolkit were aligned with functioning domains encompassed by the ICF-CY "developmental code sets" (Ellingsen & Simeonsson, 2011).

Considering the move from an impairment-based perspective towards a biopsychosocial approach as the cornerstone of the procedures revision, the consultancy model was implemented as an evolutionary process. That perspective encompassed progressive and cumulative stages – namely, (a) a document analysis of the existing practices and policies, (b) the mapping of the existing toolkit to the ICF-CY and (c) the selection and development of appropriate assessment measures.

Document analysis

A systematic comparison was made between existing policies, assessment toolkit and procedures in Armenia and current best practices regarding assessment and intervention for sustaining inclusive priorities. Documents analysed included formal steering documents (e.g. "Education Development – State Programme of the Republic of Armenia 2011–2015") and samples of the assessment toolkit and the individualised education program.

Specifically, the analysis focused on six guiding questions. (i) What domains of students' functioning are considered in assessment? (ii) How is the assessment carried out in terms of measurement and documentation of assessment results? (iii) Where does the assessment take place, in school or local setting? (iv) Who assesses the students and what is the role of professionals and parents in this process? (v) How are results/findings from assessment tools used to determine eligibility for special education services? (vi) How are assessment findings used in the development of the individualised education program?

These guiding questions were used to identify needs for the coming actions of the consultancy through systematic comparison between practices and procedures undertaken in Armenia and the current state of the art in the field.

Mapping the assessment toolkit

In order to explore and select assessment measures/tools that met requirements for holistic and dynamic assessment, the existing toolkit was mapped to ICF-CY "developmental code sets" organised into the four age groups of 0–2, 3–5, 6–12 and 13–17 years (Ellingsen & Simeonsson, 2011)

On the basis of MPPC inputs, additional codes were included in the proposed "age-group code sets", with reference to Armenian culture and indicators of functioning related to educational participation. The items included in each area of the existing toolkit were linked to ICF-CY codes, based on linking rules proposed by Cieza et al. (2005). A review of the coverage of the toolkit items and references to relevant codes in age-group code sets served as the basis for adding or changing assessment tasks and/or selecting new assessment measures.

Selecting and developing assessment tools

Based on the toolkit coverage of age-group code sets, a review was made of the methods/instruments/sources of information for collecting data for each set of codes. With the intent of developing a stronger connection between assessment practices and the person-environment fit approach, there was a broad consensus that assessment results, embodied in a functioning profile, could serve for: 1) eligibility determination, 2) identification of the nature and scope of relevant services and supports to promote student participation and 3) monitoring of students' progress.

The group used the frame of "how to assess", to identify what assessment tools to use, by whom and where. Congruent with the state of art of knowledge (e.g. Bagnato, 2007; Linder, 2008), the team based decisions on "how to assess" in terms of the need to adopt natural environments (e.g. play environments) as the vehicle to analyse students' functioning at home, school and assessment centre, and based assessment on multiple sources of information (e.g. teacher, parents and other key information providers). In light of these decisions, assessment resources/methods and tools were systematically screened within the ICF-CY framework. Based on common principles of using natural environment (routine-based assessment), attending to flexibility (considering children's interests, meaningful activities, assets, opportunities and participation) and dynamic assessment (assessing performance with and without help), measures and methods were reviewed with MPPC team of experts.

Considering the circumstances and contextual demands faced by students with more severe disabilities served by a specific curriculum, it was recognised that greater emphasis needed to be placed on the child's functional and social skills in assessment. To this end, consideration was given to alternate assessment methods and functional centred measures rather than curriculum-based measures.

In sum, the revised assessment resources were: 1) organised by age groups, 2) aligned with the main principles associated with "how to assess" decisions 3) linked to appropriate ICF-CY domains in order to identify the nature of information obtained with their use (Table 4.1).

Table 4.1 Representative screening tools/measures according by age group

Age group	Focus of the needed information	Examples of screened measures	Coverage on the ICF-CY domains
0–6 years	– Play embedded tasks for developmental observations and identification of environmental facilitators and barriers	TPBA – Transdisciplinary Play-Based Assessment (Toni Linder, 1993, 2008).	b1–b3, b7, d1–d5, d7, d8
		PEDI – Pediatric Evaluation of Disability Inventory (Haley et al., 1992).	d4, d5, d7, e1, e3, e5
		VECTOR – Vanderbilt Ecological Congruence of Teaching Opportunities in Routines (Casey, Freund, & McWilliam, 2004).	d2, d7, d8, e1, e3

Age group	Focus of the needed information	Examples of screened measures	Coverage on the ICF-CY domains
7–13 years	– Criterion-referenced measures, specifically curriculum-based assessments, for students following mainstream curriculum (with accommodations/ adaptations) – Alternate assessment methods (such as portfolios) for students with more severe disabilities, with specific curriculum	CAPE-PAC – Children's Assessment of Participation and Enjoyment & Preferences for Activities in Children (King et al., 2004). PEM-CY – Participation and Environment Measure for Children and Youth (Coster et al., 2012). CFFS – Child & Family Follow-Up Survey (Bedell, 2011).	d1, d4, d5, d7–d9 d1, d6–d9, e1, e3–e5 d1–d9, e1–e15
14–17 years	– Criterion referenced measures for students following the mainstream curriculum (with accommodations/ adaptations) – Measures of functioning for students with more severe disabilities (served with a specific curriculum), including items for independent living	SIS – Supports Intensity Scale (Thompson et al., 2004, 2012). COSA – Child Occupational Self-Assessment (Keller et al., 2005). SFA – School Function Assessment (Coster, Deeney, Haltiwanger, & Haley, 1998). ARC Self-Determination Assessment (Wehmeyer & Kelchner, 1995).	d1, d3–d9, e3 d1, d3–d7 d1, d2, d3, d4, d5, d7, d8, e1, e3

Based on a systematic approach, the MPPC expert team selected and adapted a set of tools to be used in the assessment process and developed five questionnaires directed to parents and multidisciplinary teams at the education institution.

The draft toolkit and assessment procedures were experimentally implemented through case studies, exploring validation indicators such as the congruence between information provided by the tools and the age-group code sets and the suitability of obtained information to enhance the description of dynamic functioning profiles and decision making for educational interventions.

A review was made of the difficulties perceived about the toolkit and assessment procedures, taking into consideration (i) who was involved in the toolkit implementation, (ii) how the toolkit was implemented (e.g. approach, difficulties, time consumed), (iii) how data were summarised, (iv) perceived strengths and (v) improvement needs. Positive indicators of toolkit usability and comprehensiveness as well as the nature of the adjustments made on some measures were shared with stakeholders.

Conclusion

Special education in the last three decades has been characterised by significant philosophical and conceptual changes with associated implications for policy and practice – namely, in the assessment, eligibility and intervention processes. The ICF-CY has been recognised as a conceptual framework and classification system compatible with the state of art of conceptualisations of disability and with the ethical principles and statements that founded the inclusive school. Further, its property of allowing the description of holistic and interactional functioning profiles is considered as a promising way to support the assessment of students' performance and the identification of clues for intervention. The use of the ICF-CY in education turn into reality for professionals the sharing of a common language in the assessment, eligibility and intervention processes, as well the monitoring of students' progress based on the qualifiers of their functioning profiles.

Although, the integration of changes into the routines and practices of education is a complex process. Based on experiences in Portugal where the use of the ICF-CY is compulsory as the basis for assessment and eligibility determination – and the consultation project in Armenia to develop a package of tools and methodology for special education needs assessment, the following recommendations are made for implementing the ICF-CY in education practice:

• promotion of consistent communication mechanisms within different assessment teams (school-based and external professionals) in order to comply with the holistic approach provided by the ICF-CY;
• description of functioning profiles considering students' performance with and without environmental supports in order to allow planning interventions more aligned with students' needs of supports;
• development of a set of key ICF-CY-codes related to the educational participation of students in order to be used as general organiser in the assessment and intervention processes;
• development of assessment tools that considers environmental influences on students' functioning – namely, measuring students' performance with and without environmental supports;
• use of information gathered through assessment tools (already used before), screened for the ICF-CY terminology, to contribute for a holistic view of the child's functioning;

- implementation of knowledge dissemination strategies – e.g. training programs on the use of the ICF-CY in education for professionals and stakeholders involved in different levels of assessment and creation of "sharing stations" of materials and difficulties-based problem solving strategies; and
- implementation of monitoring actions on the practical use of assessment procedures, eligibility criteria and intervention decisions at national level in order to allow the evaluation of special education policies.

Highlights from this chapter

Through the experience of two countries – Portugal and Armenia – this chapter shows the following:

- the usage of the ICF-CY in educational context allows an holistic and social-ecological approach to students' needs, supporting the description of functioning profiles that can inform not only the eligibility decision making but also the IEPs design;
- the systematic exploration and selection of assessment measures/ tools that meet requirements for holistic and dynamic assessments through their mapping into the ICF-CY taxonomy embody a useful methodology in the revision and development of assessment procedures aligned with the ICF-CY framework and Human Rights Convention; and
- the sustainability of the changes implied in the usage of the ICF-CY framework – specifically the implementation of socio-ecological and person-environment-fit approaches – depends on other supportive factors in which training and monitoring actions assume a central role.

References

Altman, B. M. (2001). Disability definitions, models, classification schemes, and applications. In G. L. Albrecht, K. D. Seelman, & M. Bury (Eds.), *Handbook of disability studies* (pp. 97–122). London: Sage Publications.

Bagnato, S. J. (2007). *Authentic assessment for early childhood intervention: Best practices.* Guilford Press, New York.

Bedell, G. M. (2004). Developing a follow-up survey focused on participation of children and youth with acquired brain injuries after discharge from inpatient rehabilitation. *Neurorehabilitation, 19*(3), 191–205.

Bijou, S. W., & Baer, D. (1978). *Behavior analysis of child development.* Englewood Cliffs, NJ: Prentice Hall.

Bronfenbrenner, U. (1979). *The ecology of human development: Experiments by nature and design.* Cambridge, MA: Harvard University Press.

Casey, A. M., Freund, P. J., & McWilliam, R. A. (1992). *Vanderbilt Ecological Congruence of Teaching Opportunities in Routines (VECTOR) - Classroom Version*. Bashville: Vanderbilt Center for Child Development.

Chiu, W.T., Yen, C.F., Teng, S.W., Liao, H.F., Chang, K.H., Chi, W.C., Wang, Y.H. & Liou, T.H. (2013). Implementing disability evaluation and welfare services based on the framework of the international classification of functioning, disability and health: Experiences in Taiwan. *BMC Health Services Research, 13*(1), 416.

Cieza, A., Geyh, S., Chatterji, S., Kostanjsek, N., Üstün, B., & Stucki, G. (2005). ICF linking rules: An update based on lessons learned. *Journal of Rehabilitation Medicine, 37*, 212–218.

Coster, W. J., Deeney, T.A., Haltiwanger, J.T., & Haley, S. M. (1998). *School Function Assessment*. San Antonio, TX: Psychological Corporation/Therapy Skill Builders.

Coster, W., Law, M., Bedell, G., Khetani, M., Cousins, M., & Teplicky, R. (2012). Development of the participation and environment measure for children and youth: conceptual basis. *Disabil Rehabil, 34*(3), 238–246.

Ebersold, S., & Evans, P. (2008). A supply-side approach for a resource-based classification system. In L. Florian & M. McLaughlin (Eds.), *Disability classification in education: Issues and perspectives* (pp. 31–44). Newbury Park, CA: Corwin Press.

Ellingsen, K., & Simeonsson, R. (2011). ICF-CY developmental code sets. Retrieved from www.icf-cydevelopmentalcodesets.com/

Farrell, M. (2010). *Debating special education*. Nova Iorque: Routledge.

Florian, L., Hollenweger, J., Simeonsson, R. J., Wedell, K., Riddell, S., Terzi, L., & Holland, A. (2006). Cross-cultural perspectives on the classification of children with disabilities part I. Issues in the classification of children with disabilities. *The Journal of Special Education, 40*(1), 36–45.

Florian, L., & McLaughlin, M. (2008). Disability classification in education. In L. Florian & M. McLaughlin (Eds.), *Disability classification in education: Issues and perspectives* (pp. 3–6). Newbury Park, CA: Corwin Press.

Fusaro, G., Maspoli, M., & Vellar, G. (2009). The ICF-based functioning profiles of school children in care with the neuropsychiatric community services in the piedmont region: Evidences for better caring and programming. *Disability & Rehabilitation, 31*, S61–S66.

Gargiulo, R. M. (2012). *Special education in contemporary society: An introduction to exceptionality* (4th ed.). Los Angeles, CA: Sage.

Haley, S. M., Coster, W., Ludlow, L. H., Haltiwanger, J. T., & Andrellos, P. J. (1992). *Pediatric Evaluation of Disability Inventory (PEDI): Development, standardization and administration manual*. Boston, MA: Trustees of Boston University.

Hollenweger, J. (2008). Cross-national comparisons of special education classification systems. In L. Florian & M. McLaughlin (Eds.), *Disability classification in education: Issues and perspectives* (pp. 11–27). Newbury Park, CA: Corwin Press.

Hollenweger, J. (2011). Development of an ICF-based eligibility procedure for education in Switzerland. *BMC Public Health, 11*(4), S7.

Hunt, P.F. (2009). Evaluation of inclusive education policies and programs in Armenia, UNICEF Armenia. Evaluation report. Retrieved from: http://www.unicef. org/evaluation/files/FINAL_Evaluation_IE_policies__programmes_Armenia_dec_15(1).pdf

Keller, J., Kafkes, A., & Kielhofner, G. (2005). Psychometric characteristics of the Child Occupational Self Assessment (COSA), Part One: An initial examination of psychometric properties. *Scandinavian Journal of Occupational Therapy, 12*(3), 118–127

King, G.A., Law, M., King, S., Hurley, P., Hanna, S., Kertoy, M., Rosenbaum, P. and Young, N (2004). *Children's Assessment of Participation and Enjoyment (CAPE) and Preferences for Activities of Children (PAC)*. San Antonio, TX: Harcourt Assessment, Inc.

Linder, T. W. (1993). *Transdisciplinary Play-Based Assessment: A functional approach to working with young children* (Revised Edition). Baltimore: Paul H. Brooks Publishing Co.

Linder, T. (2008). *Transdisciplinary play-based assessment* (2nd ed., TPBA2). Baltimore, MD: Paul H. Brooks.

Norwich, B. (2008). Perspectives and purposes of disability classification systems: Implications for teachers and curriculum. In L. Florian & M. McLaughlin (Eds.), *Disability classification in education: Issues and perspectives* (pp. 131–149). Newbury Park, CA: Corwin Press.

Poghosyan, M. (2012). *It's about Inclusion: Access to education, health, and social protection services for children with disabilities in Armenia.* Armenia: UNICEF.

Pollo, G., Pradal, M., Bortolot, S., Buffoni, M., & Martinuzzi, A. (2009). Children with disability at school: The application of ICF-CY in the Veneto region. *Disability and Rehabilitation, 31*(S1), S67–S73.

Sanches-Ferreira, M. (2007). *Educação Regular, Educação Especial – uma história de separação.* Porto: Edições Afrontamento.

Sanches-Ferreira, M., Simeonsson, R., Silveira-Maia, M., Alves, S., Pinheiro, S., & Tavares, A. (2010). *Projecto da Avaliação Externa da Implementação do Decreto-Lei n.º 3/2008: Relatório Final.* Lisboa: Direcção-Geral de Inovação e de Desenvolvimento Curricular.

Sanches-Ferreira, M., Lopes-dos-Santos, P., Alves, S., Santos, M., & Silveira-Maia, M. (2013). How individualised are the individualised education programmes (IEPs): An analysis of the contents and quality of the IEPs goals. *European Journal of Special Needs Education, 28*(4), 507–520.

Sanches-Ferreira, M., Simeonsson, R., Silveira-Maia, M., & Alves, S. (2015). Evaluating implementation of the International Classification of Functioning, Disability and Health (ICF) in Portugal's special education law. *International Journal of Inclusive Education, 19*(5), 457–468.

Silveira-Maia, M., Lopes-dos-Santos, P., Sanches-Ferreira, M., Tavares, A., Alves, S., & Pinheiro, S. (2012). The use of the International Classification of Functioning, Disability and Health (ICF) framework on educational planning: Promoting an environmental approach. *International Journal for Cross-Disciplinary Subjects in Education, 2*(2), 970–977.

Simeonsson, R. J. (2006). *Defining and classifying disability in children. Disability in America* (pp. 67–86). Washington: National Academic Press.

Simeonsson, R. J., Simeonsson, N. E., & Hollenweger, J. (2008). International Classification of Functioning, Disability and Health for Children and Youth: A common language for special education. In L. Florian & M. McLaughlin (Eds.), *Disability classification in education: Issues and perspectives* (pp. 207–217). Newbury Park, CA: Corwin Press.

Thompson, J., Bryant, B.R., Campbell, E. M., Craig, E.M., Hughes, C.M., Rotholz, D.A. et al. (2004). *Supports Intensity Scale: Users manual.* Washington: American Association on Mental Retardation.

Thompson, J. R., Wehmeyer, M. L., & Hughes, C. (2010). Mind the gap! Intellectual disability as individual-environment fit: Implications for students, teachers, and schools. *Exceptionality, 18,* 168–181.

Thompson, J. R., Wehmeyer, M. L., Copeland, S. R., Hughes, C., Little, T. D., Obremski, S., & Tassé, M. J (2012). *Supports Intensity Scale for Children Field Test Version 2.0.* Unpublished assessment instrument.

Tokunaga, A. (2008). The attempt of the practical application of International Classification of Functioning, Disability, and Health (ICF) as a tool for collaboration among various professionals: A perspective on its applicability to "individualized educational support plan". *NISE Bulletin, 9,* 1–26.

United Nations. (2006). *Convention on the rights of persons with disabilities and optional protocol.* New York: United Nations.

Ustün, B. T., Chatterji, S., Bickenbach, J., Kostanjsek, N., & Schneider, M. (2003). The International Classification of Functioning, Disability and Health: A new tool for understanding disability and health. *Disability and Rehabilitation, 25*, 565–571.

Wedell, K. (2008). Evolving dilemmas about categorization. In L. Florian & M. McLaughlin (Eds.), *Disability classification in education: Issues and perspectives* (pp. 47–64). Newbury Park, CA: Corwin Press.

Wehmeyer, M. L., & Kelchner, K. (1995). *The Arc's Self-Determination Scale.* Arlington, TX: The Arc of the United States.

WHO (World Health Organization). (2001). *International classification of functioning, disability and health.* Geneva: World Health Organization.

WHO (World Health Organization). (2007). *International classification of functioning, disability and health – version for children and youth.* Geneva: World Health Organization.

Chapter 5

The use of the ICF-CY in special needs education in Japan

Akio Tokunaga, Koji Tanaka and Yutaka Sakai

Introduction

The purpose of this chapter is to describe the implementation of the ICF-CY (WHO, 2007) in special needs education (SNE) in Japan. This chapter will provide: 1) an overview of the current status of education for students with disabilities and the use of ICF/ICF-CY in Japan, 2) a description of findings of a survey of Japanese teachers on their perspectives about the ICF (WHO, 2001) and ICF-CY in special needs education, 3) some illustrations of the use ICF/ICF-CY for SNE practice, 4) application of an ICF-CY core set of codes and an digital tool for SNE settings in Japan and 5) the challenge: the use of ICF-CY in consideration of reasonable accommodations

Overview of current condition of education for students with disabilities and the use of ICF/ICF-CY in Japan

In Japan, students with disabilities are provided educational services under al SNE. In SNE, consideration for the individual educational needs of the students, forms the basis of the efforts to fully develop their capabilities, their independence and social participation. SNE is provided in a number of different forms, including resource rooms and special classes in elementary and lower secondary schools and special schools. Additionally, various approaches are carried out in regular classes, such as instruction in small groups, team-teaching, instructions adapted to different achievement levels and the use of support assistants. Individualised Educational Support Plans (ISEPs) and Individualised Teaching Plans are obligatory for students with SEN enrolled in special schools and recommended for those in regular schools.

In 2003, the Ministry of Education, Culture, Sports, Science and Technology (MEXT) commissioned all prefectures with the implementation of the "Project for the Promotion of the Special Needs Education System". This project laid the foundation for a comprehensive education support system for children with developmental disabilities such as learning disabilities (LD) and ADHD, that were studying in elementary and secondary school classes. The project was later expanded to include preschools and high schools in addition to elementary and secondary schools, so that consistent educational support was provided to children with disabilities continuously from infancy to adulthood. MEXT has also promoted welfare education through stepped-up exchanges and joint learning of children with disabilities and those non-disabled as part of school education and through awareness-raising activities targeting local residents. One year following the implementat % ion of the SEN System by MEXT in 2014, the population of children served at the compulsory education stage (6 to 15 years old) was 69,000 students (0.67%) in special schools, 187,000 students (1.84 %) in special classes and 84,000 students (0.82 %) using special support services in resource rooms; students with special needs enrolled at regular classes often attend a tutor program (Ministry of Education, Culture, Sports, Science and Technology, 2015). Overall, students with SEN accounted for 3.33 % of all students. Elementary schools and lower secondary schools served about 6.5% of students considered to have developmental disabilities (LD, ADHD and high- functioning autism) included in regular classes (Ministry of Education, Culture, Sports, Science and Technology, 2012).

An important aspect of the history of SEN in Japan has been the introduction of the ICF in the MEXT. In 1992, the Manual of National Curriculum Standard for special schools described the utility of the conceptual framework of the ICIDH serving students with disabilities, and understanding the role of schoolteachers for working with them. In 2008, the manual further described the usage of the ICF, especially the utility of its conceptual framework for a comprehensive approach to students with disabilities, and its potential for application in sharing information between the various professions developing Individualised Educational Support Plans (IESPs).

From 2006 to 2011, a team at the National Institute of Special Needs Education Institute (NISE) led by Akio Tokunaga carried out a research project related to the use of the ICF and ICF-CY for SNE practice. The project resulted in the publication of reports and books describing proposals for practical applications of the ICF.

In 2012, the Central Committee on Education of the National Government proposed the usage of the ICF conceptual framework as the basis for undertaking reasonable accommodations for students with disabilities, within the context of the United Nations Convention for the Rights of Persons with Disabilities (UN General Assembly, 2007). A year later, the conceptual framework of the ICF was described in the *Guideline of Support Children with Special Educational Needs* as the gold standard for a comprehensive approach for children with disabilities

A survey on the visibility of the ICF and ICF-CY among educators in special needs education in Japan

I Overview of the survey

Following the availability of the ICF/ICF-CY in Japan, there was interest in determining the extent to which special education professionals were aware of these new classifications. A research project titled "The Use of ICF-CY for Special Needs Education in Japan" was carried out by the National Institute on Special Education. Specifically, a survey was developed to gather data on the visibility of the ICF/ICF-CY and their application in SNE in Japan. The project had a national scope with the survey covering all special schools (n = 1,134) in Japan. The survey was distributed to principals of each schools by post, completed and sent back to the research team by email, FAX or post, in 2009. The questionnaire covered the following information:

Part 1 Basic information

1   Name of the school
2   Number of students and their disability categories
3   With or without dormitory or residential facility

Part 2 Information of the use of the ICF/ICF-CY

1   Visibility of the ICF/ICF-CY
2   Applications of the ICF/ICF-CY in SNE practice
3   Characteristics and outcomes of the use of the ICF/ICF-CY
4   Issues in the use of the ICF/ICF-CY

2 Findings

A total of 809 schools(71.3 %)participated in the survey. 21 % (169schools) of respondents used ICF/ICF-CY and described a variety of uses. Below is a brief summary of the results on the visibility, applications, characteristics, outcomes and issues related to the ICF/ICF-CY.

(1) Visibility of the ICF/ICF-CY

The professionals' response to the question "What percentage of teachers know the ICF/ICF-CY in your school?" is presented in Figure 5.1. There was greater awareness of the ICF among teachers, more than the ICF-CY.

(2) Applications for intervention

Results related to the frequency of ICF applications for intervention purposes are presented in Figure 5.2. In responding to the questions, multiple answers could be provided. A review of the figure indicates that the application with the highest frequency related to intervention was the IESP, which is made for the purpose of collaboration among stakeholders. The second highest application was the Individualised Teaching Plan (ITP), which is made for the purpose of teaching the individualised program. The third application was identified as class planning. The fourth application involved guidance for "activities to

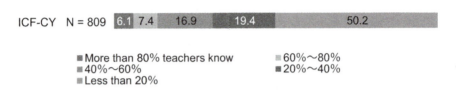

Figure 5.1 Awareness of the ICF/ICF-CY

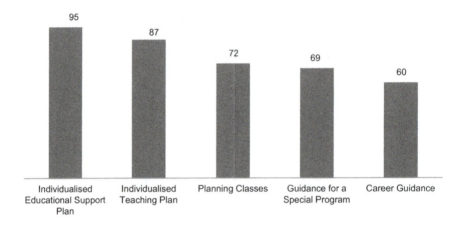

Figure 5.2 Frequency of applications of the ICF/ICF-CY for intervention

promote independence" defining a special program in SNE practice. Career guidance was the fifth most frequent application for intervention.

(3) The purpose of ICF/ICF-CY use

Results related to the frequency of purposes for the use of the ICF/ICF-CY are presented in Figure 5.3. Multiple answers were also allowed in response to this question. As shown in Figure 5.3, the use of the ICF/ICF-CY for the purpose of assessment of students was the most frequent application. The second highest purpose was for content decision making. The identification of educational targets or goals based on results of assessment was the third most frequent response. Use of the ICF/ICF-CY for decision making regarding goals and

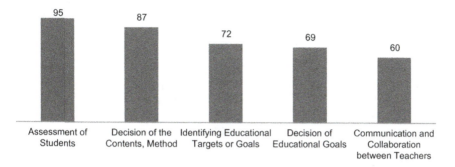

Figure 5.3 Frequency of purposes for the use of the ICF/ICF-CY

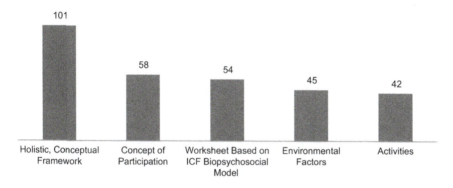

Figure 5.4 Characteristics of the ICF/ICF-CY mentioned as contributors to SNE practice

communication/collaboration between teachers were, respectively, the fourth and the fifth purposes identified in the survey.

(4) Characteristics of the ICF/ICF-CY

Results related to the nature of ICF/ICF-CY as contributors to SNE practice are presented in Figure 5.4. Multiple answers were also allowed to this question. A review of the frequencies indicates that the most frequently endorsed characteristic was the use of the ICF/ICF-CY as a holistic, conceptual framework to understand students. The next highest identified characteristic was the consideration for the status of students and intervention planning from the point of view of *participation*. The use of a worksheet based on the ICF's biopsychosocial model as a framework for collecting different sources of information about students was the third most frequent identified characteristic. The fourth was the use of environmental factors and the fifth was the use of the viewpoint of activities for consideration and planning.

(5) Outcomes of the use of the ICF/ICF-CY

Results based on multiple answers related to outcomes of using the ICF/ICF-CY in SNE are presented in Figure 5.5. The most frequently identified outcome was a more holistic understanding of students by teachers (73% of ICF/ICF-CY users). The second highest outcome was improved communication and collaboration between teachers. The third most frequent outcome was an easier approach to decide educational goals (44%). The helpfulness in developing educational goals based on assessment results and the helpfulness in assessing students were, respectively, the fourth and fifth most frequent outcomes.

(6) Issues in the use of the ICF/ICF-CY

Results related to issues in the use of the ICF/ICF-CY are presented in Figure 5.6. As for the other questions, multiple answers were allowed for this response. The issue with the highest frequency was "difficulties to understand

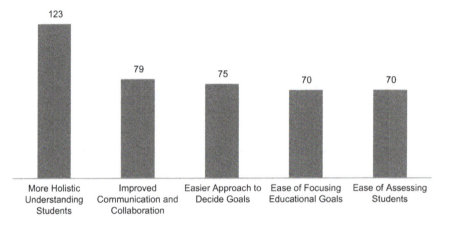

Figure 5.5 Frequency of outcomes of uses of ICF/ICF-CY

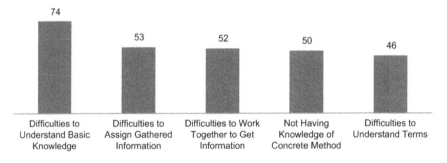

Figure 5.6 Frequency of issues in use of the ICF/ICF-CY

basic knowledge of the ICF/ICF-CY". Difficulties in assigning the information gathered about the student to the appropriate component (body functions, body structures, activity and participation, environmental factors and personal factors) was the second most frequent issue, followed by "difficulties in working together to get information". Not having the knowledge of a concrete method for using of the ICF/ICF-CY and difficulties in understanding terms, were the fourth and fifth most frequently identified issues, respectively.

(7) Descriptive comments

This survey collected also open text comments. Many comments related to expectations or issues about the use of the ICF/ICF-CY. For example, "*Wants more information about case reports in which the ICF/ICF-CY was used, with a practical method for the use*". "*Some of the teachers were interested in its use, but it its practical application was under consideration*". A detailed analysis of descriptive comments indicated that many schools that did not use the ICF/ICF-CY were aware of the need for training and enlightenment about the National Curriculum Standard Guideline. Many comments stated opinions regarding training and application of the ICF/ICF-CY to the development of IESPs or ITPs.

3 Discussion

The reason that there was greater awareness of the ICF among teachers, rather than of the ICF-CY was assumed to be related with the very recent introduction of the ICF-CY, just around the time when the survey was conducted. The ICF-CY categories are more useful SNE practice with students than the ICF categories. Therefore, it was expected that ICF-CY awareness would increase in the future.

The finding that 21% of schools used the ICF/ICF-CY was higher than expected. Even schools that did not report using the ICF/ICF-CY expressed many positive comments regarding its use in the near future. It was assumed that this was influenced by the description of the ICF in the National Curriculum Standard Guideline and that the usage rate should increase in the future. For this purpose, it was seen as useful the provision of case studies, for example, case reports on how the ICF/ICF-CY were used, practical methods and training programs.

Overall, the findings revealed variability in the nature, purpose and characteristics related to use of the ICF/ICF-CY. For example, the use of the ICF/ICF-CY for improving IESPs was considered useful, whenever there was an issue related to collaboration between teachers and therapists in hospital and in school.

The key outcomes found after using the ICF/ICF-CY in SNE were 1) the development of a holistic understanding of students with special needs, 2) the development of shared information about students between teachers and 3) the development of goals for students as guidance for intervention. The conceptual framework of the ICF/ICF-CY appears to be mainly accepted in special schools.

The major issues related to using the ICF/ICF-CY were 1) difficulties in understanding basic knowledge, 2) difficulties in coding information about students and 3) difficulties and challenges in using the ICF/ICF-CY. Most of these problems were technical in nature and a number of them were resolved by the NISE research project, after completion of the survey. It was expected that these contributions would facilitate the usage of the ICF/ICF-CY by the teachers.

Representative applications of the use ICF/ICF-CY for SNE practice in Japan

The conceptual framework of the ICF/ICF-CY is broadly accepted and used in SNE practice. Figure 5.7 illustrates the application of this conceptual framework for comprehensive assessment of a student in SNE. Summarising a range of information about a student on a single form can help teachers to efficiently integrate and share that information (see Figure 5.8). This application may be useful for stakeholder to understand the nature of the child's characteristics and to define their role in an integrated planning approach.

Figure 5.9 illustrates the five-step procedure for developing a worksheet based on the ICF/ICF-CY conceptual framework, aiming holistic comprehension of students and supported decision making, within a team.

Development of an ICF-CY core set and digital tool for SNE in Japan

Background for development of an ICF-CY core set

Early interest in the conceptual framework as well in the categories of the ICF/ICF-CY by researchers and teachers in Japan led to the translation and usage of the WHO "ICF CHECKLIST Version 2.1a Clinician Form" by the NISE research project. One goal of this research was to identify codes for effective assessment of specific characteristics of each child from different perspectives. The use of WHO Checklists of ICF codes had been reported by some schools in Japan, but a fixed core set of ICF/ICF-CY codes based on research had not been reported by then. Therefore, it was necessary to develop a specific ICF Core set for the SNE context. A research project under NISE developed an ICF-CY core set and digital tool for practical use in this context.

Methods

The participants in this project were 351 teachers of special schools who were familiar with the ICF and ICF-CY. The teachers responded to a questionnaire,

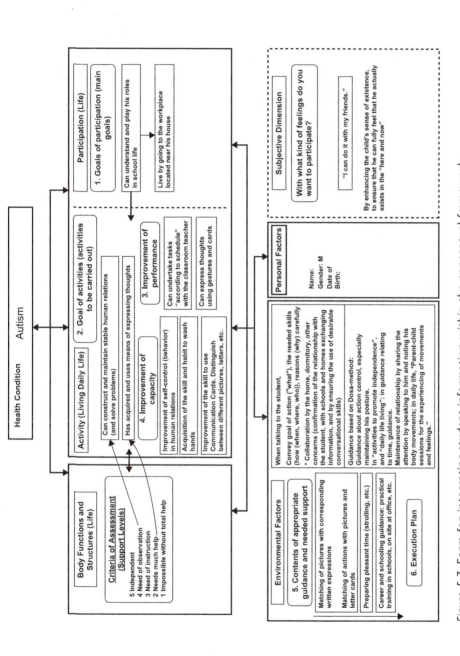

Figure 5.7 Form for integrating student information within the conceptual framework

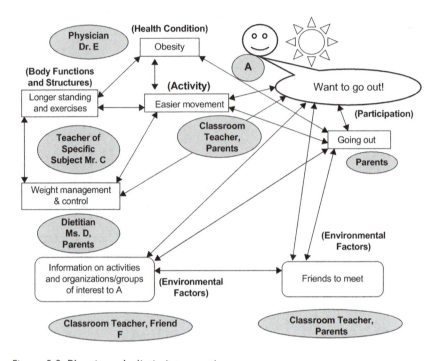

Figure 5.8 Planning a holistic intervention

(1) Describe information of the student on small cards
↓
(2) Classify cards on the work sheet, discussing with colleagues or parents
↓
(3) Confirm short of information, referring to ICF-CY book
↓
(4) Discussion for holistic comprehension considering the interaction between the information cards
↓
(5) Consider a main target, concrete goals, person in charge, method, contents and date of evaluation

Figure 5.9 Procedure for developing an worksheet based ICF/ICF-CY framework

focusing on the identification of codes that should be included in a core set from a list of 283 two-level classification codes. From this list, participants were invited to identify codes considered necessary to assess difficulty of learning and daily living of their students with disabilities, using a Visual Analog Scale. Codes selected from the four ICF-CY domains were 83 body functions, 40 body structures, 96 activities and participation and 64 environmental factors. Two steps were followed to select categories.

First step: The criteria for selection of categories were as follows:

1) Higher than average frequency of codes identified as necessary in each component (B/F, B/S, A/P, E/F) and
2) Higher than average frequency of codes identified as unnecessary in each component group

Second step: Discussion of results from first step among five experts and revision of the first core set of codes.

Results and discussion

First step: 182 categories were selected (54 on body functions, 24 on body structures, 73 on activities and participation and 31 on environmental factors).

Second step: 188 categories were selected (49 on body functions, 27 on body structures, 79 on activities and participation and 33 on environmental factors). In total, 188 categories were identified as necessary to understand students with disabilities comprehensively; these categories constitute the core set of codes for SNE settings, especially for developing IESPs.

Demonstration of core set with a digital tool for use of ICF-CY

Teachers of a special school assessed a group of students in SNE and discussed goal setting using the developed core set in the form of a digital tool. The digital tool was used as a checklist to assess student difficulty in learning and performance in daily living. The result was a comprehensive assessment and shared information about the student followed by goal setting framed by the ICF model.

Challenges in using the ICF-CY for reasonable accommodation

Our work has indicated that it is possible to use the ICF/ICF-CY conceptual framework and categories in SNE practice and for planning reasonable accommodations for students with disabilities. The conceptual framework can be useful in defining reasonable accommodations for individual students. An important issue to consider in this regard is the compatibility between reasonable accommodations made in school and the ICF-CY structure of categories. This was examined in a pilot study looking at the compatibility between reasonable accommodations in a school reported by the Central Committee on Education of the National Government and ICF–CY categories. The identified reasonable accommodations for students in the school were linked to the ICF–CY categories based on the ICF linking rules (Cieza et al., 2005). The accommodations were found compatible with the ICF–CY categories in the environmental factors component – namely, "products and technology" in Chapter 1 of the ICF, "natural environment and human-made changes to environment" in Chapter 2, "support and relationships" in Chapter 3 and "service, systems and policies in the environmental factor" in Chapter 5. Additionally, the details of reasonable accommodations were also found compatible with ICF–CY categories of body function, and activities and participation. The results confirmed that it was possible to apply the ICF–CY to define reasonable accommodations for students in SNE. Furthermore, providing reasonable accommodations according to individual student status reflects the importance of the link between body functions, activities and participation and personal factors.

A second pilot study investigated the compatibility of the components of the Design of Basic Educational Environment (hereafter the Design) with the ICF–CY. The Design came out as a report concerning students with special needs issued by the Central Committee on Education of the National Government in Japan. Using the ICF linking rules, the study examined whether the contents described in the Design could be linked to the ICF–CY categories. Results showed that the described contents could be linked to the ICF–CY categories: Chapter 1: "products and technology", Chapter 3: "support and relationships", Chapter 4: "attitudes" and Chapter 5: "service, systems and policies" of the environmental factors component. These results indicated that it was possible to arrange the contents of the Design using the ICF–CY framework, as it is the case with the reasonable accommodations made in schools in Japan. The study results also suggested that it should be possible to improve and promote the Design with reference to the ICF–CY. Furthermore, it is important to highlight that the Design, widely related to students with disabilities, should be constructed to enhance "activities and participation" from the point of view of d815 (ICF code for preschool education) and d820 (ICF code for school education).

Conclusion

In this chapter, we described the implementation of the ICF–CY in SNE in Japan.

The ICF and the ICF–CY have been accepted and used for SNE policy and practice, especially its conceptual framework, as it enables holistic understanding of students with disabilities. It is a very useful model for a comprehensive approach to students with disabilities and for sharing their between different professionals.

The key outcomes found after using the ICF/ICF-CY in SNE were 1) the development of a holistic understanding of students with special needs, 2) the possibility of sharing information about students between professionals and 3) the development of goals for students as guidance for intervention. Even schools that did not report using the ICF/ICF-CY expressed many positive opinions about its use in the near future. The ICF-CY categories also had utility in the SNE, although the conceptual framework appears to be more consensually accepted. The core set of ICF-CY codes in the form of a digital tool can contribute to facilitate the use of the categories.

It is possible to use the conceptual framework and the ICF-CY categories as a process for informed consent of children in SNE and for planning their reasonable accommodation. The Central Committee on Education of the National Government proposed the use of the ICF as the basis for reasonable accommodations to be made for students, within the context of the United Nations Convention for the Rights of Persons with Disabilities. Our studies also showed that the ICF-CY could contribute to define reasonable accommodations for students with disabilities. Furthermore, the use of the ICF/ICF-CY is expected to enrich SNE practice in Japan from this time onwards.

Highlights from this chapter

- The ICF/ICF-CY model is very useful in SNE, especially, for a holistic comprehension of students with SENs, beyond diagnosis.
- Holistic understanding of functioning of students can help school-teachers to plan their intervention and facilitate communication between stakeholders.
- It is necessary to facilitate the use of the ICF/ICF-CY, for example, with case reports where the ICF/ICF-CY were used, practical methods of application and training programs.
- The use of the ICF/ICF-CY can contribute to enrich SNE practice by helping to provide reasonable accommodations for students with disabilities, based on the United Nations Convention on the Rights of People with Disabilities.

References

Cieza, A., Geyh, S., Chatterji, S., Kostanjsek, N., Ustun, B., & Stucki, G. (2005). ICF linking rules: An update based on lessons learned. *Journal of Rehabilitation Medicine*, 37, 212–218.

Ministry of Education, Culture, Sports, Science and Technology (2012). Result of survey of students who have possibilities of developing disabilities with special educational needs, enrolled in regular classes. Retrieved from: http://www.mext.go.jp/en/

Ministry of Education, Culture, Sports, Science and Technology (2015). Documents of Special Needs Education in Japan. Retrieved from: http://www.mext.go.jp/en/

United Nations General Assembly. (2007). *United Nations convention on the rights of people with disabilities*. New York: United Nations General Assembly

World Health Organization. (2001). *International classification of functioning. disability and health*. Geneva: WHO library.

World Health Organization. (2007). *International classification of functioning disability and health for children and youth*. Geneva: WHO library.

Chapter 6

Development of the FUNDES-Child and its implications for the education of Taiwanese children

Hua-Fang Liao, Ai-Wen Hwang, Lin-Ju Kang, Ya-Tzu Liao, Mats Granlund and Rune J. Simeonsson

Introduction

Children and youth with special needs from age two to 18 years in Taiwan receive evaluation and services from both the Ministry of Health and Welfare and the Ministry of Education based on the People with Disabilities Rights Protection Act (Ministry of Health and Welfare, 2007) and the Special Education Act (Ministry of Education, 2014). On the basis of the earlier two acts, those children could apply for Disability Identification to receive related services, which are provided by the local social welfare department, and could also apply for special education services provided by the local educational department if they are going to attend preschool or higher-level school (both public and private). Special education placements range widely, from inclusion in regular classes in school to segregated setting in special education schools.

Since the launch of the People with Disabilities Rights Protection Act in 2007, the disability evaluation and social welfare services have been based on the framework of the International Classification of Functioning, Disability and Health (ICF) and its child and youth version (ICF-CY) (World Health Organization [WHO], 2001, 2007) in Taiwan. Based on the concepts of the ICF and ICF-CY, the awareness of the importance of societal participation and inclusion of children with special needs has been incorporated into service systems in Taiwan, including health, social welfare and education systems (Liao, Hwang, Pan, Liou, & Yen, 2013; Pan, Hwang, Simeonsson, Lu, & Liao, 2014; Hwang et al., 2015a). With the introduction of the People with Disabilities Rights Protection Act and a visible and steady increase of articles and workshops related to applications of the ICF in special education (Huang & Lin, 2007; Wang, 2011; Liao, Hwang et al., 2013; Liao, Yen et al., 2013), the concept of ICF seems to have received much attention in special education. However, the Special Education Act, which is more recent, does not include any ICF concepts or terminology, but is only based on the Disabilities Rights Protection Act. This chapter introduces an ICF-based assessment tool, the Functioning Scale of the Disability Evaluation System – Child version (FUNDES-Child) and its application in school settings.

The launch of the People With Disabilities Rights Protection Act in 2007

Since 1980, the Taiwanese government has applied certain legislative procedures to create and revise categories of disability. A person who fulfills the criteria for receiving disability benefits may be granted cash and in-kind services from the government. However, the criteria for eligibility were mainly based on the medical model, which considered disability as a physical and mental impairment. Thus, candidates for disability benefits were identified by physicians primarily on the basis of the degree of body impairment, without adequate evaluation of their activity, participation and environment. In 2007, the Taiwanese Legislative Yuan passed a constitutional amendment known as the "People with Disabilities Rights Protection Act" (Ministry of Health and Welfare, 2007). Under this act, the assessment of a person's eligibility for benefits was required from 2012 to be based on the ICF and ICF-CY framework (WHO, 2001, 2007).

ICF-based disability eligibility system

Based on regulations of the People with Disabilities Rights Protection Act, professionals in the medical setting and social welfare system evaluate multiple dimensions of disability within Taiwan's Disability Evaluation System (DES) (Chiu et al., 2013; Teng et al., 2013) including body structures (denoted as s), body functions (b), activities and participation (d) and environmental factors (e). The main theme of this disability service system is therefore to emphasise that people with disabilities should be evaluated by a multidisciplinary team and be provided with one-stop, individualised and diversified services. Enhancement of the societal participation of people with disabilities is thus Taiwan government policy (Ministry of Health and Welfare, 2014).

The DES is a three-stage evaluation process: (1) medical examination (body functions/structures), (2) functional assessment (participation and environment) and (3) needs assessment (Chiu et al., 2013; Teng et al., 2013; Liao, Yen, Hwang, Liou, & Chi, 2015). Figure 6.1 presents the current framework of disability evaluation and welfare services in Taiwan. People with disabilities apply for disability eligibility determination at the local district office. Then, they receive the medical evaluation, including the components of b/s/d/e by a medical team at one of the authorised hospitals. After medical evaluation, a medical evaluation report will be issued and sent to the local government. The social welfare department of the local government will organise a committee to conduct the first stage needs assessment to confirm eligibility of individuals and

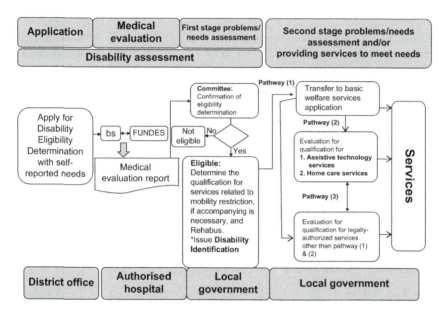

Figure 6.1 The framework of disability evaluation and welfare services in Taiwan

decide if they are qualified for four basic welfare services. The committee members are different professionals from different cities or counties, including social workers, therapists or physicians. The basic services are designed to enhance societal participation and include disability car parking priority for those with mobility restriction, accommodations necessary to access public transportation and recreation facilities and Rehabus services. Rehabus is a special transportation services for people with disabilities which requires reservation in advance and a small payment. All Rehabus vehicles are equipped with wheelchair lifts or ramps to facilitate access. If the person meets eligibility criteria, then the local government will issue the Disability Identification. With the Disability Identification, the person may enter the second stage needs assessment and receive related further services to meet their needs. The government also regulates that the Disability Identification should be issued within 45 days once the application process has started and renewed at least every five years (Liao et al., 2015; Hwang et al., 2015a). All the data collected in the DES is entered in the information system, Taiwan Databank of Persons with Disabilities (TDPD) (Chi et al., 2013), which will inform the social welfare department of the local government the due date of every Disability Identification.

Individuals with Disability Identification are qualified to receive related services and support, and equal access to participate in social, political, economical and cultural activities. The People with Disabilities Rights of Protection Act regulated that Taiwan government should provide eight types of welfare services for people with disabilities, including home care services, caregiver services, financial support, transportation services, health and medical care services, educational services, employment services and other services. In order to receive related services, they have to receive the second stage problems/needs assessments provided by the local government (Figure 6.1). On the basis of the current service framework, through pathway 2, some of those needing assistive technology services will receive assistive device evaluation at assistive device resource centres or authorised medical institutes; some needing home care services (including body care service, home affairs service, friendly visits, catering to home, etc.) have to receive home care assessment to determine their qualification (Note 1); others need other services through pathway 3 have to receive Needs Assessment Interview based on the Regulations of Needs Assessment for Welfare Services and Disability Identification Issue for People with Disabilities (Ministry of Health and Welfare, 2015).

Development of the functioning scale of the Disability Evaluation System – Child version

The Functioning Scale of the Disability Evaluation System – Child version (FUNDES-Child) was developed in 2011as the tool for assessment of functioning (body function, activity and participation) and environmental factors in the DES for children aged 6–18 years. Details of the development and initial validation for the FUNDES-Child have been described elsewhere (Liao, Yen et al., 2013; Liao, Yen et al., 2015). In brief, the FUNDES-Child is an adapted version of the Child and Family Follow-Up Survey (CFFS) (Bedell & Dumas, 2004) translated into traditional Chinese and back translated into English with approval and collaboration of the original author (Bedell, 2011). The CFFS was originally designed to monitor needs and outcomes of children and youth with acquired brain injuries (Bedell & Dumas, 2004) and later used in various settings with children and youth with a range of chronic conditions such as physical and mental dysfunctioning (Mcdougall, Wright, Schmidt, Miller, & Lowry, 2011; Weintraub, Rot, Shoshani, Pe, & Weintraub, 2011).

The FUNDES-Child utilises a proxy format in which parents or caregivers answer questions about their child's activities in the previous 6 months. In keeping with the format used in the FUNDES-Adult version interview (Chiu et al., 2013; Teng et al., 2013; Liao, Yen et al., 2015), flash cards with scoring options were used to assist parents in answering questions. In 2012, the formal implementation year of the current DES, the FUNDES 6th including both adult and child version has been developed. And in 2015, we have the FUNDES 8th (Liao, 2015).

Content of the FUNDES-Child

The FUNDES-Child contains four sections: Section I: general information, Section II: participation (adapted from the Child and Adolescent Scale of

Participation of the CFFS), Section III: body function impairment (adapted from the Child and Adolescent Factors Inventory of the CFFS) and Section IV: environmental factors (adapted from the Child and Adolescent Scale of Environment of the CFFS) (Liao, Yen et al., 2013; Liao, Yen et al., 2015). Section II and Section IV of the FUNDES-Child has been validated in studies with children with a variety of disabilities (Hwang et al., 2013; Kang et al., 2015).

An overview of the FUNDES-Child is presented in Table 6.1. The five items in Section I (physical health, emotional health and well-being, primary way of moving around, primary way of communication and whether the child lives with parents) have been used to gather general information about the child (Hwang et al., 2013; Hwang et al., 2015; Kang et al., 2015).

Child participation was assessed using FUNDES-Child Section II that contains 20 items measuring 2 dimensions, frequency and independence of participation (Hwang et al., 2013). The items from the independence dimension were translated and modified from the CFFS.

Table 6.1 Overview of the functioning scale of the Disability Evaluation System – Child 8.0 version (FUNDES – Child 8.0)

Section/Domain	Dimension	Item No.	Response Scale	Test Methods
Section I: children's health condition		5		Interview + Observation
Section II: participation (d)				
Do1. Home	frequency	6	0 ~ 3 & 9	Interview
	independence	6	0 ~ 3 & 9	Interview + Observation
Do 2. Neighbourhood and community	frequency	4	0 ~ 3 & 9	Interview
	independence	4	0 ~ 3 & 9	Interview + Observation
Do 3. School	frequency	5	0 ~ 3 & 9	Interview
	independence	5	0 ~ 3 & 9	Interview + Observation
Do 4. Home/ community living activities	frequency	5	0 ~ 3 & 9	Interview
	independence	5	0 ~ 3 & 9	Interview + Observation
Section III: body function impairment (b)	impairment	16	0 ~ 2	Interview + Observation
Section IV: environmental factors (e)	problem	19	0 ~ 2 & 9	Interview
Total item no.		76		

The frequency dimension has been designed by the Taiwan ICF team and added to each item of the FUNDES-Child Section II (Liao, Yen et al., 2015). Items are scored by the four domains describing settings (home with six items, neighbourhood and community with four items, school with five items and home/community living activities [HCLA] with five items) (Hwang et al., 2013). In the manual of the FUNDES-Child, independence was defined in terms of the child's current level of ability to participate compared to that of other children of his or her age in the same community. For each item, independence was rated as 0 (independent), 1 (with supervision/ mild assistance), 2 (with moderate assistance), 3 (with full assistance). Frequency of participation was rated as: 0 (equal to or greater than expected for age), 1 (somewhat less than expected for age), 2 (much less than expected for age) and 3 (never does). A response of not applicable (a child would not be expected to do that activity as peers of the same age and in the same community) is allowed for both dimensions. All items are rated under the condition that children used assistive devices as usual. As each item is on the same ordinal scale with the same anchor points at the extreme end (0–3 points), the two dimensions are comparable based on age-expected independence and frequency.

Section III of the FUNDES-Child consists of 15 items defining sensory, motor, cognitive and psychological functions that may be associated with problems for children with disabilities (Bedell, 2011). Each item or problem is rated on a three-point scale: No problem (0), Little problem (1) and Big problem (2).

Section IV of the FUNDES-Child is an 18-item measure of the impact of physical, social and attitudinal environment of the child's home, school and community and problems related to the quality or availability of services or assistance (Bedell, 2011). Each item is rated on a three-point scale: No problem (0), Little problem (1) and Big problem (2) and Not applicable (9).

Section scores were calculated as the sum of all "applicable" items divided by the maximum possible score of applicable items. This score then was multiplied by 100 to conform to a 0–100-point scale. A higher score means higher restriction, impaired or barrier.

Reliability and validity of the FUNDES-Child

The psychometric properties of FUNDES-Child have been examined in Taiwan with the de-identified database of TDPD provided by Ministry of Health and Welfare in 2011 (Hwang et al., 2013), and in 2012 (Hwang et al., 2013; Kang et al., 2015; Chen et al., 2017), between July 2012 and January 2014 (Hwang et al., 2015a). In addition, FUNDES-Child has been used to collect data on schoolchildren with physical disabilities (Chan, 2014) and autism spectrum disorder (ASD) (Lee, 2014) in research conducted and supported by Ministry of Science and Technology in 2013. For examining the test-retest reliability, a group of children with disabilities were tested twice with a two-week interval in 2014–2015 (Wang, 2015; Wu, 2015). A study in Canada found that youth with disabilities reported their activity/participation to be significantly higher than what their parents reported (McDougall, Bedell, & Wright, 2013). That finding led to a study to compare FUNDES-Child scores reported between parent proxy report and child self-report in Taiwan (Wu, 2015).

Cronbach's coefficient (alpha) was calculated for internal consistency, with alpha values higher than 0.80, considered excellent, 0.70–0.79 adequate and below 0.70 poor for measuring participation (Salter et al., 2005). The test-retest or inter-rater reliability was examined by intraclass correlation coefficient (ICC). Reliability coefficient $\geqq$ 0.75 is considered excellent, 0.4–0.74 adequate and $\leqq$ 0.40 poor (Salter et al., 2005). The following descriptions summarise the findings of the three sections in the FUNDES-Child.

Section II of the FUNDES-Child

This section has been examined comprehensively given the current advocacy for respect and measurement of full participation as a right of children (Granlund, 2013). Table 6.2 provides details on reliability of this section. The internal consistency of the independence and frequency dimension was adequate to excellent of total score in Section II (Cronbach's alpha = 0.81–0.96). The test-retest and inter-rater reliabilities were also adequate to excellent (ICC = 0.85–0.99). There were no significant differences between parent-report and children self-report scores in both dimensions. The school participation independence or frequency scores reported by parents were not significantly different from that by teachers.

The content validity of 20 items of FUNDES-Child Section II was demonstrated by successful linkage to all nine d chapters (Hwang et al., 2015a) (Table 6.3) using the linking rules described by Cieza et al. (2005) and Ibragimova, Pless, Adolfsson, Granlund and Bjorck-Akesson (2011). The construct validity of the two-factor structure of the independence dimension of Section II was supported by the exploratory factor analysis. Factor I and factor II were named after the "daily living" factor and the "social/ leisure/communication" factor, respectively, with 64.1% of the total variance explained (Hwang et al., 2013).

Section III of the FUNDES-Child

Moderate to high internal consistency was found in the whole Section III (Cronbach's α = 0.84) and two-factor subscales (Sensory/Motor problems α = 0.73 and Cognitive/Psychological problems α = 0.85). The third factor subscale, Visual/Auditory problems, including only two items and had low internal consistency (α = 0.31) (Chen et al., 2016).

The content validity of the 15 items of Section III was supported by successful linking to five body functions (b1, b2, b3, b4, b7) chapters of the ICF-CY (Hwang et al., 2015a). Construct validity study shows a three-factor structure:

Table 6.2 Psychometric properties of the FUNDES-Child section II

Index	Participants No. and Characteristics (Proxy/Self-Report)	Dimensions	Domains				
			Home	Neighbourhood and community	School	HCLA	Total score
Internal consistency (Cronbach's alpha)	N = 231, Disability (proxy report) (Hwang et al., 2013)	Independence	0.88	0.89	0.9	0.88	0.96
	N = 25, Physical disability (proxy report) (Chan, 2014)	Independence	0.91	0.92	0.91	0.88	0.96
	N = 28, ASD (proxy report) (Lee, 2014)	Independence	0.81	0.86	0.87	0.78	0.93
	N = 30, Intellectual disability (proxy report) (Wang, 2015)	Frequency	0.70	0.84	0.91	0.58	0.90
		Independence	0.85	0.90	0.95	0.80	0.96
	N = 30, Physical disability (self-report) (Wu, 2015)	Frequency	0.45	0.73	0.69	0.57	0.81
		Independence	0.65	0.77	0.66	0.82	0.92
	N = 30, Physical disability (proxy report) (Wu, 2015)	Frequency	0.59	0.84	0.72	0.69	0.84
		Independence	0.73	0.79	0.76	0.82	0.88
Tester-retest reliability (ICC[3.1])	N = 25, Physical disability (proxy report) (Chan, 2014)	Independence	0.86***	0.83***	0.91***	0.82***	0.93***
	N = 28, ASD (proxy report) (Lee, 2014)	Independence	0.95***	0.90***	0.91***	0.90***	0.93***
	N = 30, Intellectual disability (proxy report) (Wang, 2015)	Frequency	0.78***	0.77***	0.75***	0.81***	0.80***
		Independence	0.87***	0.88***	0.82***	0.78***	0.92***
	N = 30, Physical disability (proxy report) (Wu, 2015)	Frequency	0.52***	0.82***	0.70***	0.80***	0.85***
		Independence	0.83***	0.75***	0.81***	0.86***	0.90***
Inter-rater reliability (ICC[3.1])	N = 25, Physical disability (2 coders watch videos) (Chan, 2014)	Independence	0.97***	0.97***	1.00***	0.99***	0.99***
	N = 28, ASD (2 coders watch videos) (Lee, 2014)	Independence	0.99***	0.98***	0.99***	0.98***	0.99***
Parent-children difference (p-value)[a]	N = 30, Physical disability (parent vs. self-report) (Wu, 2015)	Frequency	1.00	0.29	0.73	0.07	0.40
		Independence	0.26	0.27	0.05	0.06	0.06
Parent-teacher difference (p-value)[a]	N = 30, Intellectual disability (parent vs. teacher report) (Wang, 2015)	Frequency	–	–	0.81	–	–
		Independence	–	–	0.78	–	–

Abbreviation: FUNDES-Child, the Functioning Scale of the Disability Evaluation System – Child version; ICC, intraclass correlation coefficient

a: paired t test, * p<0.05, ** p<0.01; *** p <0.001

Table 6.3 Scores of the FUNDES-Child and Picture My Participation in a case example

	FUNDES-Child Section II (Parent Report)			Picture My Participation (Self-Report)	
Frequency score	Independence score	Items (code)		Items (code)	Frequency score
0	1	1 Home: social, play or leisure activities with family members (d710, d7200, d7601, d7602, d7603, d8803,d9200, d9204)		9 Interact with the family (d760)	1
3	2	2 Home: social, play or leisure activities with friends (d360, d710, d7200, d7500, d7504, d8803)			
2	1	3 Home: family chores, responsibilities and decisions (d640, d650, d660)			
0	0	4 Home: self-care activities (independence)/ meals with family (frequency) d510–d560 / d550		2 Family mealtime (with usual family members) (d230, d550)	1
				1 Daily routines at home for personal care (dressing, choosing clothing, hair care, brushing teeth) (d230, d510–d560)	1
0	0	5 Home: moving around (d450, d4600, d465)			
1	2	6 Home: communicating with other children and adults (d310, d315, d320, d330, d331, d335, d340, d345, d350)			
2	2	7 Community: social, play or leisure activities with friends (d710, d7200, d7500, d7504, d8803, d9103, d920)		11 Getting together with other children in the community (d750, d920)	4
1	1	8 Community: structured events and activities (d9100, d9102, d920, d930)		16 Taking part in social activities in the community (parties, play group, parades) (d910, d920)	3

(Continued)

Table 6.3 (Continued)

FUNDES-Child Section II (Parent Report)			Picture My Participation (Self-Report)	
Frequency score	Independence score	Items (code)	Items (code)	Frequency score
			10 Family/community celebrations (birthdays, weddings, holiday gatherings) (d760, d910)	2
			12 Organised leisure activities (sports, clubs, music, art, dance) (d910, d920)	1
			14 Religious and spiritual gatherings and activities (d930)	4
0	0	9 Community: moving around (d450, d4601, d4602, d465)		
2	3	10 Community: communicating with other children and adults (d310, d315, d320, d330, d331, d335, d340, d345, d350)		
0	2	11 School: educational (academic) activities with classmates or schoolmates (d820)	18 Formal learning at school (d820)	1
1	1	12 School: social, play and recreational activities with classmates or schoolmates (d710, d7200, d7402, d7500, d7504, d880, d920)		
0	0	13 School: moving around (d450, d4601, d4602, d465)		
0	1	14 School: using educational materials and equipment (d140, d145, d150, d155, d166, d8201, d835)		
2	2	15 School: communicating with other children and adults (d310, d315, d320, d330, d331, d335, d340, d345, d350)		
2	1	16 HCLA: household activities (d6300, d6302, d640)	5 Meal preparation with or for the family (d630)	4

Item	Score
6 Cleaning up at home (clothing, household objects, laundry, rubbish, yard work) (d640)	3
4 Gathering daily necessities for the family (water, food, picking vegetables, fuel) (d620)	4
15 Shopping and errands (market) (d620, d860)	3
1 Daily routines at home for personal care (dressing, choosing clothing, hair care, brushing teeth) (d230, d510–d560)	1
20 Paid and unpaid employment (d850, d855)	5
3 Looking after his/her own health (medication) (d570)	3
7 Taking care of other family members (d660)	4
8 Taking care of animals (pet or domestic livestock) (d650)	4
13 Quiet leisure (listening to music, reading) (d880, d920)	2
17 Visit to health centre (e.g. doctor, dentist, other health care service) (d570, d470–d489)	2
19 Overnight visits and trips (d920, d470–d489)	2

Item	Score
17 HCLA: shopping and managing money (d620, d860)	2
18 HCLA: managing daily schedule (d230)	1
19 HCLA: using transportation to get around (d470, d4751)	2
20 HCLA: work activities and responsibilities (d230, d240, d850, d855)	9

(Left-margin scores: 1, 1, 2, 9)

Abbreviation: FUNDES-Child, the Functioning Scale of the Disability Evaluation System – Child version. HCLA: Home and community living activities

Note: FUNDES-Child Frequency Score, 0: the same or more than expected for age, 1 somewhat less than expected for age, 2 much less than expected for age, 3 never does; 9: not applicable. FUNDES-Child Independence Score, 0 independent, 1 with supervision/ mild assistance, 2 with moderate assistance, 3 with full assistance, 9 not applicable

Picture My Participation frequency score, 1 always, 2 sometimes, 3 not really, 4 never, 5 not applicable, 6 unsure or no answer

(1) Cognitive/Psychological problems, (2) Sensory/Motor problems and (3) Visual/Auditory problems (Chen et al., 2016).

Section IV of the FUNDES-Child

Moderate to high internal consistency was found in Section IV (Cronbach's $\alpha = 0.86$) and three-factor subscales ($\alpha = 0.74$–0.77) (Kang et al., 2015). Test-retest reliability was also adequate to excellent for the total scale (ICC was 0.85) and the three-factor subscales (ICC = 0.73–0.90) (Kang et al., 2015).

The content validity of 18 items of FUNDES-Child Section IV was supported by successful linkage to 4 ICF-CY environmental factor (e1, e3, e4, e5) chapters (Hwang et al., 2015a) except e2 (Kang et al., 2015). Evidence for construct validity was provided by a three-factor structure (family/community resources, assistance/attitude supports and physical design access) accounting for 38% variance explained (Kang et al., 2015).

Training of the FUNDES testers

Certified testers associated with 243 DES hospitals in Taiwan administered the FUNDES-Child by interviewing children's parents or caregivers (Liao, Fan et al., 2013; Liao, Yen et al., 2015). The certified testers were professionals licensed as physical therapists, occupational therapists, speech therapists, social workers, clinical psychologists, counselling psychologists, nurses, audiologists, special education teachers and vocational evaluators. To ensure the number and quality of FUNDES testers, training programs were funded by the Taiwan central government with recruitment of all the aforementioned licensed professionals, especially those in the DES hospitals.

The training programs for certified testers covered the procedures of the DES and regulations (30 minutes), introduction to ICF and ICF-CY (30 mins), introduction to assessment instruments (FUNDES-Adult [60 mins], FUNDES-Child [40 mins]), practice of assessment instruments (200 mins) and the web-based platform for entry and storage of data (30 mins). At the end of each training course, a paper-and-pencil test was administered to certify the attending professionals (Liao, Fan et al., 2013). By the end of 2014, there were about 7700 certified testers in Taiwan (Liao, Yen et al., 2015). Names, identification (ID) number and other related information of all certified FUNDES testers are kept in the FUNDES tester personnel dataset for manpower quality control in the DES (Liao, Yen et al., 2015).

Application of the FUNDES-Child for special of needs students

The ICF/ICF-CY has been recommended by WHO (2013) as a framework for nationwide services such as eligibility assessment, service planning, system-based data generated by administrative processes and needs assessment of the individual requiring environmental accommodations. Framed by the ICF-CY, the FUNDES-Child shared some important functions with the ICF-CY, but with more specific ICF-CY linked codes and utility issues. The ICF/ICF-CY is an internationally accepted standard for describing health and disability. However, the ICF/ICF-CY is a classification system, not a measure. The FUNDES-Child can measure a child's functioning status related to activity and participation and body function as well as that child's environmental barriers of the ICF/ICF-CY components. Each item of the FUNDES-Child has been linked to ICF-CY codes to facilitate interpretation. The FUNDES-Child has been used in Taiwan's DES to collect b, d and e information for children and youth with disabilities since 2012. The FUNDES-Child 8.0 manual also provides information of its clinical utility including ease of use, time, format, examiner qualification and interpretability (Liao, 2015).

As mentioned earlier in this chapter, children and youth with special needs from age 2 to 18 years receive evaluation and services from both the Ministry of Health and Welfare and the Ministry of Education. The eligibility procedures in the two systems are different. The Regulations for the Assessment of Students with Disabilities and/or Giftedness include detailed regulations of procedures in the educational system (Ministry of Education, 2013) and the Regulations for the Assessment of the Disabled describe the related regulations in the health and welfare system (Ministry of Health and Welfare, 2014b). Figure 6.1 presents the disability eligibility process in the health and welfare system. The following will introduce the eligibility procedure for students with disability. Article 24 of the Special Education Act states,

> Educational institutions at all levels shall undertake the assessment, teaching, and counseling of special needs students on the basis of an interdisciplinary team approach, and if required may combine the services of professionals in the fields of health and medical treatment, education, social work, independent living, and vocational rehabilitation to provide assistance in the form of guidance and services encompassing learning, living, psychological, rehabilitation training, occupational guidance, assessment, and transitions.

Article 2 of the Regulations for the Assessment of Students with Disabilities and/or Giftedness describes that "*the assessment of students with disabilities must be multi-source assessment, including standardized test, direct observation, interview and medical examination, or using the information in the Disability Identification as references*" (Ministry of Education, 2013). For students with Disability Identification, the information collected in the DES is useful in the special education eligibility procedure.

As evident in applications in European countries, the framework of ICF-CY has been advanced for the design of the individualised education program (De Polo, Pradal, Bortolot, Buffoni, & Martinuzzi, 2009), the establishment of context-sensitive eligibility system in education (Hollenweger, 2011) and the guidance of the implementation of education law (Sanches-Ferreira et al., 2013). The following section describes existing and expected applications of the FUNDES-Child in the Taiwan educational system.

A reference for services in the educational system

Based on linkages of FUNDES-Child to ICF-CY codes, we have captured the functional profiles of schoolchildren who have been assessed with the FUNDES-Child (Liao, Yen et al., 2013). The ICF-CY linked items scores can be transformed into ICF qualifiers. The functional profile in ICF-CY chapters or codes reflects child functioning as documented by b, s, d codes and experienced barriers measured with e codes. Goals for children and forms of service delivery can be planned with the ICF-CY profile with additional information from children and their families (Liao, Yen et al., 2013). Usually, the gap between independence (level of assistance needed in real life) and frequency (does do in real life) indicates the possible influence of environmental barriers/facilitators or other factors where intervention or support may be needed. The FUNDES-Child data has shown that the gap of higher independence ability but lower participation frequency is even wider for children with mild severity and who are of older age (Hwang et al., 2015b). This finding suggests that supports and interventions provided by welfare and educational services should be based not only on level of severity, but should also consider problems associated with the gap between frequency and independence dimensions.

In the goal setting phase, children with disabilities in school age are encouraged to express self-perceived needs and participate in decision making with or without their caregivers' assistance (Brewer, Pollock, & Wright, 2014). Children with disabilities should be respected and be given voice to express themselves with guidance strategies or a decisional support algorithm (Khetani, Cliff, Schelly, Daunhauer, & Anaby, 2014), as involvement in setting goals is a key ability of self-determination in the transition to adulthood. After assessing children's self-identified difficulties in functioning and perceived environmental barriers, our research team is now engaged in developing the strategies of supporting self-determination on goal setting for elementary school and high school (Hung, Hwang, & Kang, 2016; Liao, Hwang, Kang, & Liao, 2016).

In Taiwan, the Special Education Act (Ministry of Education, 2014), the People with Disabilities Rights Protection Act (Ministry of Health and Welfare, 2007) and the Child and Youth Welfare and Protection Act (Ministry of Health and Welfare, 2012) specified that no school can reject the enrollment of any special needs students. Although inclusive education is determined by the special education policy in Taiwan, currently, there are limited appropriate placements for inclusive education of special need students. The initial or follow-up education placement for special need student is decided by the Special Education Students Diagnosis and Placement Counseling Committee (DPCC) of the

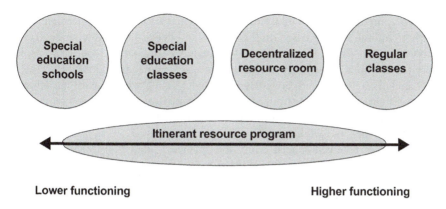

Figure 6.2 Education placements of children and youth with special needs in Taiwan (Liao, Yen et al., 2015)

local government. The members of the DPCC are scholars, experts, educational and school administrators, delegates of teacher organisations, parents, special education professionals and delegates of related institutions or groups. There are five placements for students with special needs: regular class, itinerant resource program, decentralised resource room, centralised special education class and special education schools (Ministry of Education, 2014). Students in the regular class share the same educational curriculum as their typical peers. Decentralised resource room means "students in regular class receive part-time special education and related services". Special education classes are those in which students receive full-time special education and related services and in which part of the program is carried out in the cross–class mode. Itinerant classes are provided to students who are at home, in institutions, hospitals or schools in which they receive special education and related services from itinerant teachers. The framework and level of functioning encompassed by FUNDES-Child could serves as a useful reference (Figure 6.2) in the provision and programming of special education and related services, fitting the principles of appropriateness, individualisation, localisation, accessibility and inclusion as described in Article 18 of the Special Education Act (2014).

A case example of self-determination strategy

The FUNDES-Child and Picture My Participation (Imms, Granlund, Bornman, Elliot, in prep.) are both ICF-CY framed measures for children's participation. Picture My Participation is a child self-report tool that uses pictures and guidance strategies to rate the participation and prioritise the importance of activities and related barriers/facilitators coming from environmental and personal factors. The protocol of the FUNDES-Child collects the caregiver's information about their child while the strategies of Picture My Participation gather children's voices based on their wants and needs. The following describes how to use the FUNDES-Child and Picture My Participation together to apply a self-determination strategy in the IEP for a special needs student.

Derek is a 9-year-old boy diagnosed with ASD, whose main functional limitation is verbal expression and social interaction. He uses Augmentative and Alternative Communication (AAC) for complex communication and to prompt his speech. Derek's mother is his main caregiver.

Derek has received special education services granted by Special Education Students DPCC since 2013. Prior to enrollment of elementary school, Derek applied for special education eligibility and placement with a certificate of medical diagnosis to the local educational department. At that time, Derek did not get a Disability Identification yet, otherwise the Disability Identification could replace the certificate of medical diagnosis. After application, the local department of education assigned a special education teacher to conduct a psycho-educational assessment with Derek. The content of the assessment included a parent interview, kindergarten teacher interview, onsite observation at the kindergarten and relevant reports provided by Derek's parents. The result of the assessment was reviewed by DPCC and decided to place Derek in a regular class with learning support from the special educator in the decentralised resource classroom.

From first grade to the first semester of the third grade, Derek received the inclusive education with his classmates for most of his school hours and was pulled out for one-on-one learning support by his special educator for 3–4 hours per week defined by his IEP. Instead of academic support, the special educator mainly worked on communication and social skills with Derek. In addition, Derek joined one extracurricular activity every Friday afternoon. That was a group session arranged by the decentralised resource classroom to enhance his adaptive behaviour and social skills. During the group session, students helped each other to complete homework and to do skateboard.

At the second semester of the third grade, Derek applied for the Disability Identification. His mother was interviewed with the FUNDES-Child by a clinical psychologist in one DES authorised hospital; his mother provided the results of the FUNDES-Child to the researcher. At the same time, the process of Picture My Participation was conducted in the resource classroom of Derek's school by the researcher in partnership with the special educator in the following steps: (1) Frequency, Prioritisation: Derek sorted out the participation cards on the frequency template and prioritised three activities for which he wants to make changes; (2) Level of Involvement: Derek chose "Very involved" for the first two prioritised activities and "Somewhat" in the third activity (Table 6.4); (3) Barrier and Facilitator: Derek could describe his status, the researcher then provided input to judge the barrier and facilitator factors in the suitable column. Derek described many individual strengths, such as

Table 6.4 IEP goals of Derek setting by using the Picture My Participation, the FUNDES-Child and curriculum guidelines

Top-Three Activities[a]	Level of Involvement[a]	Child Description[a]	Parent Opinions[b]	Goals of IEP[c]
(1) Organised leisure activities	Very involved (one-on-one course)	I can do violin, swimming and skating. I want to join the school team one day if I have the chance (indicating he want to have organised leisure group activities).		
I got support from teachers and mother.	Mom has to be the shadow; otherwise, it's difficult. The first priority is Derek can complete task independently, so he can join the team and communicate more by himself.	1–1. Participate and co-work with skate club classmates to complete a task.		
		1–2. Able to follow oral instructions in a group. 1–3. Able to check work progress (e.g. to tick on the checklist).		

(Continued)

Table 6.4 (Continued)

Top-Three Activities[a]	Level of Involvement[a]	Child Description[a]	Parent Opinions[b]	Goals of IEP[c]
(2) Overnight visits and trips	Very involved	I always want to go vacation with Mom and Dad.	We are not traveling as frequent as before, because Derek has heavier loads of schoolwork and learning activities.	
But I think we are okay as we arrange all kinds of outings almost every week. Family outings will be arranged by parents.	2–1. Attend and engage in the school trips.			
(3) Getting together with other children in the community	Somewhat involved	I want to take initiative.	Derek needs to work on communication skill in order to take initiative, otherwise he has to rely on Mom's accompany.	3–1. Initiate interaction with classmates in a group board games at school.

3-2. Use nonverbal communication with others properly (e.g. eyes gaze, iPad, AAC).

3-3. Able to listen to conversations and response appropriately.

3-4. Able to engage in dialogue on topics discussed.

3-5. Able to describe own life experiences and views with three sentences by iPad.

a. Child self-chosen and report from the Picture My Participation

b. Mother's main concerns from the FUNDES-Child and others

c. Goals of IEP were chosen from the capability indicators which are listed in Curriculum Guidelines for the Students with Special Needs from Elementary to Senior High Level (Ministry of Education, 2011)

Abbreviation: FUNDES-Child, the Functioning Scale of the Disability Evaluation System – Child version; AAC, Augmentative and Alternative Communication high motivation, and environmental facilitators, such as encouragement from mother and teachers, but he refused to discuss perceived barriers. The researchers linked items of the FUNDES-Child and Picture My Participation to present in a table (Table 6.4). All scores from the FUNDES-Child and Picture My Participation are showed in Table 6.4.

Derek prioritised the three activities in which he wanted to participate more: (1) organised leisure activities in group, (2) overnight visits and trips and (3) getting together with other children in the community (denoted as italic number and grey background in PMP frequency score of Table 6.3). Although Derek had participated in various kinds of organised leisure activities in a one-on-one basis (score 1 in PMP), he pointed out he wanted to join school team activities in group. The researcher further asked Derek about the level of involvement of the three activities. Derek indicated very high involvement for the first two activities meaning that he has a lot of interest in and attention to what he and others are doing during organised leisure activities and overnight visits and trips, and somewhat involvement for getting together with other children activities meaning that Derek is engaged in peer interaction activities some of the time (Table 6.4). Derek seemed to be reluctant to pick "Somewhat" as his rating of engagement with the image used to illustrate "Somewhat" as a child just sitting as an "onlooker".

The researcher, Derek's mother, Derek, class teacher and the special educator discussed and designed IEP goals and strategies together. The IEP meeting was based on the family-centred approach, a collaborative problem solving model and the ICF-CY framework (Liu et al., 2015). Related information, such as the scores of Table 6.3 were presented and discussed in the meeting. Derek's mother mentioned that the data obtained with the FUNDES-Child did reflect her concern about Derek's participation restriction in (1) social, play or leisure activities with friends in home and community and (2) communicating with other children and adults in community and school (denoted as italic number and grey background in FUNDES-Child scores in Table 6.3). For the activities in which Derek preferred to participate more according to his self-ratings, his mother had been following him in order to accommodate his needs. Derek's mother expressed concerns about his independence in social and communication skills and in completing school tasks. The class teacher had observed that Derek had relatively good compliance with classroom routine, and his social referencing skills were emerging. She also mentioned that the school had a skating club and some classmates were club members. In combining priorities from Derek and concerns of others, the special educator presented a list of Capability Indicators in the Domains of Learning Strategies and Social Skills of the Curriculum Guidelines for Students with Special Needs published by the Ministry of Education (Ministry of Education, 2011; Lu, 2011). Four indicators in the basic communication skill subdomain of the Social Skills domain were chosen as the IEP goals to meet the needs of Derek for initiating interaction with other children in the community. Two indicators in the metacognitive strategies subdomain of the Learning Strategies were chosen to meet Derek's needs for planning and executing complex task and then to be able to join some organised leisure group activities in the near future. Three participation goals were also included in the IEP, by the end of the semester Derek, 1) participate and co-work with the skating club classmates to complete one task under the guidance of his class teacher, 2) attend and engage in the school trips and 3) initiate interactions with classmates in group board games at school (Table 6.4). Appendix 1 provides an example from the records of discussion based on collaborative problem solving model.

The special educator proposed "related services and supporting strategies" in the IEP to accommodate Derek's needs. The supporting strategies for Goal 1 included 1) the class teacher and special educator provide visual cues for working process or instructions in group activities, 2) peer support, to invite and coach skating club classmates to work together with Derek, 3) special educator designs a checklist and guide Derek to do self-monitoring and 4) The supporting strategies for Goal 2 was recruiting parent volunteers for school trips and those for goals three were 1) to apply for iPad with communication apps, 2) special educator practiced with Derek using alternative communication instruction and 3) peer support, class teacher invited and coached non-disabled peers to support Derek's social needs. As a result, the special educator invited Derek skate club classmates and designed a group session with board games one hour per week, which responded to Derek's need to be more engaged in a group.

Besides the three priority activities, the researcher also stressed the FUNDES-Child items that had negative gaps between independence and frequency (means frequency restriction more than independence limitation). Pictures were used to enhance Derek's involvement in goal identification. For examples, with reference to the second item of the FUNDES-Child, Derek never participated in social, play or leisure activities with friends at home, even though he could participate with moderate assistance. Mother explained that Derek's friend never had visited their home. Derek expressed that he wanted friends to visit as one of his goals. Afterwards, one IEP goal "by the end of the semester Derek will have social or play activities with his friends at home at least once every month" was added.

Promote cross-culture comparisons

The processes of cross-culture translation and adaptation of the FUNDES-Child enabled the researchers to gather a variety of views about children's functioning internationally (Hwang, Liou et al., 2013; Hwang et al., 2015a) and also promoted further collaboration and cross-culture comparisons. The nationwide survey with the FUNDES-Child also provides empirical data to validate the developed core sets/code set for paediatric populations, such as cerebral palsy core set (Schiariti, Selb, Cieza, & O'Donnell, 2014; Liao, Hwang,

Liou et al., 2016) and ICF-CY Developmental Code Sets for children with disabilities (Ellingsen & Simeonsson, 2011; Liao, Chiou et al., 2015). The ICF/ICF-CY core or code sets resulted from the selections of a minimal number of important ICF-CY codes to define the characteristics of specific health conditions or healthcare contexts. The core/code sets are used in order to set criteria for measurement and records (Cieza et al., 2004; Stucki & Grimby, 2004; Üstün, Chatterjii, & Kostanjsek, 2004). In addition, they can support the interdisciplinary and comprehensive description of patients' functioning (Ptyushkin, Selb, & Cieza, 2012). Currently there are plans to translate the FUNDES-Child for use in the Swedish quality register system aimed at improving interventions for children with disabilities. Therefore, we can expect an international data bank for the FUNDES-Child which could contribute to international understanding of worldwide participation information for children with disabilities.

Highlights from this chapter

- An ICF-based Act activated the development of a participation measure, the Functioning Scale of the Disability Evaluation System – Child version (FUNDES-Child) in Taiwan.
- The FUNDES-Child, with acceptable reliability and validity, can be used to gather a variety of views about children's functioning internationally.
- The FUNDES-Child can be used to set IEP goals and design educational intervention strategies.
- By using the FUNDES-Child and Picture My Participation in combination it is possible to apply a self-determination strategy in the IEP setting.

Note 1: Social and Family Affairs Administration, Ministry of Health and Welfare. Resource Portal of Assistive Technology (https://repat.sfaa.gov.tw/system/subject/inside_01.asp) accessed on July 10, 2016.

References

Bedell, G. (2011). *The Child and Family Follow-Up Survey (CFFS)-administration and scoring guidelines,* Unpublished Manual.

Bedell, G., & Dumas, H. (2004). Social participation of children and youth with acquired brain injuries discharged from inpatient rehabilitation: A follow-up study. *Brain Injury, 18,* 65–82.

Brewer, K., Pollock, N., & Wright, V. (2014). Addressing the challenges of collaborative goal setting with children and their families. *Physical & Occupational Therapy in Pediatrics, 34*(2), 138–152.

Chan, S. T. (2014). *Psychometric evaluation of the Child and Adolescent Scale of Participation-Traditional Chinese Version (CASP-C) in children with physical disability.* Master's thesis, Chang Gung University.

Chen, W. C., Bedell, G., Hwang, A. W., Kang, L. J., & Liao, H. F. (2016). *Psychometric properties of the traditional Chinese version of the Child and Adolescent Factors Inventory (CAFI-C).*

Chen, W. C., Bedell, G., Yen, C. F., Liou, T. H., Kang, L. J., Hwang, A. W., Liao, H. F. (2017). Psychometric properties of the Traditional Chinese Version of the Child and Adolescent Factors Inventory (CAFI-C). *Research In Developmental Disabilities* (under revision).

Chi, W. C., Liou, T. H., Huang, W. N. W., Yen, C. F., Teng, S. W., & Chang, I. C. (2013). Developing a disability determination model using a decision support system in Taiwan: A pilot study. *Journal of the Formosan Medical Association, 112*, 473–481.

Chiu, W. T., Yen, C. F., Teng, S. W., Liao, H. F., Chang, K. H., Chi, W. C., Wang, Y. H., & Liou, T. H. (2013). Implementing disability evaluation and welfare services based on the framework of the International Classification of Functioning, Disability and Health: Experiences in Taiwan. *BMC Health Services Research, 13*, 416.

Cieza, A., Ewert, T., Üstün, T. B., Chatterji, S., Kostanjsek, N., & Stucki, G. (2004). Development of ICF core sets for patients with chronic conditions. *Journal of Rehabilitation Medicine, 44*(Suppl), 9–11.

Cieza, A., Geyh, S., Chatterji, S., Kostanjsek, N., Ustun, B., & Stucki, G. (2005). ICF linking rules: An update based on lessons learned. *Journal of Rehabilitation Medicine, 37*, 212–218.

De Polo, G., Pradal, M., Bortolot, S., Buffoni, M., & Martinuzzi, A. (2009). Children with disability at school: The application of ICF-CY in the Veneto region. *Disability and Rehabilitation, 31*(Suppl 1), S67–$73. doi:10.3109/09638280903317880.

Ellingsen, K. M., & Simeonsson, R. J. (2011). ICF-CY developmental code sets. Retrieved from http://nebula.wsimg.com/64ee51c58188874254744fc85f79778d?AccessKeyId=17 3BEF57A7BC2DE8039B&disposition=0&alloworigin=1.

Granlund, M. (2013). Participation – challenges in conceptualization, measurement and intervention. *Child: Care, Health and Development, 39*, 470–473.

Hollenweger, J. (2011). Development of an ICF-based eligibility procedure for education in Switzerland. *BMC Public Health, 11*(Suppl 4), S7.

Huang, W. H., & Lin, H. T. (2007). From the revolution of the International Classification of Function, reviewing the special education classification system in Taiwan. *Bulletin of Special Education and Rehabilitation, 17*, 89–108. (in Chinese with English abstract)

Hung, Z. J., Hwang, A. W., & Kang, L. J. (2016). Applying the UNICEF participation and environment measure to youths with disabilities. *The Sixth National ICF and ICF-CY Conferences and Workshops.* Taipei: TSICF.

Hwang, A. W., Liou, T. H., Bedell, G. M., Kang, L. J., Chen, W. C., Yen, C. F., Chang, K. H., Liao, H. F., & d Component Task Force of Disability Evaluation System. (2013). Psychometric properties of the Child and Adolescent Scale of Participation – Traditional Chinese version. *International Journal of Rehabilitation Research, 136*(3), 211–220.

Hwang, A. W., Yen, C. F., Liou, T. H., Simeonsson, R. J., Chi, W. C., Lollar, D. J., Liao, H. F., Kang, L. J., Wu, T. F., Teng, S. W., & Chiu, W. T. (2015b). Participation of children with disabilities in Taiwan: The gap between independence and frequency. *PlosOne, 10*(5), e0126693.

Hwang, A. W., Yen, C. F., Liou, T. H., Bedell, G., Granlund, M., Teng, S. W., Chang, K. W., Chi, W. C., & Liao, H. F. (2015a). Development and validation of the ICF-CY based Functioning Scale of the Disability Evaluation System – Child version (FUNDES-Child) in Taiwan. *Journal of the Formosan Medical Association, 114*, 1170–1180.

Ibragimova, N. K., Pless, M., Adolfsson, M., Granlund, M., & Bjorck-Akesson, E. (2011). Using content analysis to link texts on assessment and intervention to the International

Classification of Functioning, Disability and Health – version for Children and Youth (ICF-CY). *Journal of Rehabilitation Medicine, 43*, 728–733.

Imms, C., Granlund, M., Bornman, J., & Elliot, C. (2014). *Picture my participation.* Australian Catholoc University and Jönköping University.

Kang, L. J., Yen, C. F., Bedell, G., Simeonsson, R. J., Liou, T. H., Chi, W. C., Liu, S. W., Liao, H. F., & Hwang, A. W. (2015). The Chinese version of the Child and Adolescent Scale of Environment (CASE-C): Validity and reliability for children with disabilities in Taiwan. *Research in Developmental Disabilities, 38*, 64–74.

Khetani, M. A., Cliff, A., Schelly, C., Daunhauer, L., & Anaby, D. (2014). Decisional support algorithm for collaborative care planning using the Participation and Environment Measure for Children and Youth (PEM-CY): A mixed-methods study. *Physical and Occupational Therapy in Pediatrics, 35*(3), 231–252.

Lee, S. T. (2014). *Psychometric evaluation of the Child and Adolescent Scale of Participation – Traditional Chinese Version (CASP-C) in children with Autistic Spectrum Disorders.* Master's thesis, Chang Gung University.

Liao, H. F. (2015, March). *Functioning scale of the disability evaluation system 8.0 – manual.* Sponsored by the Ministry of Health and Welfare, Taiwan. Taipei: Taiwan Society of International Classification of Functioning, Disability and Health (TSICF).

Liao, H. F., Chiou, H. Y., Liou, T. H., Chi, W. C., Yen, C. F., Hwang, A. W., Wu, T. F., Liang, C. T., Chen, S. C., & Chiu, H. C. (2015, December). *Training programs for professionals in the Disability Evaluation System and building the personnel database system – 2015*, M04F5018 Project Report. Funded by the Ministry of Health and Welfare, Taiwan. Taipei: Taiwan Society of International Classification of Functioning, Disability and Health (TSICF).

Liao, H. F., Fan, C. J., Liou, T. H., Yen, C. F., Wu, T. F., Chang, B. S., Lu, S. J., Hwang, A. W., Chi, W. C., & Lu, L. (2013). Training programs for testers of the functioning scale of the disability evaluation system in Taiwan and outcomes. *Journal of the Formosan Medical Association, 17*(5), 368–380. (text in Chinese with English abstract)

Liao, H. F., Hwang, A. W., Liou, T. H., Yen, C. F., Chi, W. C., Schiariti, V., Hung, H. C., & Teng, S. W. (2016, June 1–4). Validating the ICF core set for cerebral palsy by using national disability sample in Taiwan. *International Conference on Cerebral Palsy and other Childhood-onset Disabilities.* Stockholm, Sweden.

Liao, H. F., Hwang, A. W., Pan, Y. L., Liou, T. H., & Yen, C. F. (2013). Application of ICF/ICF-CY to physical therapy and the ICF Mobility Scale in Taiwan. *Formosa Journal of Physical Therapy, 38*(1), 1–15.

Liao, H. F., Yen, C. F., Hwang, A. W., Liou, T. H., Chang, B. S., Wu, T. F., Lu, S. J., Chi, W. C., & Chang, K. H. (2013). Introduction to the application of the functioning scale of the disability evaluation system. *Journal of the Formosan Medical Association, 17*(3), 317–331. (text in Chinese with English abstract)

Liao, H. F., Yen, C. F., Hwang, A. W., Liou, T. H., & Chi, W. C. (2015). The development and application of the Functioning Disability Evaluation Scale. *Community Development Quarterly, 105*, 77–98. (text in Chinese)

Liao, Y. T., Hwang, A. W., Kang, L. J., & Liao, H. F. (2016, March 19). Applying the UNICEF Participation and Environment Measure (UNICEF-PEM) to self-determination among children with disabilities in elementary school. *The Six National ICF and ICF-CY Conferences.* Taipei: Taipei Medical University.

Liu, W. Y., Pan, Y. L., Su, H. C., Hung, J. H., Liao, H. F., Huang, S. Y., Yang, J. Z., Sun, S. H., & Chuan, Y. F. (2015). A family-centered collaborative problem-solving process for a child with cerebral palsy and the family. *Formosa Journal of Physical Therapy, 40*(1), 18–26.

Lu, T. H. (2011). The connections of individual differences, curriculum adaptations, and differentiated instructions with the newly revised curriculum guidelines for the students with special needs. *Special Education Quarterly, 119*, 1–6. (in Chinese)

McDougall, J., Bedell, G., & Wright, V. (2013). The youth report version of the Child and Adolescent Scale of Participation (CASP): Assessment of psychometric properties and comparison with parent report. *Child: Care, Health and Development, 39*(4), 512–522.

McDougall, J., Wright, V., Schmidt, J., Miller, L., & Lowry, K. (2011). Applying the ICF framework to study changes in quality-of-life for youth with chronic conditions. *Developmental Neurorehabilitation, 14*, 41–53.

Ministry of Education. (2011). Curriculum guidelines for the students with special needs from elementary to senior high level. Retrieved July 10, 2015, from http://sencir.spc. ntnu.edu.tw/site/c_principle_001/index/process_t_key/212/mode_t_key/-1/data_t_ key/-1/code/001/kind_code/001). (In Chinese)

Ministry of Education. (2013). The regulations for the assessment of students with disabilities and/or giftedness. Retrieved June 30, 2016, from http://law.moj.gov.tw/LawClass/ LawAll.aspx?PCode=H0080065. (in Chinese)

Ministry of Education. (2014). Special Education Act. Retrieved April 30, 2016, from http:// law.moj.gov.tw/Eng/LawClass/LawContent.aspx?PCODE=H0080027.

Ministry of Health and Welfare. (2007). People with Disabilities Rights of Protection Act. Taiwan. Retrieved April 30, 2016, from http://law.moj.gov.tw/Eng/LawClass/LawContent.aspx?PCODE=D0050046

Ministry of Health and Welfare. (2012). Child and Youth Welfare and Protection Act. Retrieved from http://glrs.moi.gov.tw/EngLawContent.aspx?Type=C&id=163.

Ministry of Health and Welfare. (2014). Ministry of health and welfare report. Retrieved April 30, 2016, from www.mohw.gov.tw/MOHW_Upload/doc/%E4%B8%AD%E8 %8F%AF%E6%B0%91%E5%9C%8B103%E5%B9%B4%E7%89%88%E8%A1%9B%E7 %94%9F%E7%A6%8F%E5%88%A9%E5%B9%B4%E5%A0%B1_0047784001.pdf. (in Chinese).

Ministry of Health and Welfare. (2014b). The regulations for the assessment of the disabled. Retrieved June 30, 2016, from http://law.moj.gov.tw/LawClass/LawContent. aspx?PCODE=L0020020. (in Chinese)

Ministry of Health and Welfare. (2015). The regulations of needs assessment for welfare services and disability identification issue for people with disabilities. Retrieved July 10, 2016, from http://law.moj.gov.tw/LawClass/LawContent.aspx?PCODE=D0050050. (in Chinese)

Pan, Y. L., Hwang, A. W., Simeonsson, R. J., Lu, L., & Liao, H. F. (2014). ICF-CY Code Set for infants with early delay and disabilities (EDD Code Set) for interdisciplinary assessment: A global experts survey. *Disability and Rehabilitation, 21*, 1–11.

Ptyushkin, P., Selb, M., Cieza, A., Bickenbach, J., Cieza, A., Rauch, A., & Stucki, G. (2012). *ICF core sets: The ICF core set manual for clinical practice*. (pp. 14–21). Gottinggen: Hogrefe Publishing.

Salter, K., Jutai, J. W., Teasell, R., Foley, N. C., Bitensky, J., & Bayley, M. (2005). Issues for selection of outcome measures in stroke rehabilitation: ICF participation. *Disability & Rehabilitation, 27*, 507–528.

Sanches-Ferreira, M., Simeonsson, R. J., Silveira-Maia, M., Alves, S., Tavares, A., & Pinheiro, S. (2013). Portugal's special education law: Implementing the International Classification of Functioning, Disability and Health in policy and practice. *Disability and Rehabilitation, 135*(10), 868–873.

Schiariti, V., Selb, M., Cieza, A., & O'Donnell, M. (2014). International Classification of Functioning, Disability and Health Core Sets for children and youth with CP: Contributions to clinical practice. *Developmental Medicine and Child Neurology, 29*, 582–591.

Stucki, G., & Grimby, G. (2004). Applying the ICF in medicine. *Journal of Rehabilitation and Medicine, 44*(Suppl), 5–6.

Teng, S. W., Yen, C. F., Liao, H. F., Chang, K. H., Chi, W. C., Wang, Y. H., Liou, T. H., & Taiwan ICF Team. (2013). Evolution of system for disability assessment based on the International Classification of Functioning, Disability, and Health: A Taiwanese study. *Journal of the Formosan Medical Association, 112*, 691–698.

Ustün, B., Chatterji, S., & Kostanjsek, N. (2004). Comments from WHO for the Journal of Rehabilitation Medicine special supplement on ICF core sets. *Journal of Rehabilitation Medicine, 44*(Suppl), 7–8.

Wang, K. Y. (2011). From the perspective of changing paradigm on disability study to discuss the implication of ICF and ICF-CY in special education. *SpecialItalic Education Quarterly, 118*, 1–12 (in Chinese with English abstract).

Wang, W. H. (2015). *The reliability and validity examining of Part II of Functioning Scale of the Disability Evaluation System- Child version in junior high school students with intellectual disability.* Master's thesis, University of Taipei.

Weintraub, N., Rot, I., Shoshani, N., Pe, J., & Weintraub, M. (2011). Participation in daily activities and quality of life in survivors of retinoblastoma. *Pediatric Blood and Cancer, 56*, 590–594.

World Health Organization. (2001). *International Classification of Functioning, Disability and Health (ICF).* Geneva: WHO.

World Health Organization. (2007). *International Classification of Functioning, Disability and Health: Children & Youth Version (ICF-CY).* Geneva: WHO.

World Health Organization. (2013). *How to use the ICF: A practical manual for using the International Classification of Functioning, Disability and Health (ICF).* Geneva: WHO.

Wu, Y. C. (2015). *The reliability and validity of part II of Functioning Scale of the Disability Evaluation System – Child version in youth with physical disabilities.* Master's thesis, University of Taipei.

Records of discussion based on collaborative problem-solving model – an example

Step 1: Problem identification: Derek is unable to participate in the activities of school music, swimming or skating club.

Step 2: Problem explanation and strength identification:

1) Derek's school does not have music and swimming clubs, it does have a skating club (some Derek classmates are club members).
2) School skating club never has special needs students with aide to join the club.
3) School skating club coach is a contractual skating expert, not a professional teacher; he might have limited knowledge on how to get along with special needs students.
4) Unpredictable and unstructured activities in the skating club are not easily followed by Derek.
5) Derek has difficulties in following oral instructions in a group.
6) Derek has difficulties in planning and execution in complex task, such as group practice for a task with sequential skating moves. He usually needs a lot of structured instructions or cues.

Step 3: Goal setting: Derek will participate and co-work with the skating club classmates to complete one task under the guidance of his class teacher by the end of the semester.

Step 4: Intervention strategies (related services and supporting strategies):

1) Peer support, to invite and coach skating club classmates to work together with Derek and support Derek's social needs.
2) Class teacher and special educator provide visual cues and checklist for working process or instructions in group activities.
3) Special educator designs a checklist and guide Derek to do self-monitoring.
4) Special educator discusses with the skating coach about the possibility of Derek's joining.

Part III

Contribution of the ICF to education and care – applications in professional practice

Chapter 7

The ICF goes to school

Contributions to policy and practice in education

Kirsten Ellingsen, Eda Karacul, Meng-Ting Chen and Rune J. Simeonsson

Introduction

The school, as the universal setting for children in every country in the world, has needed a definitional and classification system to guide policy and practice in defining the match between child functioning and performance and characteristics of the learning environment. The ICF-CY provides a standard approach to define the characteristics and needs of children relative to the demands of the educational environment. The ICF-CY offers a framework and taxonomy to provide comprehensive documentation of the dimensions of learning and performance needs of students and the corresponding school environment to meet those needs through instruction and individualised support. Characteristics of attending, responding, learning, social interaction and the acquisition of skills included in the ICF-CY are relevant to the instruction of all students and have particular significance for practices in special education and school psychology. The purpose of this chapter is to describe application of the ICF-CY as a common language for administrators and practitioners in education and related services and provide recommendations for future use to support educational participation and inclusion for all children.

Background

Access to education is now widely recognised as a universal right for children. Over the past couple of decades, several global initiatives have aimed to promote access to quality education for all children, including children with disabilities. International agreements and conventions have identified access to education as a human right and advocated for inclusive educational practices for children with disabilities (UN CRPD, 2006; United Nations Conventions on the Rights of the Child (CRC), 1989; Salamanca Statement, UNESCO 1994). However, providing an accessible and appropriate education for children with disabilities and SEN presents challenges at many different levels. Achieving this goal requires educational policy and practice that will not only allow children to attend school it will also facilitate students successful engagement in a learning environment. It will require 1) identifying individual and school-wide educational support needs, 2) examining the relationship of child functioning with characteristics of the learning environment, 3) enhancing student success by understanding the barriers and facilitators that influence learning and participation in school and 4) implementing effective instruction and interventions that enhance performance and result in positive educational outcomes for all students.

This universal aim of inclusive education is reflected in recent national legislation and educational policy initiatives of many countries. However, there is considerable variability in the focus of national education policy and the level of implementation and approaches used to achieve inclusive education (Maxwell & Granlund, 2011). There is variability in how disability is defined and documented and how SENs are identified and met. There are differences in the provision of disability benefits and the methods to provide school-based interventions (Raggi et al., 2014). Eligibility decisions often still rely on categorical decisions that provide limited information about functioning and contextual variables that can influence school success. There is also variability in the process used to monitor intervention effectiveness and the type of information collected to assess progress towards educational goals for individual students. A shared goal for universal and inclusive education is an important starting point, but translating this into practice requires policy that is informed and adequately supported. A common framework and documentation system, such as the ICF-CY that aligns with the CRPD and CRC, would support global efforts to establish educational policy and guide practice so that all children are able to participate and learn in school.

Rationale for applying the International Classification of Functioning, Disability and Health for Children and Youth in education

A universal standard framework and system, such as the ICF-CY, could contribute to the successful inclusion of all children in school and guide educational policy and practice by providing a common language and shared system to document the school experiences of children with SEN worldwide. Derived by the International Classification System (ICF) and endorsed by the WHO in 2007, the ICF-CY is the first universal classification system of child health and disability. It provides a shared conceptualisation of child disability across disciplines and countries using a biopsychosocial model. The ICF-CY includes content to describe multidimensional aspects of child health and functional consequences of disabilities or underlying health conditions. Within this framework, *functioning* is explained as an "umbrella term that encompasses all body functions/structures, activities, and participation", whereas *disability* is defined as an "umbrella term for impairments, activity limitations and participation restrictions" (Gan, Tung, Yeh, Chang, & Wang, 2014, p. 25). The ICF-CY was designed to record the characteristics of developing children for multiple purposes, such as use in program planning, surveillance, research and documentation of intervention outcomes (WHO, 2007). Until the ICF-CY, there was no standard universal health classification available to document human functioning and health status. A review of the ICF application by the EU MHADIE project endorsed the ICF as a framework "to provide comparable health applications across settings and countries" (Bruyere, Van Looy, & Peterson, 2005, p. 114).

One of the major life roles for children is to be a student who performs successfully in school. Gaining access to an educational setting is the first step to help children assume this societal role. However, "providing equitable access to education for all children requires reliable prevalence data on childhood disability, documentation of factors limiting access to education and identification of necessary supports and resources" (Ellingsen & Thormann, 2011, p. vii). The ICF-CY offers a new way to conceptualise, implement and document characteristics of children and youth with disabilities in learning environments. It includes categories that describe social, educational and functional needs of children as well as medical needs (Ibragimova, Bjorck-Akesson, Granlund, Lillvist, & Eriksson, 2005).

The ICF-CY structure allows for documentation of children's participation in important daily life activities, such as school. It can be used to record environmental barriers and facilitators that influence the level and quality of student learning and engagement. Identifying environmental factors that promote or hinder functioning is an important component in the provision of inclusive education, as "inclusion . . . requires that schools adapt and provide the needed support to ensure that all children can work and learn together" (UNICEF, 2007, p. 1). Simeonsson, Simeonsson and Hollenweger (2008) identified the following potential applications of the ICF-CY in special education:

1   Serve as a standard reference for defining the rights of children and basis for documenting rights;
2   Provide a framework for integrating multidisciplinary efforts for assessment, intervention and progress monitoring;
3   Identify student problems within body function, body structure and activities and participation to derive profiles of child functioning and document environmental factors that serve as facilitators or barriers to functioning;
4   Define the nature and extent of functional limitations in meeting the demands of the school environment and match child characteristics with needed supports or resources to plan individualised interventions;
5   Guide the selection of measures for assessment or outcome monitoring;
6   Document change of child functioning with the use of severity qualifiers and codes; and
7   Increase the precision of statistical databases.

Application of the ICF-CY in education

The ICF-CY has had limited application for work with children who have SEN and in school settings, particularly in comparison to implementation in medical and rehabilitation fields (Aljunied & Frederickson, 2014; Benson & Oakland, 2010). Nevertheless, countries have started implementing the ICF-CY as part of assessment practice and eligibility determination procedures in special education. Studies are underway to examine and enhance the feasibility of the application of the ICF-CY in schools. Some countries have even incorporated the ICF-CY in national disability policy. A review of these efforts is presented in the following section. The chapter concludes with recommendations for future application of the ICF-CY to promote inclusive education based on these experiences.

National policy

Portugal was the first country to mandate the use of the ICF-CY in national special education policy (Sanches-Ferreira, Silveira-Maia & Alves, 2014). The Decree-Law No.3/2008 was published in January 7, 2008 and called for the use of ICF-CY to determine the eligibility of students for special educational services and the development of IEPs for students with special education needs (de Miranda-Correia, 2010). The ICF-CY was required be used as a reference when reporting evaluation results and to use these results to develop IEPs for students. Taiwan adopted the ICF/ICF-CY framework in its DES under the People with Disabilities Rights Protection Act and as such the "country can be viewed as one of the first to specifically identify the ICF's b chapters [body functions codes] in a legislative act" (Hwang et al., 2015, p. 1171). Switzerland began to implement a multidimensional procedure to determine eligibility in education based on the ICF-CY starting in 2011. ICF tools and procedures were used in schools at local and cantonal levels prior to the implementation in the national educational system (Hollenweger, 2013). Currently, Switzerland has also been one of the few countries to "officially adopt the ICF as the guiding classification for disability in education and as the foundation to develop a common language" (Hollenweger, 2013, p. 1088).

Assessment practice

(1) Eligibility determination

Obtaining a diagnosis is often the key to accessing intervention and special education services in many countries. In fact, "most education systems require that children be matched with vaguely defined disability categories despite the endorsement of the ICF by their governments" (Hollenweger, 2013, p. 1089). This process is problematic because there is limited information gained by diagnosis and many disabilities present overlapping symptoms and that makes it challenging to identify specific needs of individual students. The use of the ICF-CY framework was selected to guide special education assessment procedures and eligibility determination in Portugal because the ICF-CY aligns with the principles and values in accepted human rights documents and emphasises students' functioning rather than using a traditional medical approach (Sanches-Ferreira et al., 2014). Decisions about eligibility for special education services under the new special education law are based on student profiles of functioning and the severity of limitations and restrictions in activities and participation and impairments in body functions (Sanches-Ferreira et al., 2013).

In Italy, although lawmakers have not incorporated the ICF-CY into formal assessment processes in education, and researchers have started testing the efficacy of using the ICF-CY at school. The ICF-CY was introduced as a conceptual framework in the school inclusion process for students with disabilities in the Vento region of Northwest Italy. Three territorial Health Unit Agencies in Treviso implemented a project that used the ICF-CY language to help integrate children and adolescents with disabilities in schools (De Polo, Pradal, Bortolot, Buffoni, & Martinuzzi, 2009). They piloted a four-step system incorporating the ICF-CY body functions and activity and participation codes into functional assessments for eligibility determination and educational objectives in IEPs. Professionals reported that the integration between various documents for the school inclusion of children with disabilities improved with the ICF-CY, because it allowed different disciplines to share a common language and helped professionals to capture contextual factors and to understand how the environment affects students' performance (De Polo et al., 2009).

(2) Understand functional limitations and determine needs

The ICF-CY can be used to provide a functional profile of children in school to identify where problems exist. A functional approach may encourage professionals to focus on children's participation. For example, Kovac and Simeonsson (2014) mapped the clinical features of Agenesis Corpus Callosum documented across several studies to the ICF-CY. The reported characteristics of the disorder highly linked with brain structures, body structures and intellectual functions components of the ICF-CY. There were a few codes for the activities and participation and environmental factors. The researchers suggest that use of ICF-CY would strongly guide the evaluation and intervention development phases. In Brazil, the ICF-CY was used to help classify students functioning and neuropsychomotor development to identify the contextual conditions of health. Findings of the study were found to support the applicability and use of the ICF-CY in the school environment to classify an expanded health perspective of children and adolescents (da Silva et al., 2016).

The ICF-CY has been used to examine the documentation of service needs for children with disabilities. Many aspects of functional problems that are formally considered in ICF-CY are missing in the determination processes of eligibility for students with special needs in schools, if the assessment is done with other existing tools. A biased determination may affect and potentially distort the documentation of children's educational needs and the plans for meeting those needs in IEPs. Tantilipikorn and colleagues (2012) reviewed the medical and school records of children with cerebral palsy (CP) up to age 14 in Thailand to consider the extent ICF-CY components are covered. A review of medical and school records revealed important existing gaps in information collected about students.

(3) Measurement selection and mapping measures to ICF-CY

The ICF-CY has been used as a standard for content comparisons and examination of standardised instruments, in order to select the most appropriate items or measures and report functioning with a standard language for clinicians and researchers (Hwang et al., 2014; Krasuska et al., 2012; Sommer, Bullinger, Rohenkohl, Quitmann, & Brütt, 2015). Mapping items from reliable and valid measures with ICF-CY codes serves as a basis for determining the nature and extent of impairments within a common cross-culturally consistent taxonomy and inform professionals (Sommer et al., 2015). For instance linkage of meaningful concepts in identified environmental factors in studies on infants and toddlers with or at risk for motor delays revealed their impact on developmental outcomes and informed early intervention services (Hwang et al., 2014). Studies on linking standardised instruments with the ICF-CY aim to "raise awareness in clinicians and researchers about relevant domains from a well-being and functioning perspective" as well as making it easier to compare and better understand the domains of the instruments (Sommer et al., 2015, p. 439).

The same linkage rules by Cieza et al. (2005) are used to connect existing tools to the ICF-CY framework. Recently, published rules by Cieza et al. (2016) require 1) thorough understanding of the ICF, 2) identifying the main and 3) additional concepts in the item 4) identifying the perspective 5) categorisation of responses 6) linking meaningful concepts to the most precise ICF category 7) use "other specified" or "unspecified" as appropriate. In the recent research, the ICF-CY has been used as a framework to examine how quality of life measures are represented as well as providing a basis for a standard language for comparing and contrasting the nature and extent of the health conditions (Krasuska et al., 2012). The linkage of a health-related quality of life measure to the ICF-CY proved the scope and comparability of parent and child forms and helped estimating the prevalence of the related disabilities (Sommer et al., 2015). Linking common ASD diagnostic measures improved documentation of child functioning, informed interventions, identified functional characteristics of the tool and provided a common language for professional practices (Castro, Ferreira, Dababnah, & Pinto, 2013).

(4) Development of new assessment tools

Another area of application involved the development of new tools to document disabilities using the ICF-CY framework. An initiative commissioned by UNICEF-Armenia was implemented to assist in the revision of SENs assessment and educational planning to align with the ICF-CY and UN Conventions on the Rights of Persons with Disabilities (2006) www.inclusive-education-in-action.org/example-109.html. The ICF-CY served as a guiding framework to develop new assessment tools and procedures focusing on the difference between student needs and environmental supports. This was a departure from existing procedures that focused on medical diagnosis and standardised developmental testing. Existing measures used in Armenia were evaluated and adapted using the Ellingsen and Simeonsson (2011) ICF-CY Developmental Code Sets as reference to determine what to assess and identify what was missing. A new toolkit and procedural manual was created with national and international expert consultants. In addition, the initiative developed a methodology to translate assessment results into IEPs based on functional profiles. This new toolkit can be used for eligibility determination and identifying the support and services needed for student participation and intervention monitoring.

The ICF-CY consists of numerous potential characteristics to code. The application of the ICF-CY is important to unify functional data, but the complexity and time required to use it limits its feasibility. The ICF-CY Core Sets and Development Code Sets were developed as abridged sets of key functional dimensions of development, which intended to reduce the time necessary to use the ICF-CY in practice. In 2004, field trials of age-based questionnaires (i.e. younger than 3, 3–6 and 7–12 years) were conducted at Mälardalen University in Sweden (Ibragimova, Bjorck-Akesson, Granlund, Lillvist, & Eriksson, 2005). Study participants reported several challenges using the ICF-CY; feedback was used to revise ICF-CY questionnaires in 2005 with the I-CY-HAB project. Reduced item forms were developed and organised by ICF-CY domain and used to examine the utility of the ICF-CY within Swedish habilitation services (Adolfsson, Pless, Ibragimova, Granlund, & Björck-Åkesson, 2007).

ICF-CY core sets

Researchers in Sweden have conducted studies to design an interdisciplinary assessment tool of child participation in daily life situations (Adolfsson, Granlund, Björck-Åkesson, Ibragimova, & Pless, 2010). Under development are the core sets for ASD and ADHD. The Karolinska Institute in Sweden and the ICF Research Branch in collaboration with an international, multiprofessional Steering Committee have developed the ICF core sets that can be used in the assessment and follow-up of persons with ASD. The core sets are shortlists of ICF categories that are considered most relevant to individuals with a disability. The ICF core sets for ADHD aim to provide a standardised method to classify functioning in individuals with a diagnosis of ADHD (Bolte et al., 2014a). (See www.icf-research-branch.org/icf-core-sets-projects2/other-health-conditions/icf-core-set-for-autism-spectrum). Gan et al. (2014) also developed an ICF-CY based questionnaire consisting of 118 items for children with ASD between the ages of 3 to 6, containing items for domains of body functions, activities, participation and environment. The ICF-CY provides a useful model to understand the factors effecting children's participation from a whole-child perspective, making the intervention design based on needs more convenient.

ICF-CY developmental code sets

The ICF-CY Developmental Code Sets were developed to increase the utility and accessibility of the ICF-CY by identifying essential items by child age for use in research, policy and practice. A professionally diverse sample of 151 international experts representing all major world regions completed a series of iterative online surveys to rate the most important categories of child functioning to include in brief universal age-based "ICF-CY Developmental Code Sets" (Ellingsen, 2011). The Delphi technique was used to obtain participant consensus. A reduced number of categories (between 37 and 60 items) from the ICF-CY representing essential characteristics of children's functioning for four different age groups were created to be used as a standard minimal for documenting children's functioning (Ellingsen & Simeonsson, 2011). They have been translated into different languages and are available for free at www.icfcydevelopmentalcodesets.com/home.html.

Intervention and the provision of support services

(1) Set educational objectives or IEP goals

The categorical approach used by many countries to determine eligibility for special education provides limited information for intervention planning and does not identify environmental factors that may affect student functioning and performance. However, a disability diagnosis does not predict child functioning or inform specific areas to target as intervention outcomes and very rarely includes important environmental factors as part of the diagnostic criteria (Simeonsson et al., 2006; Florian et al., 2006). In Italy, using the ICF-CY in the development of IEPs was positively received because it highlights the role of the environmental factors and was seen to help recognise the role of environments to influence student functioning (de Polo et al., 2009). An important innovation of this tool was viewed to be the continuity with the other tools of the project and that the IEP now completes a profile of functioning for students in a global and multi-perspective way, underlining the environmental factors which may facilitate or hinder the functioning in the various situations of life. In Portugal, the ICF-CY was reported by professionals to support a better understanding of students' functioning and the development of assessment processes that more accurately capture students' needs beyond impairments and deficits. (Sanches-Ferreira et al., 2014). Klang et al. (2016) chose 43 students' IEPs and coded them by ICF-CY codes in terms of environmental factors, activity and participation. Castro, Pinto and Maia (2011) linked students' existing curricula to ICF-CY domains, including body functions and body structures, activities and participation and environmental factors. Raggi et al. (2014) developed an ICF-CY-based schedule for individualised education programs named the ICF-PEI Schedule. Cramerotti and Ianes (2016) developed a web-based system to draft IEP for students with SENs in school in Italy.

(2) Inform intervention planning

The ICF-CY has been used to determine impact of different types of impairment on student activity and participation at school. McCormack, Harrison, McLeod and McAllister (2011) investigated the association between communication impairment and activities and participation outcomes for 4,329 children between ages of 7 to 9 in Australia. Researchers suggested that understanding this connection provided a valuable tool for service implementation, by illustrating how the classification may be used in documenting assessment outcomes and in planning and monitoring interventions. The ICF-CY was used to understand the characteristics and needs of the adolescents with neurological and cognitive disabilities (primarily CP) in a neuro-rehabilitation program and determined to improve the medical, school and family collaboration with increased understanding and providing a common ground for patient centred services (Martinuzzi, De Polo, Bortolot, & Pradal, 2015). The ICF-CY was also used to understand the characteristics and needs of the adolescents with neurological and cognitive disabilities in a neuro-rehabilitation program and was found to improve the medical, school and family collaboration with increased understanding and providing a common ground for patient centred services (Martinuzzi, De Polo, Bortolot, & Pradal, 2015). A study in Singapore of the ICF evaluation system for use by educational psychologists to apply the ICF framework for children with ASD provided further support that ICF framework can be used to work with children who have ASD (Aljunied & Frederickson, 2014).

Andrade, Haase and Oliveira-Ferreira (2012) used an ICF-based instrument for cerebral palsy (IBI-CP) and pre-existing instruments to assess the activity and participation of children with cerebral palsy relative to motor and cognitive impairments in Brazil. Findings from the study suggested that using an ICF-based approach can help to systematise the use of the biopsychosocial approach endorsed by WHO rehabilitation services for youth with CP and illustrates the feasibility of developing a measure using the ICF-CY framework to create a profile of functioning for intervention planning. Ajovalasit et al. (2009) presented the possible social, emotional and behavioural concerns of children and adolescents with brain tumour by using the ICF- based instruments besides other assessments. The researcher demonstrated the importance of the role of environmental factors for reducing disability and to demonstrate the complexity of life conditions for children and adolescence particularly for social inclusion and participation and found that the ICF-CY provided a convenient way to present the nature and severity of the disability.

(3) Measure outcomes

The ICF-CY's emphasis on documenting the impact of environmental factors has important implications for prevention and intervention efforts. According to Benson and Oakland (2011) the "ICF's emphasis on intervention planning, execution, and evaluation are highly compatible with current federal efforts to minimize diagnosis and maximize efforts that lead to meaningful and permanent changes in achievement and social/emotional behaviours" (p.9). The ICF-CY classification system applied in schools would provide a profile of child functioning reflecting the degree of difficulty performing specific behaviours or activities related to learning and participation in school. The collection of functional status information with the ICF-CY could facilitate more effective evaluation of treatment outcomes and comparisons of treatment approaches. A list of ICF-CY codes that may be particularly applicable to educational settings is included in Tables 7.1, 7.2 and 7.3.

(4) Case management and interdisciplinary collaboration

The ICF-CY has been used to support multidisciplinary communication and understanding about the functional impairments of different disabilities and medical conditions. The ICF-CY can facilitate interdisciplinary communication and promotes comprehensive and consistent service. The use of ICF-CY to understand the characteristics and needs of the adolescents with neurological and cognitive disability, (CP being the main disorder) in a neuro-rehabilitation program had a meaningful impact improving the medical, school and family collaboration as well as within medical team because they were able to understand each other and had a common ground especially in patient centred services (Martinuzzi, De Polo, Bortolot, & Pradal, 2015). It could also assist with the integration of mental health and education agendas (Benson & Oakland, 2011).

(5) Promote participation

Success at school for children with disabilities "begins with accessing an educational program, but it depends on adequate policy, facilities, teaching, and sustained child participation" (Ellingsen & Thorman, 2011, p. 8). Participation is an important concept that relates to learning and development and reflects a child's actual experience in school. According to Maxwell and Granlund

Table 7.1 Potential activities and participation codes

	Activities and Participation

CHAPTER 1 – Learning and applying knowledge

Purposeful Sensory Experiences

d110	Watching
d115	Listening

Basic Learning

d132	Acquiring information
d137	Acquiring concepts
d140	Learning to read
d145	Learning to write
d150	Learning to calculate

Applying Knowledge

d160	Focusing attention
d161	Directing attention
d163	Thinking
d166	Reading
d170	Writing
d172	Calculating
d175	Solving problems

CHAPTER 2 – General tasks and demands

d210	Undertaking a single task
d220	Undertaking multiple tasks
d250	Managing one's own behaviour

CHAPTER 3 – Communication

d310	Communicating with – receiving – spoken messages
d315	Communicating with – receiving – nonverbal messages
d330	Speaking
d350	Conversation (e.g. starting, sustaining and ending a conversation; conversing with one or many people)
d355	Discussion

CHAPTER 4 – Mobility

d440	Fine hand use
d440	Fine hand use
d450	Walking
d455	Moving around

CHAPTER 7 – Interpersonal interactions and relationships

d710	Basic interpersonal interactions
d720	Complex interpersonal interactions
d740	Formal relationships
d750	Informal social relationships

Table 7.2 Potential ICF-CY environmental factors

Environmental Factors	
CHAPTER 1 – Products and technology	
e130	Products and technology for education
e140	Products and technology for culture, recreation and sport
CHAPTER 2 – Natural environment and human-made changes to environment	
CHAPTER 3 – Support and relationships	
e320	Friends
e325	Acquaintances, peers, colleagues, neighbours and community members
e340	Personal care providers and personal assistants
CHAPTER 4 – Attitudes	
e420	Individual attitudes of friends
e425	Individual attitudes of acquaintances, peers, colleagues, neighbours and community members
CHAPTER 5 – Services, systems and policies	
e585	Education and training services, systems and policies

(2011), the "concept of participation has been used both to describe goals for policies and as an outcome for individual students in education; that is, the outcome of policy on individuals" (p. 252). However, little guidance exists in the international conventions and documents about how to promote participation in education (Maxwell & Granlund, 2011). Maxwell and Granlund (2011) used the ICF-CY as a framework to investigate how environmental dimensions that influence student participation (i.e. availability, accessibility, affordability, accommodations and acceptability) are documented in national, regional and local levels in Scotland and Sweden. Both countries had more references to participation opportunities at the national level when compared to regional and local levels. They suggest that although there is a common aim to promote participation and inclusive practice at the national level, the application has not been widely achieved at lower levels (Maxwell & Granlund, 2011).

Challenges

Lack of professional knowledge, awareness and time to use and learn the ICF-CY have been identified as challenges applying the ICF-CY to educational practice. The need for adequate training and support, improved mechanisms for

Table 7.3 Potential ICF-CY body functions codes

Body Functions	
Global mental functions	
b110	Consciousness functions
b117	Intellectual functions
b122	Global psychosocial functions
b125	Dispositions and intra-personal functions
b126	Temperament and personality functions
b130	Energy and drive functions
Specific mental functions	
b140	Attention functions
b144	Memory functions
b147	Psychomotor control
b152	Emotional functions (emotions regulation and range of emotion)
b156	Perceptual functions
b160	Thought functions (pace, form, content, control of thought)
b163	Basic cognitive functions
b164	Higher-level cognitive functions
b167	Mental functions of language
b172	Calculation functions
b176	Mental function of sequencing complex movements
Sensory functions and pain	
b210	Seeing functions
b230	Hearing functions
Voice and speech functions	
b310	Voice functions
b320	Articulation functions
b330	Fluency and rhythm of speech functions

collaboration and development of assessment measures were challenges documented in the implementation of the ICF-CY in Portugal (Sanches-Ferreira, Silveira-Maia & Alves, 2014). In Portugal, Miranda-Correia (2010) also found 54% of psychologists, regular teachers and special education teachers lacked training on the ICF-CY, despite legislation requiring it for eligibility determination. Given the extensive scope of the ICF-CY, the clinical feasibility and ready integration of this important tool into research and policy is restricted. New instruments require time and effort, and may need a redefinition of roles and responsibilities of professionals. The comprehensive view of the ICF-CY on students' functioning demands collaborative work from school professionals and services. The ICF-CY has been viewed as a useful tool for data analysis, but "lacks details to describe the pedagogical situation well" (Maxwell & Granlund, 2011, p. 266). Awareness of the ICF-CY is limited in some countries. For example, Klang and her colleagues (2016) found 41 out of 43 (about 95.3%) special education teachers and speech-language pathologists from 17 states in the United States indicated that they had no or little knowledge about ICF and only the rest 2 (4.7%) report having moderate knowledge. Professionals have expressed concerns about the implications and consequences of the use of the ICF-CY to determine eligibility of a student with a SEN and in the development of IEP (Miranda-Correia, 2010).

Conclusion

The ICF-CY provides a standard framework and system to document and define the needs and functioning of children relative to the characteristics and demands of their educational environment. It holds great promise to contribute to the successful inclusion of all children in school by guiding educational policy and practice that aligns with a whole-child perspective and functional model of disability. The ICF-CY offers a framework and taxonomy to provide comprehensive documentation of the dimensions of learning and performance needs of students and the corresponding school environment to meet those needs through instruction and individualised support. It also provides a tool to examine the impact of the physical and social environment on school participation and educational achievement. The use of severity qualifiers can help categorise the severity of impairments in functioning and document if these levels change over time or with interventions and support.

The ICF-CY can serve as a valuable tool for service implementation by documenting assessment outcomes and in planning and monitoring interventions. Furthermore, the use of the ICF-CY is compatible with current psychological assessment methods, tools and data sources, yielding a functional profile for summarising a child's functional status within a child-environment interaction perspective. The ICF-CY model is feasible and useful for research, educational and policy purposes to develop effective interventions by using a whole-child approach instead of focusing solely on the disability diagnosis. The underlying assumption that disability is a universal phenomenon and manifestations of a health condition or disability are a consequence of interactions among the body, personal and societal levels supports a functional model of disability and encourages consideration of the role of environmental factors in mediating functioning (Lollar & Simeonsson, 2005). This may be of particular importance for children in school settings. ICY-CY is a function-focused model, and addresses the level of ability in functional areas, such as learning, mobility, communication, self-care, social relationships and other similar characteristics. It encourages the development of interventions that targets at the development of individual' functioning in relation to their environment and personal conditions.

The application of the ICF-CY in schools could facilitate the documentation of comparable and consistent information about the SEN and performance of students. The International Classification of Functioning, Disability and Health (ICF-CY) provides a common language for administrators and practitioners in education and related serves. The ICF-CY as a standard tool would provide a common language and framework to facilitate inclusive and participatory education. It offers a new way to conceptualise and document characteristics of children and youth with disabilities in learning environments. It provides a classification tool to guide global efforts in achieving the shared goal of education for all children. As such, the ICF-CY has the potential to enhance educational policy and practice to support and promote the successful inclusion of all children in school settings. Determining how to use the ICF-CY effectively for school-based psychological services for assessment, intervention planning and research is strongly warranted. Table 7.4 presents a synthesis of recommendations for the application of the ICF-CY in school settings.

Table 7.4 Recommendations for the application of the ICF-CY in school settings

- GUIDE EDUCATION POLICY
  - Inform special education resource allocation decisions
  - Provide standard framework and content to analyse policy
  - Establish the type of information to collect for IEPs and service eligibility
- ASSESSMENT
  - Guide Eligibility Decision Guidelines
  - Provide a functional profile for children in need of special support
  - Select measures for special education assessment
  - Unify assessment information and guide measurement selection
  - Provide a framework and content to develop new assessment tools that reflect recommended practice and international human rights perspective
  - Provides both a framework and detailed taxonomy that would comprehensively capture functioning to organise or combine standardised diagnostic measures by mapping the content of standardised measures to a shared bio-psych-social
- INTERVENTION PLANNING
  - Set educational objectives or IEP goals. It can guide IEP goals by providing a map of areas that are relevant to student learning and educational performance
  - Inform intervention planning. The ICF-CY has been used to help establish IEP goals and educational objectives for students with SEN. Gain parent, child, teacher, professional perspectives on educational needs and intervention goals for students
  - Identify barriers at different levels that can be addressed to support children in school settings, including environmental factors. Contextual factors are seldom accounted for in the diagnostic criteria of a disability, but they are important areas to target for interventions
  - Provide diagnostic clarification
- INTERDISCIPLINARY COLLABORATION AND CASE MANAGEMENT
  - Facilitate interdisciplinary communication and case management
- MONITOR SERVICE IMPLEMENTATION AND INTERVENTION OUTCOMES
  - Document and monitor intervention and educational outcomes

---

Highlights from this chapter

- The ICF-CY provides a global framework and classification system to help countries achieve inclusive education by providing a standard approach and common content to document and understand the learning and educational needs of all students.

- The ICF-CY allows for documentation of functional profiles of students that can be used to identify school-wide and individual special education needs, determine resource allocation, develop educational goals and demonstrate intervention outcomes. Documenting environmental facilitators and barriers can also promote participation of students with disabilities in school and match their needs.

- Although there has been limited global application of the ICF-CY in schools, there have been important recent efforts to incorporate the ICF-CY in national educational policy and special education practice within different countries including to determine eligibility for special education services and guide the development of individualised education programs. Research examining these efforts identified several benefits and barriers of using the ICF-CY, as well as promising areas for future application that will support education for all children.

References

Adolfsson, M., Pless, M., Ibragimova, N., Granlund, M., & Björck-Åkesson, E. (2007). *Användbarhet av ICF/ICF-CY inom Barn-och ungdomshabilitering.* Paper presented at ICF-ökad delaktighet för barn och unga i behov av särskilt stöd.

Adolfsson, M., Granlund, M. Björck-Åkesson, E., Ibragimova, N., & Pless, M. (2010). Exploring changes over time in habilitation professionals' perceptions and applications of the International Classification of Functioning, Disability, and Health version for children and Yourh. *Rehabilitation Medicine, 42*(7) 670–678.

Ajovalasit, D.,Vago, C., Usilla, A., Riva, D., Fidani, P., Serra,A., . . . Leonardi, M. (2009). Use of ICF to describe functioning and disability in children with brain tumours. *Disability and Rehabilitation, 31*(Suppl 1), S100–S107. doi:10.3109/09638280903317856

Aljunied, M., & Frederickson, N. (2014). Utility of the International Classification of Functioning, Disability and Health (ICF) for educational psychologists' work. *Educational Psychology in Practice, 30*(4), 380–392.

Andrade, P. M. O., Haase,V. G., & Oliveira-Ferreira, F. (2012). An ICF-based approach for cerebral palsy from a biopsychosocial perspective. *Developmental Neurorehabilitation, 15*(6), 391–400. doi:10.3109/17518423.2012.700650

Benson, N., & Oakland, T. (2011). International classification of functioning, disability, and health: Implications for school psychologists. *Canadian Journal of School Psychology, 26*(1), 3–17. doi:10.1177/0829573510396982

Bruyere, S. M., Van Looy, S. A., & Peterson, D. B. (2005). The International Classification of Functioning, Disability, and Health, contemporary, literature overview. *Rehabilitation Psychology, 50*(2), 113–121.

Castro, S., Ferreira, T., Dababnah, S., & Pinto, A. I. (2013). Linking autism measures with the ICF-CY: Functionality beyond the borders of diagnosis and interrater agreement issues. *Developmental Neurorehabilitation, 16*(5), 321–331. doi:10.3109/17518423.2012.733438

Castro, S., Pinto, A. I., & Maia, M. (2011). Linking the Carolina curriculum for preschoolers with special needs to the ICF-CY. *The British Journal of Development Disabilities, 57*(113), 133–146.

Cieza, A., Fayed, N., Bickenbach, J., & Prodinger, B. (2016, April). Refinements of the ICF Linking Rules to strengthen their potential for establishing comparability of health information. *Disability and Rehabilitation, 8288*, 1–10. http://doi.org/10.3109/09638288.2016.1145258

Cieza A, Geyh S, Chatterji S, Kostanjsek N, Üstün B, Stucki G. (2005). ICF linking rules: An update based on lessons learned. *Journal of Rehabilitation Medicine, 37*, 212–218.

Cramerotti, S., & Ianes, D. (2016). An ontology-based system for building Individualized Education Plans for students with Special Educational Needs. *Procedia-Social and Behavioral Sciences, 217*, 192–200.

Da Silva, A., Z., Vojciechowski, A. S., Ribas Mélo, T., Yamaguchi, B., Touchan, A. S., Serio Bertoldi, A., & Israel, V. L., (2016, January/April). Neuropsychomotor evaluation and functional communication in schoolchildren between the ages of 10 and 12 from the public school system. *Rev Ter Occup Univ San Paulo, 27*(1), 52–62. http://dx.doi.org/10.11606/issn.2238-6149.v27i1p52-62

de Miranda-Correia, L. (2010). Special education in Portugal: The new law and the ICF-CY. *Procedia-Social and Behavioral Sciences, 9*, 1062–1068.

De Polo, G., Pradal, M., Bortolot, S., Buffoni, M., & Martinuzzi, A. (2009, May). Children with disability at school: The application of ICF-CY in the Veneto region. *Disability and Rehabilitation, 31*(Suppl 1), S67–S73. doi:10.3109/09638280903317880

Ellingsen, K. M. (2011). *Deriving developmental code sets from the international classification of functioning, disability and health, for children and youth (ICF-CY).* Unpublished doctoral dissertation, University of North Carolina at Chapel Hill, Chapel Hill.

Ellingsen, K. M., & Simeonsson, R. J. (2011). ICF-CY developmental codes sets. Retrieved from www.icfcydevelopmentalcodesets.com/

Ellingsen, K., & Thormann, M. S. (2011). Access to quality education for children and youth with disabilities in conflict, crisis, and stable countries: Background report. *USAID and EQUIP.* Retrieved from http://pdf.usaid.gov/pdf_docs/pnaea969.pdf

Florian, L., Hollenweger, J., Simeonsson, R. J., Wedell, K., Riddell, S., Terzi, L., & Holland, A. (2006). Cross-cultural perspectives on the classification of children with disabilities part I. Issues in the classification of children with disabilities. *The Journal of Special Education, 40*(1), 36–45. doi:10.1177/00224669060400010401

Gan, S.-M., Tung, L.-C., Yeh, C.-H., Chang, H.-Y., & Wang, C.-H. (2014). The ICF-CY-based structural equation model of factors associated with participation in children with autism. *Developmental Neurorehabilitation, 17*(1), 24–33. doi:10.3109/17518423.2013.835357

Hollenweger, J. (2013). Developing applications of the ICF in education systems: Addressing issues of knowledge creation, management and transfer. *Disability and Rehabilitation, 35*(13), 1087–1091. doi:10.3109/09638288.2012.740135

Hwang, A.-W., Liao, H.-F., Granlund, M., Simeonsson, R. J., Kang, L-J., & Pan, Y-L. (2014). Linkage of ICF-CY codes with environmental factors in studies of developmental outcomes of infants and toddlers with or at risk for motor delays. *Disability and Rehabilitation*, *36*(2), 89–104. doi:10.3109/09638288.2013.777805

Ibragimova, N., Bjorck-Akesson, E., Granlund, M., Lillvist, A., & Eriksson, L. (2005, May 19). ICF version for children and youth (ICF-CY). *Fourth Nordic-Baltic Conference on ICF*, Tallin.

Klang, N., Rowland, C., Fried-Oken, M., Steiner, S., Granlund, M., & Adolfsson, M. (2016). The content of goals in individual educational programs for students with complex communication needs. *Augmentative and Alternative Communication*, *32*(1), 41–48. doi:10.3109/07434618.2015.1134654

Kovac, M. L., & Simeonsson, R. J. (2014). Agenesis of the corpus callosum: Classifying functional manifestations with the ICF-CY. *Disability and Rehabilitation*, *36*(13), 1120–1127. doi:10.3109/09638288.2013.833299

Krasuska, M., Riva, S., Fava, L., von Mackensen, S., & Bullinger, M. (2012). Linking quality-of-life measures using the International Classification of Functioning, Disability and Health and the International Classification of Functioning, Disability and Health – Children and youth version in chronic health conditions: The example of young people with hemophilia. *American Journal of Physical Medicine & Rehabilitation*, *91*(13), S74–S83. doi:10.1097/PHM.0b013e31823d4f35

Maxwell, G., & Granlund, M. (2011). How are conditions for participation expressed in education policy documents? A review of documents in Scotland and Sweden. *European Journal of Special Needs Education*, *26*(2), 251–272.

Martinuzzi, A., De Polo, G., Bortolot, S., & Pradal, M. (2015). Pediatric neurorehabilitation and the ICF. *NeuroRehabilitation*, *36*(1), 31–36. doi:10.3233/NRE-141188

McCormack, J., Harrison, L. J., McLeod, S., & McAllister, L. (2011). A nationally representative study of the association between communication impairment at 4–5 years and children's life activities at 7–9 years. *Journal of Speech, Language, and Hearing Research*, *54*(5), 1328–1348. doi:10.1044/1092-4388(2011/10-0155)

Moretti, M., Alves, I., & Maxwell, G. (2012). A systematic literature review of the situation of the International Classification of Functioning, Disability, and Health and the International Classification of Functioning, Disability, and Health – Children and Youth version in education: A useful tool or a flight of fancy? *American Journal of Physical Medicine & Rehabilitation*, *91*(13), S103–S117. doi:10.1097/PHM.0b013e31823d53b2

Raggi, A., Meucci, P., Leonardi, M., Barbera, T., Villano, A., Caputo, M. R., & Grassi, A. (2014). The development of a structured schedule for collecting ICF-CY-based information on disability in school and preschool children: An action research from Italy. *International Journal of Rehabilitation Research*, *37*(1), 86–96. doi:10.1097/MRR.0000000000000042

Sanches-Ferreira, M., Lopes-dos-Santos, P., Alves, S., Santos, M., & Silveira-Maia, M. (2013). How individualised are the Individualised Education Programmes (IEPs): An analysis of the contents and quality of the IEPs goals. *European Journal of Special Needs Education*, *28*(4), 507–520. doi:10.1080/08856257.2013.830435

Sanches-Ferreira, M., Silveira-Maia, M., & Alves, S. (2014). The use of the International Classification of Functioning, Disability and Health, version for Children and Youth (ICF-CY), in Portuguese special education assessment and eligibility procedures: The professionals' perceptions. *European Journal of Special Needs Education*, *29*(3), 327–343. doi:10.1080/08856257.2014.908025

Sanches-Ferreira, M., Simeonsson, R. J., Silveira-Maia, M., Alves, S., Tavares, A., & Pinheiro, S. (2013). Portugal's special education law: Implementing the International Classification of Functioning, Disability and Health in policy and practice. *Disability and Rehabilitation*, *35*(10), 868–873. doi:10.3109/09638288.2012.708816

Simeonsson, R. J., Simeonsson, N. E., & Hollenweger, J. (2008). International Classification of Functioning, Disability and Health for Children and Youth: A common language for special education. In L. Florian & M. J. McLaughlin (Eds.), *Disability classification in education: Issues and perspectives* (pp. 207–226). Thousand Oaks, CA: Corwin Press.

Sommer, R., Bullinger, M., Rohenkohl, A., Quitmann, J., & Brütt, A. L. (2015). Linking a short-stature specific health-related quality of life measure (QoLISSY) to the International Classification of Functioning – Children and Youth (ICF-CY). *Disability and Rehabilitation, 37*(5), 439–446. doi:10.3109/09638288.2014.923528

Tantilipikorn, P., Watter, P., & Prasertsukdee, S. (2012). Identifying assessment measures and interventions reported for Thai children with cerebral palsy using the ICF-CY framework. *Disability and Rehabilitation, 34*(14), 1178–1185. doi:10.3109/09638288.2011.637603

UNICEF. (2007). Promoting the rights of children with disabilities innocenti digest No. 13. The United Nations Children's Fund (UNICEF). Retrieved from www.un.org/esa/socdev/unyin/documents/children_disability_rights.pdf

World Health Organization. (2007). International Classification of Functioning, Disability, and Health: Children & Youth Version: ICF-CY. Retrieved from http://apps.who.int/iris/bitstream/10665/43737/1/9789241547321_eng.pdf?ua=1

Chapter 8

The ICF-CY and collaborative problem solving in inclusive Early Childhood Education and Care

Eva Björck-Åkesson

Introduction

The wide-ranging educational, economic and social benefits of Early Child-hood Education and Care (ECEC), at both individual and societal levels, are increasingly acknowledged in large parts of the world. Major changes in physi-cal, socio-emotional and cognitive areas of development occur during these years, and meaningful educational experiences have been shown to have long-lasting effects upon a child's cognitive development, socio–emotional develop-ment and learning (Pianta, Barnett, Burchinal, & Thornburg, 2009; Shonkoff & Phillips, 2000; Sylva, 2010). International and European communities (EU, 2011; OECD, 2014; UNESCO, 2015; UN, 2015) regard quality of ECEC as a foundation for later school achievement, success in the modern knowledge based economy and lifelong learning.

In inclusive ECEC all children in a neighbourhood attend a nearby pre-school together (European Agency, 2016). Inclusion may be defined as

> an ongoing process aimed at offering quality education for all while respecting diversity and the different needs and abilities, characteristics and learning expectations of the students and communities, eliminating all forms of discrimination.
>
> (UNESCO IBE, 2008, p. 18)

Inclusion for the child means to be in the preschool, and being engaged in everyday life in the preschool (Granlund & Lillvist, 2015). Since ECEC is the first part of the educational system in most countries the children's strengths and needs for support may be identified early. In assessment of needs for sup-port, both the child and the everyday environment in preschool should be the focus. The ICF-CY (WHO, 2007) may be used to structure and facilitate collaborative problem solving centred on children in need of support in the preschool. This chapter shows how the biopsychosocial interactive model of ICF-CY can be used as a frame in collaborative problem solving in assessment of children's needs of support, focusing both on the child's needs and the social and physical environment in the preschool. When referring to the workforce in preschool, the term preschool staff is used. The preschool staff includes preschool teachers with a university degree in education, preschool assistants and assistant to children in need of special support, and child-minders.

Background

ECEC spans the period from birth to the start of compulsory schooling. Policies and curricula are most often applied to children from 3 years old to the start of compulsory schooling (OECD, 2013). During the last decade, many governments have promoted research on their own national early years programmes. Economists such as James J. Heckman, a Nobel prize winner and an expert on the economics of human development, has shown that the quality of early childhood development has a massive impact on health, economics and social outcomes for individuals, families and society (Heckman, 2006). In the United States, for example, an evaluation of the state-funded Head Start program, which focused on poor children, found that participation in an ECEC-programme increased the possibility of obtaining a secondary diploma by 9% and decreased the likelihood of dropping out of school by 7% (Garces, Thomas, & Currie, 2002; Heckman & Masterov, 2007).

A central element in ECEC is the inclusion and participation of all children. The EU 2020 Strategy goals for example state that at least 95% of children between the age of four and the age of compulsory primary education should participate in early childhood education. Also in the UN goals for sustainable development, SDG2030 (UN, 2016) pre-primary education is highlighted as a goal of itself. At the same time, there are concerns about the accessibility and quality of ECEC provisions for all children. In spite of the positive growth of ECEC, it may be questioned if all children do receive the support needed for development and learning in the preschool environment. In particular, it may be questioned if children with disability and fragile and vulnerable children at developmental risk receive the support they need, and if early intervention is provided to the extent needed for those children. In line with this, it is important to point out the essential role of assessment in the preschool, which is the everyday environment of many children today.

Participation – being in preschool and being engaged

Early childhood researchers have proposed that children's engagement in preschool is a strong predictor for learning as well as well-being in later school years (Belsky et al., 2007; Hamre & Pianta, 2001). Studies have shown that participation and engagement is especially important for inclusion and learning of children in need of special support (Dunst, Bruder, Trivette, & Hamby, 2006). Participation can be conceptualised as "attendance" ("being there") and "involvement" ("experience of participation while attending") (Imms, Adair et al., 2016a). Inclusion of all children requires both attendance and involvement. Learning and development is assumed to be enhanced if the "optimal, positive participation" of each child is ensured (Imms, Granlund et al., 2016b). Involvement is closely related to engagement. Child engagement has been referred to as the amount of time the child is actively involved with other persons, material or in a situation (McWilliam & Casey, 2011). Engagement processes are enabled through surrounding inclusive structures, which consist of the physical, social, cultural and educational environment. The structures surrounding the children in preschool affect the process quality that children directly experience that in turn influences their development and learning (Pianta, 2009). The European Agency of Special Needs and Inclusive Education envision an approach to assessment in mainstream settings where policy and practice are designed to promote the learning of all pupils. The overall goal of inclusive assessment is that all assessment policies (structures) and procedures (process) should support and enhance the successful participation and inclusion of all children (outcome) (Barolo, Björck-Åkesson, Giné, & Kyriazopoulou, 2016). In order to work with assessment and intervention for children in need of special support the WHO International Classification of Functioning, Disability and Health, Child and Youth version (ICF-CY) (2007) can be used as a frame for assessment in the inclusive preschool, coordinating information, knowledge and competence from the different stakeholders, i.e. the preschool staff, the parents, external experts (if needed) and also the child.

The inclusive preschool

With the recent developments in ECEC, where many children spend a large part of everyday life in preschool, the preschool environment becomes a central part of the child's everyday environment. Seeing development as a transactional process (Sameroff & Fiese, 2000) developmental outcomes depend on the continuous dynamic interactions of the child and the experiences provided by the close environment. As a result, the focus for assessment should be the child, the proximal social environment and the interactions between them, and the physical environment. ICF-CY, through the interactive model, may be used to structure information in collaborative problem solving in the assessment process promoting inclusion in ECEC (Björck-Åkesson et al., 2010; Castro, 2012).

In a European project, initiated by the European Agency of Special Needs and Inclusive Education (2014–2017) (www.european-agency.org/agency-projects/inclusive-early-childhood-education/) the goal is to identify and analyse factors that enable high quality and equitable early childhood education of all children, including the most vulnerable ones, in inclusive settings. Here, processes, structure and outcomes are regarded. Inspired by an ecological systems model (Bronfenbrenner, 1979; Bronfenbrenner & Ceci, 1994) the outcome is engagement of the children in the preschool, and the process factors are involvement in daily activities, a child-centred approach, personalised assessment for learning, accommodation adaptation and support and positive social interaction. Structures in the proximal environment include among others leadership, curriculum, family involvement and collaboration. On a higher level, structures such as interagency collaboration and in-service training are important, and on the highest level national factors such as governance and funding, monitoring and national curriculum. All those factors are to be found in the different parts of the ICF model. In the version for children and youth ICF-CY (2007) the items, on the different levels describe child functioning and components important for participation. In using this model of collaborative problem solving in the assessment and intervention processes, the outcome on child-level is participation in everyday life of the preschool.

The International Classification of Functioning, Disability and Health, Child and Youth version

In the International Classification of Functioning, Disability and Health, Child and Youth version (ICF-CY), the construct of participation is defined as a child's involvement in life situations (WHO, 2007). This interactive model was developed to "provide a unified and standard language and framework for the description of health and health related states" (WHO, 2001, 2007, p. 3) (see the Figure 8.1).

As a biopsychosocial model with focus on functioning in everyday life ICF-CY integrates a medical and social model providing a conceptual framework

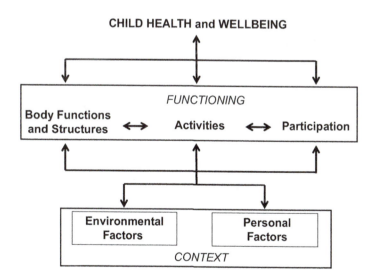

Figure 8.1 The interactive ICF model (WHO, 2001, p. 17) adapted for use with children

and terminology for describing functioning in children and youth. It was developed to "provide a unified and standard language and framework for the description of health and health related states" (WHO, 2001, 2007, p. 3). WHO defines health in a very broad perspective related to quality of everyday life. The ICF-CY system can be regarded as a system providing building blocks to study aspects of a child's functioning in various everyday life contexts and the relationships between functioning and contextual factors important for children, i.e. environmental factors and personal factors. Child health and well-being is described as a health condition (disorder or disease) in the original model (WHO, 2001), but in using a wider perspective it can be described as health and well-being, or the quality of a child's everyday living. The functioning of the child in everyday life is described in a broad manner including body functions and structures, activities and participation, and in a context defined by environmental and personal factors. Activity is defined as an action by the child, and participation means the child's involvement in a life situation.

The assessment and intervention process

In an inclusive preschool, the focus in assessment should be on participation in the natural environment in the preschool, including the physical and social context. The perspective is mainly functional even if developmental aspects are relevant as well (Björck-Åkesson, Brodin, & Fälth, 1997; Björck-Åkesson and Granlund (submitted) (see Table 8.1). The assessment process involves the child, individuals in the proximal environment and the physical environment.

Table 8.1 Characteristics of a developmental and functional perspective in assessment

Perspective	Developmental Perspective	Functional Perspective
Relation to ICF-CY	Body functions and structures Activity	Activity Participation Environment
Focus of assessment	Optimal performance Specific domains Knowledge and skills of the child	Everyday life functioning of the child Interaction Social environment Physical environment
Assessment methods	Norm-referenced tests Criterion-referenced tests Interview about child Observation of child Profession specific assessment	Observations of the child, interaction and play and of the social and physical environment Interview about and with the child and the social and physical environment the child

Perspective	Developmental Perspective	Functional Perspective
Criteria	Normal development	Individual development Child in social context and natural environment
Outcome	Maximal/optimal level . Specific domains Complexity "Best performance"	Context competence Everyday functioning Mostly used behaviour
Goals	"Milestones"	Competencies needed for everyday life, empowerment

It encompasses everyday life functioning of the child in the preschool context and proximal processes, such as interaction with and between the child and the peers and adults. The assessment methods involve observations of play, activities and interactions and the environment, interviews about and with the child, and interviews about the social and physical environment with staff and parents. It can be related to all components of ICF-CY.

Assessment traditionally has been conducted from a developmental perspective (see Table 8.1). The child's optimal performance in specific domains of development has been emphasised by professionals using profession specific instruments based on "normal" development in children. Norm-referenced assessment instruments have been used. Those tests compare the development of the child in need of support to that of typically developing children. Informal interviews and observations are often part of child assessment. Maximal level of performance and complexity is often emphasised in assessment regardless of method for assessment. The outcome from assessment has a tendency to describe the best performance of the child and be based on developmental "milestones". With a functional perspective everyday functioning and the social and physical context is in focus for assessment. Functional scales and behaviour measures are used and systematic observation of the child in interaction with the social environment are carried through. Structured interviews with parents and staff in preschool are done with the aim to discover needs, strengths and weaknesses in both the child and the social and physical environment. The uniqueness of each child is emphasised and the physical environment is included.

The outcome of functional assessment describes everyday functioning with a focus on context competence with the aim of generalisation over contexts. Frequency of behaviour is accentuated and the most used functions are sought. Factors in the environment, barriers and facilitators are stressed. The functional perspective is close to the ICF-CY model, even if a developmental perspective is included. The two perspectives on assessment and intervention are related to different roles in the process and to different knowledge about the child and the environment. The parents and/or other people in the close proximal environment of the child are most qualified to describe their family and their life with the child including culture, roles, structures, routines and activities and the child's participation. The preschool staff are knowledgeable about the pre-school environment, the child's everyday life in preschool and the interactions between children, routines, structures and activities. They also have knowledge about child development and learning and the preschool as a natural environ-ment for learning. External experts, from the community social services, child health services or re/habilitation services may also be part of the assessment and intervention process depending on the difficulties a child experiences. Their role is to provide information and competence from their respective fields of knowledge representing different areas in the ICF-CY-model.

Collaborative problem solving

Assessment is understood as part of a problem-solving process which starts with the selection of initial difficulties experienced by the child to be solved through collaboration between those who work with the child in the preschool, the parents and sometimes external professional experts. In adopting an inclusive perspective on ECEC some of the general assumptions behind early childhood intervention, where a diagnosis has been a dominant factor, are questioned. With the focus on inclusion functioning in everyday life and functional char-acteristics of the child become the focus and not a diagnosis (Björck-Åkesson et al., 2010). This leads to a problem-solving process where ICF-CY can assist with a structure for assessment based on participation in preschool as the goal.

The model for collaborative problem solving, based on systems theory, where assessment is regarded as a learning process for preschool staff, parents and pro-fessionals and where the roles of the preschool staff, parents and the child are highlighted, can be used together with the ICF-CY. At the core of collaborative problem solving is that explanations to difficulties or problems, based on dif-ferent components, lead to different goals and methods of intervention that are discussed by the preschool staff, the parents and if possible the child. Basic is that strengths and difficulties in everyday life are recognised and that multiple expla-nations for problems are highlighted in the assessment. Explanations can be sought in different components corresponding to the ICF-CY model, both in terms of the child, the social and physical environment and interaction between the child and the environment per se. This means that assessment instruments describing functioning are needed, both informal and formal to reach a good view of the child's resources and needs of support.

In the model for collaborative problem solving, the assessment and interven-tion process is seen as a learning process for parents, preschool staff and exter-nal professionals that sometimes are involved. Also the child may be involved guaranteed that the child can contribute with her or his thoughts and expe-riences five (Björck-Åkesson et al., 2010). The knowledge of preschool staff, parents and professionals and if possible the child is in focus. The assessment

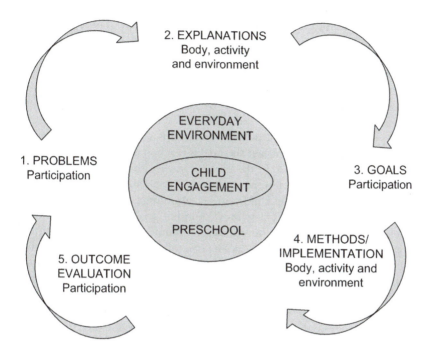

Figure 8.2 The model for collaborative problem solving related to ICF-CY

and intervention-circle used in collaborative problem solving involves five steps recurring over time: (1) problem description, (2) problem explanations and priority, (3) goal setting, (4) methods and intervention design, (6) implementation, (5) evaluation of outcome (Björck-Åkesson & Granlund, 2004).

Figure 8.2 shows the collaborative problem solving model involving the ICF-CY. The first step in the model for collaborative problem solving is to describe concrete problems in everyday life for the child in words that are easy to understand. Problems may concern positive actions and events that happen too seldom, negative actions and events that happen too frequently or should not occur at all. For each problem, multiple explanations are used to guide assessment. Explanations for problems are selected both in relation to the child, in terms of the social and physical environment and in interaction between the child and the environment. In the ICF-CY framework, the explanations may concern the body, activities and environmental factors. For example, explanations to why a child too seldom takes part in play with other children can be that the child has few means to express him or herself and take initiatives due to physical limits (body), or that the child has difficulties in timing turn-taking in play (activity). It can also depend on that other children do not wait long enough for the child to start interaction or take a turn or do not respond (social environment). It can also be related to the child's possibilities to be physically close and follow other children in play (activity) or the other children's actions towards the child or the type of play (social environment). Those are just a few possible explanations to the problems. In most cases, there are multiple explanations to problems, and an analysis must be made where those are prioritised and ranked in relation to possibilities of solving them and a discussion about what problem to solve first. Problems can also be general or specific and related to each other. This process builds on the knowledge of the participants, their capacity to listen to each other end collaborative logic reasoning.

The goal is described as a desired state and is closely linked to the problem that should be solved. When the goal is reached, the problem should have decreased or ceased to exist. In the example earlier, the goal could be that the child initiates communication more often the earlier and could be expressed in a concrete way such as "the child initiates communication with another child three times during free-play activities". Another goal could be that the child uses a communication device to initiate communication in a specific situation and that the other children respond. The core of the model is to use the different problem explanations in the assessment to design intervention methods in a collaborative process involving the preschool staff, the parents, the child and, if needed, the external professionals. After implementation of the intervention, the outcome should be evaluated against the goal. Next, a case study is presented that shows how the assessment process using the ICF-CY model can be implemented.

Case study

The child, Carol, is 4 years old. She is mostly a happy and curious child, and in a one-to-one situation with adults and some peers, she is participating and engaging in different activities. Her speech is sometimes difficult to understand. She was born prematurely and has had a slow development. At 4 years old, she has been catching up with other children, but still she has difficulties participating in play situations with other children. She experiences difficulties in moving fast and has some problems with fine-motor tasks. She often ends up sitting by herself looking at the other children, especially in free-play situations. In structured situations with a preschool teacher, she participates in activities most of the time.

One problem in everyday life in preschool formulated by the parents and the preschool teacher is about the interaction between Carol and other children. Carol seldom participates in play with other children and she becomes unhappy when she is not invited to play with other children. To start the process of trying to find out in what situations this happens and the reasons why, the parents, preschool staff and child meet and talk about it. All of those persons have information that may help to solve the problem. First, the child is in focus and describes her view of the situation. She may say that she wants to be with the other children in a specific situation. This may lead to that preschool teacher recognising the situation and provides a wider picture of what is going on. The parents can also contribute with their view reflecting on that the one-to-one playing situation is easier, since this happens at home. They all agree that this problem mainly occurs in free play, which actually happens many times during the day at preschool. At home, Carol plays with other children her age sometimes, but most often she plays with a younger sister.

Now the problem is described in a more concrete way, and they decide that there is one special free-play situation that happens frequently where Carol would like to participate – i.e. when the children play zoo. The children in the preschool play zoo, in-doors and out-doors, pretending that they are different animals and take care of animals. Teddy bears and other toys are also involved in this play situation. Now it is possible to make a concrete description of the problem: Carol is too seldom engaged in playing zoo with the other children. Consequently, the goal should be that Carol participates in playing zoo with the other children more often.

The next step is to look at explanations to why Carol does not participate in this play situation. Her own description of the day in preschool and her experiences is the starting point. Of course how this is done needs to be adapted to the age of the child. After Carol has described her view, it is evident that she tries to follow the other children when they play zoo and tries to be part of this play situation, but that she is too slow following them, and the other children do not always pay attention to her. Explanations to why there is a problem can be found at all levels in the ICF-CY model. For problems with interaction, there are a number of explanations at the body-structure level, for example, related to the ear, producing sounds and cognition and motor difficulties. At body-function level there may be problems with the reception and production of language, hearing and moving around. There are also explanations associated with activity, i.e. communication skills, use of speech or motor skills like running and fine-motor activities. Explanations can be found in the environment, i.e. the other children do not pay enough attention to Carol and do not see that she wants to participate in the zoo-play. It could also be related to the actions of the preschool teachers, i.e. they do not pay enough attention to strategies that may help Carol to make other children engaged in her activities or Carol invited to their activities. At the environmental level, also a lack of adapted toys or products and technology for communication, support and relationships and individual attitudes and actions of friends may be relevant.

The goal for Carol is to be engaged in interaction with other children, and methods can be found at all levels of ICF-CY. Each explanation to a problem points to a possible method. For example, if the problem is to start interactions, the method would be that Carol is engaged in play activities that trigger the curiosity of other children. The preschool teacher could help Carol to start an interesting activity making the other children join. If the explanation is that the other children do not pay attention to Carol, the method would be that the preschool teacher initiates a role for Carol in the play encouraging the other children to include her. The explanation may be related to contextual factors, for example the attitudes of the children or the design of the playground.

In reality, a number of methods will be given priority in collaborative problem solving, involving both the child, the peers and the preschool staff. The most important factor is the careful and continuous monitoring provided by the preschool staff in order to promote that all children are active and interacting with other children and adults in preschool. Inclusion means not only being in preschool but also being engaged while being there.

Highlights from this chapter

- For inclusion of all children in ECEC, the environment should be available and accessible for all children an environment that can meet the needs of all children should be provided.
- Assessment should focus both on the child and on the environment, as well as on the interactions between the child and the environment. The intervention process should be collaborative, involving the preschool staff, the parents and the child and, if needed, the external experts.
- The biopsychosocial interactive model of the ICF-CY can be used as a frame in collaborative problem solving, in the assessment of children's needs of support, focusing on the child's needs and on the social and physical environment in the preschool.
- As an interactive model, the use of the ICF-CY for assessment provides a structure and framework for looking at functioning and participation of the child in everyday life at preschool, including the social and physical environment.
- Collaborative problem solving involves the preschool staff, the parents, the child and the external experts are needed in the assessment and intervention process, providing different information, knowledge and expertise in describing problems, explaining the sources of problems in a multifaceted way, setting goals, designing methods and monitoring progress and following up goal attainment.
- Involvement in everyday life activities together with other children in a preschool based on a holistic curriculum and careful follow-up is the basis for inclusion of all children in ECEC. Children need not only to be present in preschool but also to be actively involved and engaged in the preschool activities.

References

Bartolo, P., Björck-Åkesson, E., Giné, C., & Kyriazopoulou, M. (2016). Ensuring a strong start for all children: Inclusive early childhood education and care. In A. Watkins & C. Meijer (Eds.), *International perspectives on inclusive education*. Bingley, UK: Emerald Group Publishing Limited.

Belsky, J., Burchinal, M., McCartney, K., Vandell, D. L., Clarke-Stewart, K. A., & Owen, M. T. (2007). Are there long-term effects of early child care? *Child Development*, 78(2), 681–701. doi:10.1111/j.1467-8624.2007.01021.x

Björck-Åkesson, E., Brodin, J., & Fälth, IB. (1997). *Åtgärder, samspel, kommunikation.* (Intervention, interaction and communcation) WRP International Förlag, Rockneby.

Björck-Åkesson, E., & Granlund, M. (2004). Early intervention in Sweden: A developmental systems perspective. In M. Guralnick (Ed.), *The developmental systems approach to early intervention* (pp. 571–592). Baltimore, MD: Paul H. Brookes Publishing Company.

Björck-Åkesson, E., Granlund, M., & Olsson, C. (1996). Collaborative problemsolving in communication intervention. In S. von Tetzchner & M. H. Jensen (Eds.), *Augmentative and alternative communication: European perspectives* (pp. 324–341). London: Whurr Publishers.

Björck-Åkesson, E., Wilder, J., Granlund, M., Pless, M., Simeonsson, R., Adolfsson, M., Almqvist, L., Augustine, L., Klang, N., & Lillvist, A. (2010). The International Classification of Functioning, Disability and Health and the version for children and youth as a tool in child habilitation/early intervention – feasibility and usefulness as a common language and frame of reference for practice. *Disability and Rehabilitation*, 32(S1), 125–138.

Björck-Åkesson, E., & Granlund, M. (submitted). Early childhood education and care in Sweden – an inclusive preschool? *Infants and Young Children*.

Bronfenbrenner, U. (1979). *The ecology of human development: Experiments by nature and design.* Cambridge, MA: Harward University Press.

Bronfenbrenner, U., & Ceci, S. J. (1994). Nature-nurture reconceptualised in developmental perspective: A bioecological model. *Psychological Review*, 101, 568–586.

Castro, S. (2012). *The assessment intervention process of young children with Autism Spectrum Disorders: Contributions of the ICF-CY.* Unpublished doctoral dissertation, Porto University, Porto.

Dunst, C. J., Bruder, M. B., Trivette, C. M., & Hamby, D. W. (2006). Everyday activity settings, natural learning environments, and early intervention practices. *Journal of Policy and Practice in Intellectual Disabilities*, 3(1), 3–10.

EU (European Commission, 2011). Strategic framework – education & training 2020. Retrieved January 22, 2017, from http://ec.europa.eu/education/policy/strategic-frame work_en

European Agency for Special Needs and Inclusive Education. (2016). European Commission (2011). Retrieved January 23, 2017, from www.european-agency.org/agency-projects/inclusive-early-childhood-education

Garces, E., Thomas, D., & Currie, J. (2002). Longer-term effects of head start. *American Economic Review*, 92(4), 999–1012.

Granlund, M., & Lillvist, A. (2015). Factors influencing participation by preschool children with mild intellectual disability in Sweden: With or without diagnosis. *Research and Practice in Intellectual and Developmental Disabilities*, 2(2), 126–135.

Hamre, B. K., & Pianta, R. C. (2001). Early teacher – child relationships and the trajectory of children's school outcomes through eighth grade. *Child Development*, 72(2), 625–638. doi:10.1111/1467-8624.00301

Heckman, J. (2006). Skill formation and the economics of investing in disadvantaged children. *Science*, 312, 1900–1902.

Heckman, J., & Masterov, D. (2007). The productivity argument for investing in young children. *Review of Agricultural Economics*, 29, 446–493.

Imms, C., Adair, B., Keen, D., Ullenhag, A., Rosenbaum, P., Granlund, M. (2016). 'Participation': A systematic review of language, definitions, and constructs used in intervention research with children with disabilities. *Developmental Medicine and Child Neurology*, 58(1), 29–38.

Imms, C., Granlund, M., Wilson, P., Steenbergen, B., Rosenbaum, P., & Gordon, A. (2016). Participation – both a means and an end: A conceptual analysis of processes and outcomes in childhood disability. *Developmental Medicine and Child Neurology, 59*(1), 16–25.

McWilliam, R. A., & Bailey, D. B. (1992). Promoting engagement and mastery. In D. B. Bailey & M. Wolery (Eds.), *Teaching infants and preschoolers with disabilities* (2nd ed., pp. 229–256). New York: Merrill.

McWilliam, R. A., & Casey, A. M. (2011). *Engagement of every child in the preschool classroom.* London: Pall H. Brookes Publishing Company.

OECD. (2013). How do early childhood education and care (ECEC) policies, systems and quality vary across OECD countries? Education Indicators in focus – 2013/02. Paris: OECD. Retrieved January 22, 2017, from www.oecd-ilibrary.org/docserver/download/5k49czkz4bq2-en.pdf?expires=1485115393&id=id&accname=guest&checksum=A7D056C476FD8473FC2C60B40DFB918C

OECD. (2014). Education: Quality standards essential to boost child learning and development. Retrieved January 22, 2017, from www.oecd.org/edu/school/educationquality standardsessentialtoboostchildlearninganddevelopmentsaysoecd.htm

Pianta, R. C., Barnett, W. S., Burchinal, M., & Thornburg, K. R. (2009). The effects of preschool education: What we know, how public policy is or is not aligned with the evidence base, and what we need to know. *Psychological Science in the Public Interest, 10*(2), 49–88.

Sameroff, A. J., & Fiese, B. H. (2000). Transactional regulations: The developmental ecology of early intervention. In J. P. Shonkoff & S. J. Meisels (Eds.), *Handbook of early childhood intervention* (2nd ed., pp. 135–159). Cambridge: Press Syndicate of the University of Cambridge.

Shonkoff, J. P., & Phillips, D. A. (2000). *From neurons to neighborhoods: The science of early childhood development.* Washington, DC: National Academy Press.

Sylva, K. (2010). Quality in early childhood settings. In K. Sylva, E. Melhuish, P. Sammons, I. Siraj-Blatchford, & B. Taggart (Eds.), *Early childhood matters evidence from the effective preschool and primary education project* (pp. 70–91). Abingdon: Routledge.

UNESCO, (2008). *Inclusive education: The way of the future.* Genève: International Conference on Education.

UNESCO, (2015). Ingeon Declaration. Equitable and inclusive quality education and lifelong learning for all by 2030. Transforming lives through education. World Education Forum 2015. Republic of Korea. Retrieved January 23, 2017, from http://en.unesco.org/world-education-forum-2015/incheon-declaration

United Nations. (2016). Sustainable Development Goals (SDG 2030). Retrieved January 22, 2017, from www.un.org/sustainabledevelopment/sustainable-development-goals/

WHO. (2001). *International Classification of Functioning, Disability and Health ICF.* Geneva: World Health Organization.

WHO. (2007). *International Classification of Functioning, Disability and Health, version for Children and Youth (ICF-CY).* Geneva: World Health Organization.

Chapter 9

ICF-CY in early childhood intervention

A step-by-step model for assessment-intervention processes

Vera Coelho, Susana Castro, Catarina Grande and Ana Isabel Pinto

Early childhood intervention (ECI) has been defined as a system of coordinated services and resources for young children (ages 0 to 6) with disabilities or at risk for developmental delay and their families (e.g. Meisels & Shonkoff, 2000). Within a biopsychosocial approach, ECI aims to empower children and their environments in order to ensure children's full participation and development in their natural settings. This chapter presents a research project designed to understand the contribution of the ICF-CY (WHO, 2007) as a procedure that operationalises the biopsychosocial approach to ECI in Portugal. First, ECI legislation and practices in Portugal are briefly described. Then the project's goals, methods and main outcomes are presented, highlighting how the ICF-CY was used in the research. Finally, a case study illustrates how the ICF-CY can be used to support embedded intervention in mainstream settings.

ECI in Portugal

In Portugal, substantial changes in ECI in the last decades are closely connected with the development of health, education and economic policies and services that occurred after the democratic revolution (Pinto et al., 2012). Portuguese ECI has evolved from segregated special education services for children in need of special support in the 1980s (Bairrão, 1999; UNESCO, 2010), to policies where inclusion is assumed as an educational principle. The current nationwide policy for Preschool Education (Ministry of Education, 1997) is strongly based on the Salamanca Statement assuring accessibility and accommodation of preschool settings to all children, including those with additional support needs. Issues related to inclusion and special support services are regulated by two legislation acts – Decree-Law 3/2008 (Ministry of Education, 2008) and Decree-Law 281/2009 (Ministry of Education, Ministry of Social Security & Ministry of Health, 2009) which are based on inclusive principles, emphasizing children's right to access care and education (Simeonsson, Bjorck-Akesson, & Bairrão, 2006) and determining that support services are to be provided in children's natural settings. Both legislation acts are framed by the biopsychosocial per-spective and thus underline the relevance of a multidimensional approach to the assessment-intervention process and regulate the ICF-CY as a central tool in determining the child functioning. Rather than diagnosis, the child's func-tioning is regarded as the basis for eligibility decisions. A recent study aiming to evaluate the implementation of the legal guidelines mentioned earlier, affirms that professionals are, indeed, taking a functional approach to assess children's disabilities by documenting their limitations in activities and restrictions in par-ticipation (Sanches-Ferreira, Simeonsson, Silveira-Maia, & Alves, 2015). Addi-tionally, results show that Portuguese professionals – namely, special education teachers and regular teachers – consider the ICF-CY a useful resource to guide policy and practice in the provision of special education, while also facilitat-ing the congruence across professionals in eligibility decision-making processes (Sanches-Ferreira et al., 2015) and supporting a more comprehensive under-standing of children. However, Portuguese ECI professionals still face some challenges in the use of the ICF-CY – namely, regarding (a) training in the ICF-CY framework, (b) difficulty in finding measures to assess environmental factors and/or focused on functionality and (c) challenges in achieving a real partnership and collaborative work between the different professionals and dis-ciplines involved in planning and conducting assessment-intervention processes (Sanches-Ferreira, Silveira-Maia, & Alves, 2014).

In fact, the implementation of the ICF-CY theoretical framework in ECI practice is still a major challenge for professionals (e.g. Castro, Pinto, & Simeon-sson, 2014). Any demands placed on ECI teams seem to require that empirical evidence is gathered and specific guidelines are provided to professionals in order to promote their proficiency in implementing assessment-intervention processes in natural environments, within a biopsychosocial approach.

With these in mind, this chapter illustrates the relevance of planning inter-ventions within a biopsychosocial approach by presenting a step-by-step model to conduct assessment-intervention processes using the ICF-CY and by provid-ing evidence of gains on child outcomes when intervention is carried within the child's daily routines.

The project "contribution of the ICF-CY to the study of participation in children with disabilities at early ages"

In the context of the aforementioned policy changes in the ECI and special education services for early years in Portugal, it became necessary to gather evidence on how the ICF can be a useful tool to support assessment and inter-vention in the scope of interdisciplinary teams. This was the overall purpose of a two-year funded research project (FCT -RIPD/CIF/109664/2009), which has profoundly impacted participant professionals' practice by introducing a step-by-step model on how to use the ICF-CY in ECI. To pursue this overall aim, specific goals were designed to gather this evidence systematically and in collaboration with services/practitioners – namely, 1) to identify the most commonly used instruments for the assessment of young children with disabilities and/or at risk of developmental delay, 2) to identify activity limitations, participation restrictions and associated environmental barriers in inclusive preschool settings, 3) to develop an ICF(CY)-based tool to support embedded interventions in preschool settings and 4) to study the factors associated with children's participation in inclusive preschool settings, in order to better predict facilitators and barriers to children's full participation.

Thus, aiming to introduce a step-by-step model on how to use the ICF-CY in ECI, an action research based approach was designed to facilitate the implementation of high quality practices according to the current Portuguese legislation and to international guidelines (Brown, & Guralnick, 2012; Carr and Kemmis, 1986; McNiff, 2013). The study design approach was inspired in the action research method as a *"reciprocal challenging of professional knowledge and experiences, rooted in everyday practices within schools, in collaboration arenas populated by researchers and practitioners, and in the interchange of knowledge of different kinds"* (Rönnerman, Moksnes Furu, & Salo, 2008, p. 277). In fact, likewise the action research, the study aimed to advance science and practice, promoting changes in the community, with the collaboration of community members. The project started with an action research based design within an outsider perspective, as the researchers initiated the study and invited the professionals to join. However, along the study, researchers became closer to professionals – in fact, the research design was gradually changed along the intervention to include both regular preschool teachers and ECI professionals leading them to collaborate in planning and monitoring interventions. Through this process researchers became familiar with the context where the study was taking place, thus getting nearer to an insider orientation (Titchen, 2015). This was particularly evident during the intervention and monitoring phases. However, the outsider perspective was predominant, as the researchers decided the research questions, gathered and analysed the data and gave feedback to the professionals/participants in order to inform their actions/practices (Titchen, 2015).

A convenient sample of 50 inclusive preschool settings from three cities in the north of Portugal was invited to join the project. In order to capture the diversity of the Portuguese inclusive settings, public, private for-profit and non-profit centres and teachers with different levels of experience in ECI were included in the sample. Families, regular teachers and professionals from ECI teams (e.g. special education teachers, speech therapists and physiotherapists) agreed to participate. The study involved three phases: baseline assessment, intervention/monitoring and post-intervention assessment. Figure 9.1 provides an illustration of the assessment-intervention trajectory implemented in the 50 preschool children/classrooms participating. In the baseline assessment, the following measures were used: (i) Abilities Index (Simeonsson & Bailey, 1991) – a screening measure of children's overall functioning profile, was used to account

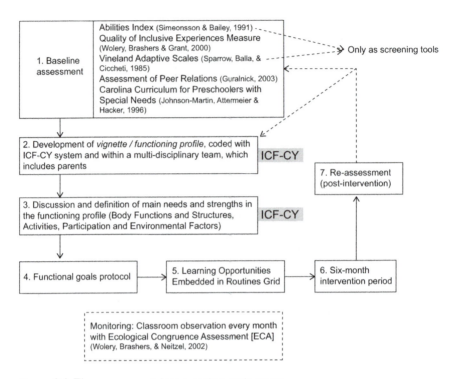

Figure 9.1 The assessment-intervention trajectory

for different abilities and their influence on intervention outcomes; (ii) Quality of Inclusive Experiences Measure (QIEM; Wolery, Paucca, Brashers, & Grant, 2000), assessed the quality of individualisation, accessibility of preschool space/ materials, children's participation and engagement, teacher interactions and peer interactions; (iii) Assessment of Peer Relations (APR; Guralnick, 2003) assessed child's relationships within the group/peers; (iv) Vineland Adaptive Scales (Sparrow, Balla, & Cicchetti, 1985) measured child's adaptive behaviour regarding communication, socialisation and daily living skills; and (v) Carolina Curriculum for preschoolers with Special Needs (CCPSN; Johnson–Martin, Attermeier, & Hacker,1996), a curriculum-based measure assessed diverse areas of children's development.

The ICF–CY was used as a framework in the assessment-intervention process, between the first assessment and the intervention phases of the project, as a way of translating the information obtained through the measures into a common language, based on child functioning in everyday life. So, the items of the baseline assessment measures (e.g. APR and CCPSN items), which had been previously linked to the ICF–CY coding system (Castro, Pinto & Maia, 2011; Ferreira, 2011) provided initial information on preschool environment and on children's development. This baseline assessment was documented in a *vignette* format − a brief narrative summarizing the assessment information about the child and her/his environments' characteristics. The *vignette* was then divided into units of meaning and the ICF-CY classification system was used to code such units of meaning. Because the APR and CCPSN items had been linked to the ICF system, the coding process had improved rigour and was described as "easier" by the professionals involved in the project. The final coded narrative for each child provided a functioning "portrait", based on the ICF-CY universal language; more than a description of the child performance on each measure item (a common way previously used by professionals to describe the child assessment results), the *vignette* that resulted from this assessment process was a portrait of the child functioning profile in several domains.

The next step was to identify the main needs and strengths of the child, based on the child's functioning profile and as a result of a discussion with teachers, ECI professionals and parents. The main needs and strengths could be identified at any level – it could be an issue of body functions or structures, an ability or restriction at the activity or participation level and/or an environmental factor barrier or facilitator. The goal of this step was to reach consensus within the team of professionals, along with parents, on what comprised a major need or ability for the child, highlighting not only needs but also strengths, both regarded as fundamental for planning the intervention.

Information on the quality of the inclusive preschool experience was also gathered with the QIEM measure comprising aspects such as programme purpose and goals, staff supports, accessibility, depth of interventions' individualisation, overall level of child participation and engagement, frequency and quality of adult–child interactions and frequency and length of child-to-child interactions. This information was particularly useful for planning specific interventions targeting change in the preschool environment characteristics.

Using a wide range of measures enables gathering different sorts of evidence – objective and subjective – a useful approach for a deeper knowledge about children's characteristics and about the demands posed their environmental. Some of the measures used were objective and required the researcher to observe and perform ratings (e.g. QIEM), while others were completed by proxy, often by the classroom teacher (e.g. APR) or even have an open-ended format (e.g. interviews). In this study, it has been observed that there were discrepancies between staff perceptions and objective observations. These differences were discussed within the team, while agreeing on the final functioning profile of each child, to obtain a consensus and accurate description.

After the team meeting where the final functioning profile was settled, the researcher together with the ECI team designed functional goals for the child. These goals targeted the main needs previously identified by the team based on the *vignette*. To design the goals, a Functional Goals Protocol (Figure 9.2) was used (adapted from Adolfsson & Klang, 2013). In the first column of this protocol, excerpts of the functioning profile are compiled; these excerpts provide the description of the main needs and strengths of the child, decided by the team. The second and third columns provide the respective ICF-CY code and descriptor ascribed to that portion of information, in order to facilitate the ECI team, including parents, comprehension of the ICF-CY codes and qualifiers'

	Actual Situation/ Problem Explained			Functional Problem	Functional Goal	Intervention (Who, With Whom, Where)
	Actual situation/ problem explained	Functional problem				
		(ICF-CY code and qualifier)	Descriptor			
Activities and participation						
Environmental factors						
Body functions and body structures						

Figure 9.2 Functional Goals Protocol (adapted from Adolfsson, 2008)

meaning. Following a problem-solving systematic approach, the team, along with the researcher, tries to formulate hypothesis that might explain the functional problem underlying the child's specified need and design appropriate goals for each hypothesised problem. Intervention strategies (columns 3, 4 and 5) were also defined aligned with the identified functional problem. Once the goals and overall strategies had been agreed upon, the intervention was planned, by embedding these goals and strategies in the natural daily routines of the preschool setting. In order to do this, the Learning Opportunities Embedded in Routines Grid was developed (Pinto, Grande, & Coelho, 2016). Figure 9.3 illustrates this grid. The first column contains the main routines of the child's typical day in the preschool, identified by the teacher. The designed goals were then assigned to one or to several routines. This means that often the same goal and respective strategy was used several times in one day, in different routines. Additionally, within the same routine, more than one goal can be targeted, allowing the child multiple opportunities during the day to develop main competencies. This planning exercise proved to be very useful for classroom staff as the grid can easily be put up in the classroom wall, so that all professionals interacting with the child in daily routines can easily be aware of when and how to target a specific goal.

This assessment-intervention planning procedure reflects a systematic, planned and intentional intervention. Intervention is embedded in natural daily routines, as ECI quality practices recommend (e.g. Dunst, Bruder, Trivette, &

Intervention Plan for _____

Routines	Activities		Intervention Dimensions		
	Functional goal				Engagement 1 2 3 4 5
	Strategies				
		Not achieved			Independence 1 2 3 4 5
		Emergent			
	Evaluation	Achieved			Social relations 1 2 3 4 5
	Functional goal				Engagement 1 2 3 4 5
	Strategies				
		Not achieved			Independence 1 2 3 4 5
		Emergent			
	Evaluation	Achieved			Social relations 1 2 3 4 5
		Participation in the routine			
		Engagement 1 2 3 4 5 Independence 1 2 3 4 5 Social relations 1 2 3 4 5			

Figure 9.3 Learning Opportunities Embedded in Routines Grid

Hamby, 2006; McLaughlin, Snyder, & Hemmeter, 2011; McWilliam, 2010). This procedure does not require major changes in the preschool global organisation, as the intervention strategies are simple and closely aligned with the classroom routine and agenda. Additionally, it is asked to professionals that are implementing the plan across routines, to rate the observed levels of child engagement, independence and social relationships during intervention, as these are considered the pillars of development and learning (de Kruif & McWilliam, 1999), the ultimate outcome of any childhood intervention.

After the intervention grid was completed, the intervention phase lasted six months. Once a month, the researcher visited the preschool setting for monitoring purposes. At this stage, the researcher checked whether the intervention strategies were being implemented in the assigned routines and targeting the pre-defined goals. An adaptation of the Ecological Congruence Assessment (ECA; Wolery, Brashers, & Neitzel, 2002) was used during this monitoring process. Every two months a team meeting took place and potential revisions of the intervention plan were agreed by the team in order to improve the fit between the child and context characteristics and the defined functional goals defined, as illustrated in Figure 9.1.

After the intervention period, all children and settings were reassessed with the QIEM and APR measures for identification of changes in both the quality of the inclusive experiences provided and the quality of the relationships with peers. Besides the quality of inclusive experiences, peers interactions were chosen as an outcome as it is widely accepted and documented that it is through frequent and continuous interactions in their natural environments that children participate, learn and develop (Bronfenbrenner & Morris, 2006; Granlund, 2013). Additionally, interviews and focus groups with the teachers were conducted to obtain more detail on their views about the assessment-intervention model introduced and its impact in promoting children's participation.

Outcomes of the intervention study

When analysing the project results on the quality of the inclusive experiences provided in the 50 preschool contexts, some important outcomes should be highlighted.

First, the levels of individualisation, which were initially quite low, improved significantly after the intervention period; individualisation of service provision is a recognised good practice in ECI (Dunst, Bruder, Trivette, & Hamby, 2006; McLaughlin, Snyder, & Hemmeter, 2011; McWilliam, 2010) and refers to the extent to which personalised and specific goals and interventions are planned and implemented for each child. It is considered essential for ECI success once each child has different and unique needs and abilities, and responds differently to the environment. The implementation of the earlier described assessment-intervention model with individualised goals systematically targeting specific child competences during daily routines and according to a pre-planned agenda, had significant impact on teachers' ability to target the child idiosyncratic needs and to adjust the characteristics of the natural settings and resources, resulting in developmentally more adequate interventions to children's unique characteristics.

Second, the time spent by children with disabilities in the same activity as their typically developing peers has also increased substantially after the intervention period. This may indicate that, by embedding interventions in the routines, ECI professionals tended to provide less extra support outside the classroom, which resulted in increased joint activities between children with disabilities and their peers. Results also show a slight increase in children's engagement, an important dimension of participation (WHO, 2007). "Being present in their natural contexts" and "being engaged" are considered two main dimensions of children's participation (Granlund, 2013). Moreover child engagement in everyday activities is related to learning and development at present and in the future (e.g. Aydogan, 2012) and it is considered a proximal process, as it involves children's interactions with their immediate physical and social contexts (Dower, Rimm-Kaufman, & Pianta, 2007; Pinto, 2006). These results seems to reflect an improvement in quality of inclusion as measured at the child's level (through better levels of participation) after the intervention period. One main limitation of this study was the short duration of the intervention. It is possible that, with a more prolonged intervention period the reported positive outcomes would be more apparent.

Regarding interactions and relationships with classroom peers, although the length of interactions remained approximately the same after the intervention period (i.e. there was a very slight, but non-significant increase in the number of turn-takings), the number of interactions in which the child with disabilities was engaged increased significantly. Additionally, there was a significant reduction in the display of inappropriate emotional responses towards peers.

In the scope of a focus group conducted just after the end of the project, the professionals who had experienced this step-by-step model for assessing and planning intervention within an ICF-CY framework, expressed several positive contributions of the process – namely: (1) Improvement in consistency and rigour regarding the translation of the child assessment contents into the functionality profile as a means to design and implement intervention plans that are adjusted to children's characteristics and meaningful within the preschool classroom daily routines. (2) Enhancement of communication among team members and parents through their involvement in the definition of the intervention plan and by using a common language depicted in the intervention grid (both excerpts of the functional profile and ICF-CY codes), such documentation was described by the professionals as simultaneously simple and rigorous. (3) The project's assessment-intervention methodology assured that internationally recommended practices in ECI were implemented, by embedding interventions into the classroom ongoing activities; moreover, professionals found these practices to be simple to implement as part of daily routines. They also highlight that, as the plan was so aligned with the classroom routines, it was extensible to all children in the group. (4) Improvement of professionals' ability to observe and assess, not only the child with disabilities but also other children in the classroom; the regular monitoring observations by researchers and team meetings between the project members and the professionals were highlighted as positive aspects that contributed to enhance such ability. According to teachers and ECI professionals, these moments were opportunities for joint reflection about the child and about the intervention process. By not focusing exclusively on the child specific competences, the monitoring process set the foundations for a deeper and more comprehensive understanding of child participation and relations in the classroom. Although the project did not include generalisation and follow-up phases, which would be desirable in future implementation – these results may indicate that professionals gained understanding on how to implement the new legal guidelines and models for ECI, as well as on how such intervention models can positively impact children's outcomes.

How the ICF-CY contributed to the study outcomes

This intervention research showed that the use of a functional approach to assess and document developmental outcomes in young children with disabilities can support the systematic implementation of intervention strategies embedded in typical daily routines. The ICF-CY was used as the framework and its coding system provided a common language to document changes in child functionality, from the initial/baseline assessment, through the intervention, to the final assessment. Moreover, as the ICF-CY is regarded as a common language between different disciplines (Lollar & Simeonsson, 2005), its use is highly relevant for professionals involved in multidisciplinary ECI team work. Multi-agency networking has been recognised as a recommended practice in ECI and for that, a common language across disciplines – that is, simultaneous accessible to parents – is of crucial importance. In the present project, as information was obtained through different sources (observation measures, professionals and parents' coding, interviews and meetings), the ICF-CY was a fundamental resource in unifying and synthesizing such diverse information into one single document describing each child's unique functioning profile. This profile was then the starting point of a systematic and individualised intervention process. Additionally, as also shown in previous studies (Björck-Åkesson et al., 2010), the ICF-CY provided the framework and the system to facilitate discussions within the interdisciplinary team. By using this common language, professionals from different fields could more easily discuss and arrive to a consensus on the child main strengths and needs. Lastly, using the ICF-CY coding system enables the documentation of children's progress over time. Every time the functioning profile is reviewed, it is possible to obtain graphical representations of the overall changes in functioning, using the ICF-CY classification. The aforementioned study results provide evidence to affirm the usefulness of the ICF-CY framework in obtaining a comprehensive assessment of the child, family and other developmental contexts, thus contributing to a higher quality inclusion. By developing a step-by-step model on how to use the ICF-CY in ECI and by introducing a problem solving systematic approach to the assessment-intervention process, the present project contributed to support professionals in overcoming the challenges placed on them by the introduction of the ICF-CY framework as a legal requirement, thus contributing to a more efficient intervention.

A case study exemplifying how the ICF-CY can be used to support embedded early childhood interventions in mainstream settings

Mary is a 41-month-old girl attending an inclusive classroom in a public Portuguese preschool for the first time. Before entering preschool, she had ECI services at home. Her profile, as measured by the Abilities Index tool, is close to the normal range with suspected or mild disabilities at the level of limbs and communicating with others.

Based on Mary's assessment conducted with the APR and the CCPSN a narrative (/vignette) was developed to describe Mary's functioning profile, and the ICF-CY coding system was used to code its content. Figure 9.4 illustrates this profile where it is highlighted the source (e.g. APR measure, observation data) of the described information which had been previously linked with the ICF-CY codes, as sated before. The ECI team has jointly discussed this profile and has identified dimensions of learning and applying knowledge (d1 chapter of the activities and participation component of the ICF-CY) as Mary's main strengths. On the other hand, aspects related to mobility (d4 chapter), self-care (d5 chapter) and interpersonal interactions (d7 chapter) were identified as the child's main needs. In terms of environmental factors, issues related to preschool architecture, care providers' attitudes and products for mobility were identified as potential barriers to participation. As environmental facilitators, aspects related to supports and relationships and health and education services were highlighted by the ECI team during the case discussion. The assessment of Mary's inclusive experience in her preschool setting was initially evaluated with the QIEM. Results of this assessment showed a *poor* level of programme *individualisation* regarding Mary's specific needs and *mediocre* levels of *engagement* in the preschool routines and activities. Therefore, these are changes that should also be targeted in the embedded opportunities intervention plan, for Mary. By focusing the intervention on improving the level of individualisation of the programme (ensuring a better fit between the child characteristics, the context characteristics/resources and the defined intervention goals), as well as on increasing the level of Mary's engagement in her daily activities in preschool, a more positive functioning profile should be achieved, as described by the ICF-CY system. Additionally, Mary's initial assessment revealed that 27.3% of the interactions initiated by her peers

Mary has 3 years of age and her family has low socio-economic status. Although her parents seem to lack knowledge of educational issues, they are receptive and they collaborate with the preschool and health professionals that have been working with Mary. (OBS) [e310+2].

Mary is a child with Down syndrome, with a mild developmental delay, especial in terms of cognitive and language development. She attends preschool since the beginning of the current academic year. She has special support and is very adjusted and integrated to this setting, where she also has weekly support from the special education teacher. (OBS) [e5850+3; e5854+1].

Mary seems to enjoy her daily life at preschool. She is very well adjusted to the preschool classroom routines, performing all daily activities with her peers. (OBS) [d2300.0; d8151.0]. Sometimes she tends to be unoccupied, however, spends most of her time interacting with objects and peers. (APR) [d131.1; d880.0]. Sometimes shows difficulty in complying with rules and in remaining in large group activities, specially, during structured activities. (OBS) [d2303.1].

Usually Mary engages in social exchanges with peers, however, these are often short and unsophisticated. (APR) [d71040.3; d71041.2]. Usually, her social initiations with peers are aimed at obtaining attention, acquiring objects, stopping an action of a peer and asking for or giving affect.(APR) [d71040.1]. Such initiations are almost always successful. (APR) [e325+3].

She has good social interaction competencies and is almost always able to talk with peers, turn-taking and responding adequately to social contacts. (CC) [d350.1; d2503.1; d7106.1]. She's able to recognise feelings in others and to act in consonance with such feelings. (CC) [b11421.2]. Mary shows some difficulty at the level of emotional regulation functions, sometimes rejecting social approaches by peers or being angry or hostile during interactions. Such difficulties may be due to the high frequency of conflict observed – namely, conflicts related with ownership, space and social control. (APR) [b1521.1; d7202.2]. Mary is the one who usually initiates the conflicts she has with peers, having a hard time solving such conflicts. The strategy that Mary uses the most is rejecting the request without reason. (APR) [b1251.2]. In free play, she particularly like puzzles and block-boxes, playing on her own at times with these materials. With some support from the teacher, she can carefully complete a structured activity. She has low ability to remain in an activity autonomously. (OBS) [d2102.1; d2105.3].

Figure 9.4 Mary's vignette/functioning profile

did not obtain any response from her, and Mary initiated few interactions with her peers. It was our expectation that the embedded opportunities intervention would have some positive effects on these aspects of Mary's daily interactions, once peer interactions are found to be crucial for children's development. Figure 9.5 illustrates some examples of the intervention that was planned for Mary. Overall, a total of seven dimensions were selected for Mary's intervention plan, from which only two of them will be illustrated here – namely, *directing attention* (d161.3) and *initiate interactions* (d71040.3) – by describing how they

Intervention Plan for Mary			
Routines	Activities	Maintaining Attention (D161.3)	Initiate Interactions (D71040.3)
Free play	Functional goal	Mary participates in a simple play script in the pretend play area (e.g. cooking and eating dinner), maintaining activity and developing actions according to the theme.	Mary participates in the pretend play area, approaching her peers and responding to their requests (at least two).
	Strategies	Adult suggests different scripts that children can perform in pretend play. Introduce new objects or elements related to Mary's interests and direct her attention in order to engage the child with her peers.	Adult supports children's play by assigning complementary roles to child and peers (e.g. let's ask your friend if she wants to cook dinner). Give verbal encouragement for the child to repeat.
	Evaluation	Not achieved	
		Emergent	
		Achieved	
		Engagement 1 2 3 4 5	
		Independence 1 2 3 4 5	
		Social relations 1 2 3 4 5	
Participation in the routine			
Engagement 1 2 3 4 5 Independence 1 2 3 4 5 Social relations 1 2 3 4 5			

Figure 9.5 Mary's Learning Opportunities Embedded in Routines Plan (excerpt)

were translated into functional goals embedded within the preschool classroom daily routines. Having these two intervention dimensions in mind, the ECI team had to decide which routines naturally provided opportunities for the child to practice and develop each competence – the team agreed that free play was the routine to privilege in order to enhance Mary's competence to engage in peer interactions. Moreover, the team also agreed that by promoting peer interactions during free play, the child was simultaneously developing other competencies, for instance, by becoming more autonomous in this routine over time, by making pretend play themes more complex and by developing her language skills while communicating and interacting with peers.

By focusing on a single key intervention dimension for Mary – initiate interactions – several other competencies were generated while the child got more proficient in the competence that was the direct intervention focus. Moreover, we highlight that the embedded opportunities plan identifies several moments/opportunities, along the day, for the child to develop peer interactions, such as mealtime and transitions. This is particularly relevant once children learn and develop while playing in their natural environments. Particularly for children with disabilities or at risk of developmental delay, it is essential that their natural settings provide, systematically and intentionally, multiple opportunities to learn and practice. Multiple learning opportunities within the daily routines, along with the professionals adequate supports (also in the natural context), are fundamental so that children can engage in play and, simultaneous, develop the identified and targeted competencies stated in the intervention plan. In Mary's example, the child had a severe difficulty in initiating interactions (d71040.3, as coded by the ECI team in the initial child functionality profile). Both the transcript of the *vignette* and the corresponding ICF-CY codes and qualifiers were of crucial relevance, not only to document Mary's pre-intervention functioning profile and compare it with the post-intervention profile but also to plan the embedded intervention in natural settings. In Mary's plan, this can be checked in the column where the competence/dimension that was being targeted is defined (Figure 9.5). Then, specific functional goals were defined for different routines aiming to improve Mary's specific competence (initiating interactions with peers) and overall participation in the routines – namely, in terms of engagement, social relations and independence. Note that each goal has to be followed by intervention strategies so that all professionals working with the child (and the family when the plan is extended to home routines) can understand what kind of supports/strategies are adequate for the specific goal defined for the child/routine. After the plan is completed – with the goals and strategies defined and matched with the routines where the opportunities would naturally emerge for the child – it is implemented and monitored by all professionals working with the child in her everyday natural routines (e.g. regular teacher, assistants, special education teacher and therapists). In this project, researchers were engaged in all the steps of the assessment-intervention design and monitoring process.

Monitoring included feedback by the researcher to teachers' comments and records about (i) how Mary was progressing in goals acquisition and (ii) how they evaluated Mary's engagement, social relations and independence in pre-school routines. Moreover the researcher observed Mary's classroom once a month using the ECA to collect information on Mary's performance in the activities and the degree of participation and engagement in the routines, as well as on how consistently the adults were implementing the defined strategies. This observation was particularly relevant for the team meetings, which happened once every two months, in the scope of which the intervention plan was reviewed based on child progresses and on professionals' evaluation about their own practices and about difficulties in implementing the strategies to support the child performance, participation and engagement.

After a six-month intervention period (comprising six observations with ECA and three team meetings, with the researcher), Mary's inclusive experience in preschool was assessed with QIEM and the quality of her peer relations and competences was documented based on the APR. In line with the project global results, the quality of individualisation improved, as well as Mary's engagement in the preschool routines. Mary's functionality profile was then reviewed, considering the final assessment, in order to document the intervention results and developmental changes. Professionals agreed that Mary's competences in initiating interactions with her peers had improved, as she was then able to initiate and respond to a higher number of interactions. ICF-CY qualifiers were updated so that Mary's progresses were reflected in her functionality profile. Although some important additional information was added in the final functionality profile, the ICF-CY dimensions that were selected for intervention by the team (based on the initial assessment) and targeted during the plan implementation, were also documented in the final profile, with updated qualifiers, based on the reassessment results. This documentation process allowed professionals to clearly visualise and understand how the assessment and intervention processes are closely connected and deeply related. Although it's mandatory that the assessment informs the intervention planning as well as that results from interventions inform subsequent assessments and interventions, studies show that this is not the case in most Portuguese preschool education plans (Boavida, Aguiar, McWilliam, & Pimentel, 2010; Castro, Pinto, & Simeonsson, 2014; Ferreira, Coelho, & Pinto, 2012).

Conclusion

By placing professionals and researchers together in an action based approach to research, it was possible to build on professionals' knowledge and needs to design a process aligned with both the contexts/professionals needs and with internationally recommended models as well as with legal requirements. This allowed improving professionals knowledge about the models defined in the legislation while also providing procedures to translate them into practice, thus bridging theory, legislation and practice. As a result, children experienced higher quality interventions and better inclusion practices which, in turn, resulted in improved developmental outcomes. Based on their involvement in the aforementioned step-by-step, assessment-intervention model, ECI professionals acknowledged the benefits of the ICF-CY framework for planning and evaluating their practice and originated strategies for a better team functioning and collaboration with families. Although follow-up analyses would be needed, the aforementioned results seem to indicate that, by the end of the project, participant professionals were using the ICF-CY as a working tool useful for everyday planning, progress documentation and team communication.

Highlights from this chapter

• The ICF-CY has been used in early childhood intervention (ECI) services in Portugal. This chapter describes a step-by-step model according to which the ICF-CY is used as a tool to support assessment and intervention procedures.

• The model described shows how to create opportunities for the interventions to take place in preschool contexts without implementing any changes in the daily routine, with the support of the ICF-CY.

• A case study illustrates the step-by-step model for ECI using the ICF-CY, showing the development of a child with special educational needs over time, as documented by the ICF-CY classification system.

References

Adolfsson, A. (2008). *A problem-solving approach to children's habilitation.* Presentation delivered at Porto University.

Adolfsson, M., & Klang, N. (2013). *MATRIX – A problem solving process related to the ICF-CY.* Unpublished document, CHILD Research Group. Jönköping University, Sweden.

Aydogan, C. (2012). *Influences of instructional and emotional classroom environments and learning engagement on low-income children's achievement in the prekindergarten year.* Unpublished doctoral dissertation, Vanderbilt University.

Bairrão, J. (1999). Early intervention in Portugal. In E. Björck-Åkesson & M. Grandlund (Eds.), *Proceedings of the international research symposium: Excellence in early childhood intervention.* Västeras, Sweden: Mälardalen University.

Björck-Åkesson, E., Wilder, J., Granlund, M., Pless, M., Simeonsson, R., Adolfsson, M., . . . Lillvist, A. (2010). The International Classification of Functioning, Disability and Health and the version for children and youth as a tool in child habilitation/early childhood intervention – feasibility and usefulness as a common language and frame of reference for practice. *Disability & Rehabilitation, 32,* 125–138.

Boavida, T., Aguiar, C., McWilliam, R. A., & Pimentel, J. S. (2010). Quality of individualized education program goals of pre-schoolers with disabilities. *Infants and Young Children*, 23(3), 233–243. doi:10.1097/IYC.0b013e3181e45925

Bronfenbrenner, U., & Morris, P. A. (2006). The ecology of developmental processes. In W. Damon & R. M. Lerner (Eds.), *Handbook of child psychology, Vol. 1: Theoretical models of human development* (6th ed., pp. 793–828). New York: John Wiley and Sons, Inc.

Brown, S., & Guralnick, M. (2012). International human rights to early intervention for infants and young children with disabilities: Tools for global advocacy. *Infants & Young Children*, 25(4), 270–285.

Carr, W., & Kemmis, S. (1986). *Becoming critical: Education, knowledge and action research*. London: Falmer Press.

Castro, S., Pinto, A. I., & Maia, M. (2011). Linking the Carolina curriculum for preschoolers with special needs to the ICF-CY. *British Journal of Developmental Disabilities*, 57(113, 2), 133–146. doi:10.1179/096979511798967043

Castro, S., Pinto, A., & Simeonsson, R. J. (2014). Content analysis of Portuguese individualized education programmes for young children with autism using the ICF-CY framework. *European Early Childhood Education Research Journal*, 22(1), 91–104.

de Kruif, R. E. L., & McWilliam, R. A. (1999). Multivariate relationships among development age, global engagement and observed child engagement. *Early Childhood Research Quarterly*, 14, 515–536.

Downer, J. T., Rimm-Kaufman, S. E., & Pianta, R. C. (2007). How do classroom conditions and children's risk for school problems contribute to children's engagement in learning? *School Psychology Review*, 36(3), 413–432.

Dunst, C. J., Bruder, M. B., Trivette, C. M., & Hamby, D. W. (2006). Everyday activity settings, natural learning environments, and early intervention practices. *Journal of Policy and Practice in Intellectual Disabilities*, 3(1), 3–10. doi:10.1111/j.1741-1130.2006.00047.x

Ferreira, D. (2011). *Temperamento e participação social com pares em crianças com perturbação do espectro do autismo (PEA)*. Unpublished master's thesis. Faculty of Psychology and Educational Sciences of Porto University.

Ferreira, T., Coelho, V., & Pinto, A. I. (2012). Early childhood intervention practices based on evidence: The case of Participation. In Medimond International Proceedings (Ed.), *European conference on developmental psychology* (pp. 485–490). Bologna, Italy.

Granlund, M. (2013). Participation – challenges in conceptualization, measurement and intervention. *Child: Care, Health and Development*, 39(4), 470–473. doi:10.1111/cch.12080

Guralnick, M. J. (2003). *Assessment of peer relations: Child development and mental retardation center*. Washington, DC: University of Washington.

Johnson-Martin, N. M., Attermeier, S. M., & Hacker, B. J. (1996). *The Carolina curriculum for preschoolers with special needs* (2nd ed.). Baltimore, MD: P. H. Brookes Pub. Co.

Lollar, D., & Simeonsson, R. (2005). Diagnosis to function: Classification for children and youths. *Developmental and Behavioral Pediatrics*, 26(4). doi:10.1097/00004703-200508000-00012

McLaughlin, T., Snyder, P., & Hemmeter, M. L. (2011). Using embedded instruction to support young children's. *Learning Exchange Magazine*, 49–52.

McNiff, J. (2013). *Action research: Principles and practice*. New York: Routledge.

McWilliam, R. A. (2010). *Routines-based early intervention supporting young children and their families*. Baltimore, MD: Paul H. Brookes Publishing Co.

Meisels, S. J., & Shonkoff, J. P. (2000). Early childhood intervention: A continuing evolution. In J. P. Shonkoff & S. J. Meisels (Eds.), *Handbook of early childhood intervention* (2nd ed., pp. 3–31). Cambridge: University Press.

Ministry of Education. (1997). *Lei-quadro da Educação Pré-Escolar [Preschool Education law]*. Diário da República, série-A, 34.

Ministry of Education. (2008). *Decreto-Lei n.° 3/2008 de 7 de Janeiro [Decree-Law No.3/2008 of January 7].* Diário da República, 1. série, N.° 4.

Ministry of Education, Ministry of Social Security, & Ministry of Health. (2009). *Decreto-Lei n.° 281/2009 de 6 de Outubro [Decree-Law No. 281/2009 of October 6].* Diário da República, 1.série, N.° 193.

Pinto, A. I. (2006). *O envolvimento da criança em contexto de creche: efeitos de características da criança, da qualidade do contexto e das interações educativas [Child engagement in child care: Effects of child characteristics, child care quality and learning interactions].* Unpublished doctoral dissertation, Porto University, Porto, Portugal.

Pinto, A.I., Grande, C., Aguiar, C., de Almeida, I.C., Felgueiras, I., Pimentel, J.S., Serrano, A.M., Carvalho, L., Brandão, M.T., Boavida, T. & Santos, P. (2012). Early childhood intervention in Portugal: An overview based on the developmental systems model. *Infants & Young Children, 25*(4), 310–322. doi:10.1097/IYC.0b013e31826d8242

Pinto, A. I., Grande, C., & Coelho, V. (2016). *Planeamento de intervenções: Oportunidades de Aprendizagem Inseridas nas Rotinas [The Learning Opportunities Embedded in Routines Grid].* XII Congresso Nacional de Intervenção Precoce. Lisboa. Portugal.

Rönnerman, K., Moksnes Furu, E., & Salo, P. (Eds.). (2008). *Nurturing praxis: Action research in partnership between school and university in a nordic light.* Rotterdam: Sense Publishers.

Sanches-Ferreira, M., Silveira-Maia, M., & Alves, S. (2014). The use of the International Classification of Functioning, Disability and Health, version for Children and Youth (ICF-CY), in Portuguese special education assessment and eligibility procedures: The professionals' perceptions. *European Journal of Special Needs Education, 29*(3), 327–343. doi:10.10 80/08856257.2014.908025

Sanches-Ferreira, M., Simeonsson, R. J., Silveira-Maia, M., & Alves, S. (2015). Evaluating implementation of the international classification of functioning, disability and health in Portugal's special education law. *International Journal of Inclusive Education, 19*(5), 457–468. doi:10.1080/13603116.2014.940067

Simeonsson, R. J., & Bailey, D. B. (1991). *ABILITIES index.* Chapel Hill, NC: Frank Porter Graham Development Center, University of North Carolina.

Simeonsson, R. J., Bjorck-Akesson, E., & Bairrão, J. (2006). Rights of children with disabilities. In G. Albrecht (Ed.), *Encyclopedia of disability* (pp. 257–259). Thousand Oaks, CA: Sage Publications.

Sparrow, S. S., Balla, D. A., & Cicchetti, D. V. (1984). *Vineland adaptive behavior scales.* Circle Pines, MN: American Guidance Service.

Titchen, A. (2015). Action research: Genesis, evolution and orientations. *International Practice Development Journal, 5*(1), 1–16.

United Nations Educational, Scientific and Cultural Organization – UNESCO. (2010, September). Early childhood care and education regional report Europe and North America. *World Conference on Early Childhood Care and Education.* Moscow: Russian Federation.

Wolery, M., Brashers, M. S., & Neitzel, J. C. (2002). Ecological congruence assessment for classroom activities and routines: Identifying goals and intervention practices in childcare. *Topics in Early Childhood Special Education, 22*(3), 131–142. doi:10.1177/0271121402022 0030101

Wolery, M., Paucca, T., Brashers, M. S., & Grant, S. (2000). *Quality of inclusive experiences measure.* Chapel Hill, NC: University of North Carolina, FPG Child Development Center.

World Health Organization. (2007). *International Classification of Functioning, Disability and Health for Children and Youth (ICF-CY).* Geneva: World Health Organization.

Chapter 10

"Let us be prepared, but wait and see"

The use of ICF-CY in early childhood intervention and paediatric social care in Germany and neighbouring countries

Manfred Pretis

It is not about information; it is about usage and implementation

The aim of this specific chapter is to provide a critical analysis of the usage of the ICF-CY in German-speaking countries (Germany, Austria, Switzerland, German-speaking community in Belgium). In addition to the description of concrete initiatives in the field of ECI, Social Pediatric Care and inclusive kindergartens, the issue of usability and transferability into daily practice is highlighted.

The implementation of the ICF-CY in Germany, Austria and Switzerland can be compared to the overall situation of vulnerable preschool children and their families: in both areas (service delivery and implementation of the ICF-CY) a "wait and see" strategy is followed (Pretis, 2014). Information is available relating to both service delivery and implementation of the ICF-CY: transdisciplinary services are defined by federal laws, parents are entitled to obtain services, there is a systematic network of more than 1000 ECI Services for disabled or at-risk children age 0–3 years, and there are 157 Pediatric Social Clinical Centres all over Germany. However, the age of referral to programmes remains relatively high: Pretis (2015a) describes the mean intake age of 30.11 months (SD = 9.32) for vulnerable children into early intervention programs. A comparable "waiting strategy" is found in relation to the ICF-CY: numerous training sessions on the ICF-CY were carried out in Germany (mainly by Camargo and Simon, 2015). The ICF-CY has been addressed through annual practitioner conferences from 2013 to 2016, and there are books available on how to use it in daily practice (Camargo & Simon, 2015; Pretis, 2016).

Despite this information and training campaigns, only a handful of centres in the German-speaking area implemented the ICF-CY into their daily practice (e.g. two in Austria use an Internet-based version within the www.icf-training.eu tool), and one rehabilitation centre implemented an electronic version as a mainstream tool within transdisciplinary therapy planning and evaluation (Reutlinger, Isermann, & Niebuhr, 2016). A mapping process is currently being performed by Simon and colleagues (Simon, Kindervater, & Irmler, 2016), in all-inclusive kindergartens and Early Intervention Centres in Nordrhein-Westfahlen (one German state out of 17) will be trained. It can be hypothesised that professionals are interested in knowing what the ICF-CY is about, but they seem to be reluctant to use it. Alternatively, they remain in a passive position and wait to see the extent to which the use of the ICF-CY will be implemented (e.g. through top-down strategies by political decision makers or financial bodies such as health insurance companies, comparable to the situation in Portugal (Sanches-Ferreira et al., 2014).

It is important to note, that Germany, Switzerland and Austria are all federal countries (and the German-speaking community of Belgium is part of a federal system). This means that most of the regulations – namely, concerning the use of a common language in service provision in general – are based at the state level; within each national context, a diversity of approaches concerning legislation, service delivery, documentation and evaluation can be observed. Therefore, when we refer to "Germany, Austria or Switzerland" we mostly address the situation of some states within these federal nations. Concerning the ICF-CY, this state of diversity collides with national strategic papers concerning the ICF (CY): the German Federal Bundesarbeitsgemeinschaft Rehabilitation (BAR) recommended the use of the ICF for clinical assessment of people with disabilities. Already in 2004, the guidelines on how to use ICF (CY) in medical rehabilitation were published on the basis of legal recommendations (Gemeinsamer Bundesausschuss, 2004). However, due to a lack of concrete empirical mapping data, it seems difficult to assess the extent to which the ICF-CY is implemented in daily practice. Similarly, at the European level, strategic papers (e.g. European Commission, 2010) highlight the need for empirical data, comparability, harmonisation of assessment and call for future data analysis to rely on the ICF. In Germany, it remains unclear the ongoing discussion on the impact that the *Bundesteilhabegesetz (Law on Participation)* has on the assessments of needs by applying comparable ICF-criteria (Deutscher Bundestag, 2014).

As mentioned earlier, the general political will in Germany and Austria (mostly based on the ratification of the UN Convention on the Rights of Persons with Disability UN 1986), is not reflected in the use of ICF or ICF-CY in daily practice. It can be hypothesised that political decision makers foresee possible socio-demographic, efficiency or transparency effects through the use of the ICF-CY, but usually delegate the concrete implementation of tools to experts. This step towards an operationalisation or theory-practice discourse of the general WHO-approach is still missing and service providers might therefore face a lack of concrete transferability.

ICF-CY: an interesting approach but too complex, too "bulky", too "technocratic"

Despite its conceptual background as a biopsychosocial model and its ethical guidelines to describe and not stigmatise or "label" children and young people, the ICF-CY is still seen by the majority of (non)-users as a complex, time-consuming coding system with unclear goals (Wolf, Berger, & Allwang, 2016). Parents are afraid that the ICF-CY represents a new "secret" professional language and that their situation might be reduced to "codes". Professionals often do not see the added value of using the ICF-CY alongside existing clinical description systems. Transparency and comparability of observations or having a common descriptor language in transdisciplinary teams are also considered as potential threats to existing open (almost un-monitored) services. The ICF-CY language – often considered to be technocratic and difficult to understand (e.g. by parents) also represents a barrier for teams and requires extensive (mostly) in-house-training (Pechstädt & Svaton, 2016). It is not only about reading the book but also about creating a common understanding within teams on what the ICF-CY is about. These preparatory processes are time consuming and require a strategic decision as to whether to use ICF-CY over the long term or "wait and see". In addition to issues regarding how to connect existing laws with the ICF-CY, the issue of practicability is seen as a major obstacle for clinical transfer (Bering, 2013).

Some "glimpses" of ICF-CY use in Germany and Austria

Using selected examples, the concrete use of the ICF-CY in the field of ECI will be described. However, as mentioned earlier, no systematic approach towards the ICF-CY can be observed. The rare examples of its implementation (within a hierarchical structure of complexity) focus on

1   Structuring anamnestic information using the ICF-CY (Espei, 2014);
2   Development of code sets, mainly age lists (Amorosa & Keller, 2012);
3   Development of core sets concerning defined health status;
4   Defining areas of intervention (Kraus de Camargo & Simon, 2015b);
5   Planning, documentation and evaluation of interventions (Pretis, 2015b, 2016); and
6   ICF-CY as a continuously developing, problem solving tool in Pediatric Social Care (Pretis & Stadler, 2016).

Structuring anamnestic information using ICF-CY

Comparable to the situation in Italy (Francescutti, Martinuzzi, Leonardi, & Kostanjek, 2009) where the implementation of the ICF-CY is assessed as a "success story", some Pediatric Social Centres in Germany – in terms of an initial step towards implementing the ICF-CY in their clinical practice – associate clinical (narrative) anamnestic data with ICF-CY codes, as described in Figure 10.1. Therefore, the ICF-CY provides additional data to enable statistical

(✓) Postnatal Situations		Tick If Relevant
Without complications		0
With complications		0
Artificial respiration necessary	b449	0
Coronary disease	b429	0
Enteral nutrition (PEG)	b510	0
(✓)		0
Intermediate Diseases		
Asthma	s430	0
Seizures	s110	0
(✓)		0
Child takes medication	e115	0
Child obtains special financial allowances due to disability	e199	0
Vaccinations	e355	0
Activities		
Child likes to talk	d350	0
Preferred play	d9200	0
Attends kindergarten	d815	0

Figure 10.1 Example of anamnestic data collection introducing ICF-CY codes to pre-defined categories (Pretis, 2016, translated and modified)

analysis of the situation of children; however, it might only represent "additional" information to existing clinical information.

Development of checklists, mainly age related (Amorosa & Keller, 2012)

In order to reduce the complexity of more than 1700 codes, a German working group identified relevant codes for different age groups (0–3 years, 3–6 years, 6–12 years and 12–18 years). These checklists however, are only available in paper form and lack easily accessible electronic tools. The idea of these checklists consists mainly in reducing the number of items when describing a family. It means the user will only choose relevant ones from reduced lists (e.g. the age list 0–3 consists of 200 items) instead of approximately 1700 items of the full version. However, users need to be trained to understand the meaning of the codes.

Development of core sets concerning defined health status

A step forward towards clinical usage can be seen in the development of clinical core sets. This means that – for specific conditions (ADHD) or diagnoses

(CP), lists of ICF-CY items were developed, which are regarded as relevant to describe the respective symptoms. These sets aim to focus on relevant aspects of a health condition (e.g. children with ASD, as in Castro & Pretis, 2016) and might serve as qualitative and quantitative roadmaps towards information management and planning or intervention and evaluation. Castro and Pretis (2016) highlight that core sets might "broaden" the professional view by focusing on other aspects (e.g. environmental factors), which the specific diagnostic view might not address: most of the professionals focus on the narrative and assessment of the child and "neglect" carers, the relevance of attitudes, the availability of services or the surrounding politics. It is no wonder that only 3%–5% of ICF-CY items used during the description process of a child and family focus on environmental factors (Pretis, 2014). Most of the core sets developed in the German-speaking areas can be assessed as still in the "pilot stage". As an example, an ICF-CY based questionnaire might be used when assessing aspects of functioning in children with brain cancer or other chronic diseases (Pletschko et al., 2013).

A list of ongoing activities to extract core sets can be found under www. dimdi.de/static/de/klassi/icf/projekte/index.htm.

However, core sets are also seen critically, as they might not always reflect the biopsychosocial approach of the ICF-CY as a common language within teams around the child (mainly if professional groups define their own "core sets") and as such, they might be easily misinterpreted as diagnostic tools (Castro & Pretis, 2016).

Checklists or code sets to reflect ongoing intervention processes and define goals

To increase usability and meaningfulness for teams and parents, the group around Olaf Kraus de Camargo (2007) tried specifically to reduce the complexity of the codes. They used two strategies:

a) To create specific code sets for defined services (e.g. ECI services addressing disabled or at-risk preschool children, mainly within home visiting services); and

b) To reduce the complexity of the proposed WHO qualifier. This numeric system intends to assess the severity of a "problem" (of each child and family relevant ICF-CY-item) by using codes between 0 and 4. Alongside this ordinal scale, other (non-ordinal) categories such as 8 = "more information necessary" and 9 = "not relevant" have been introduced (Kraus de Camargo & Hollenweger, 2011).

Using both strategies, a pool of 150 items was created for preschool children in ECI programs. This reduction aimed to promote easier usability (due to a limitation of codes) and higher practicability by reducing the complexity of the qualifier. The authors replaced the WHO qualifier (0 = no difficulty, 1 = mild difficulty, 2 = moderate difficulty, 3 = severe difficulty and 4 = complete difficulty) by a new (categorical) grouping: 1 = no difficulty, 2 = difficulty, F = goal of intervention, I = further information necessary and N = not relevant. This amended checklist in the field of ECI mainly serves as a basis to reflect ongoing processes within teams: team members develop a (video-supported) narrative of a child or family and are asked to describe by means of selected ICF-CY codes the current situation and to evaluate (based on the aforementioned modified qualifier) the ongoing support process. This descriptive process leads to joint definitions of goals for further intervention. However, the modification of the WHO qualifiers decreases the possibilities for quantitative evaluation.

The introduction of electronic tools

Even though some preliminary initiatives use electronic versions of the ICF-CY, only the European initiatives www.icf-training.eu and www.icfcy-meduse.eu were able to bridge the gap between the complexity of the items and the use of information and communication technology. Comparable electronic tools are now being used such as the recently introduced one in Helios rehabilitation clinics in Geesthacht, Northern Germany (Reutlinger et al., 2016). These initiatives can be seen as pioneering the introduction of electronic or Internet-based solutions for the highly complex ICF-CY in the German-speaking area.

Taking into account issues of personal data storage on the Internet, these electronic attempts followed the comparable logic of existing paper versions by

a) associating relevant anamnestic or observation data with ICF-CY codes;
b) evaluating relevant information/codes – based on indicators – with WHO qualifiers (in terms of a baseline);
c) deducing intervention goals based on the aforementioned WHO-qualifier evaluation;
d) combining this information with relevant clinical documentation systems; and
e) re-evaluating post-intervention data concerning the pre-intervention baseline.

Three issues arose from the electronic use of these tools, which are implemented in two kindergartens and one ECI centre in Austria:

a) Data protection issues have to be respected, as in some projects – especially when using peer-to-peer learning tools – Internet-based storage of personal data is still perceived as a big challenge.
b) It is important that the ICF-CY be easy to use and connected to existing clinical documentation systems.
c) The ICF-CY as a problem-solving tool will only be successful if the use of the tool itself will make life easier for professionals in their daily practice.

Relevant Observations	Source	Associated ICF-CY Codes	Observing Team Member
M. obtains physiotherapy	Parental report	e355	MD
Kindergarten teacher report certain helplessness regarding their strategies	Report	e455	Special educator
Parents react timely towards the needs of M.	Own observation	e410	Special educator
M. often is playing alone	Parental report	d8803	Special educator
The family reports 1–2 close friends	Parental report	d7402 e320	Psychologist
M. follows the rhythm of music	Report educator	d469	Special educator
M. is walking short distances	Own observation	d450	Physiotherapist
M. is willed to perform the CPM	Test	b1301	Psychologist
The results of the CPM represents the sixtieth percentile	Own observation	b117	Psychologist
Mobility of tarsal bones is restricted	Own observation	b7203	MD
Musculus gastrocnemius and soleus are contracted	Own observation	b7351	MD
Supination of the right leg can be observed	Own observation	s75012	MD

Figure 10.2 Step 2: associating observation data with ICF-CY codes

Figure 10.2 illustrates one example of associating observation records with the ICF-CY codes. At the moment, usage in clinical practice is still seen as a critical issue. The added value of using the ICF-CY is not yet fully appreciated, due to the complexity of the tools. Particularly within the Erasmus plus project www. icfcy-meduse.eu "peer-to-peer learning systems" (comparable to social media) were included in order to increase the usefulness of the ICF-CY. This means that the system develops itself based on its usage, as indicated in Table 10.1. ICF-CY tools are therefore understood as "living" (growing and learning) within a

Table 10.1 Peer to peer learning processes within the ICF-CY-MedUse project

Challenges for the User	Examples	Hypothesised Impact on Usage
Users wish to associate own observation data (while observing a child or a family) with relevant ICF-CY codes. Professionals therefore have to know codes "by heart" or look for them within code-lists. The system provides a "full-text search function".	The user is able to search for relevant "key words" within approximately 1700 items during anamnestic data collection. A full text search for "play" achieves 35 hits: b1521, d110, d131, d1313, d1314, d155, d1551, d163, d172, d2101, d2102, d2103, d2105, d3503, d620, d6200, d650, d750, d880, d8800, d8801, d8802, d8803, d8808, d8809, d9103, d920, d9200, d9202, e1152, e11520, e11521, e11528, e11529, e3.	Looking for appropriate codes within the whole list or selection is assessed as challenging and time-consuming for professionals. A full text search therefore saves time and increases usability.
Users wish to know, which codes other professionals used concerning a given diagnosis. By using the system, users "learn" from the search history of "others".	Professionals who used a certain diagnosis (e.g. F.84) chose the following ICF-CY items (most frequently used items are listed).	This function reduces individual effort in code selection and therefore saves time for the team and increases the efficiency/costs of anamnestic processes.
Users wish to describe the complex situation of a child – especially for a better understanding – by a graphical representation. The system provides a translation of the individual "narrative" of the child and family into an ICF-CY "picture".	Without entering personal data onto the Internet, relevant aspects of the individual narrative are linked with ICF-CY codes (the child, 5 years old, often (more than 50% of the time) plays alone.	Regulations regarding protection of personal data on the Internet are not an issue, as only an anonymous ICF-CY related picture of the child and the family is created by the tool.
Users wish to assess the quantity/quality of the health problem. The system facilitates evaluation by using WHO qualifiers and by providing graphical representations.	Based on the indicator-related (Pretis, 2016) evaluation, a graphical representation (a comprehensive picture) is provided.	This graphical representation can be re-imported into the existing (medical) documentation system. Individual narrative and ICF-CY based comprehensive picture.

community of practice and allow for quick, intuitive access to useful methodology, based on the relevant consultancy (information, feedback and assessment) of other professionals with similar areas of work.

Based on their own narratives (diagnosis, anamnestic data, observations, tests . . .), professionals record this information using ICF-CY- based processes and create a graphical representation of these narratives, which can transferred into their own clinical documentation system. In this context, no personal data is used or stored on the Internet, because only abstract ICF-CY code representations reflect the situation of the child and family. Furthermore, this user can also benefit from the experience of others (the search history of others): for example, the electronic tool includes the option "other professionals who were in contact with a child with the diagnosis F83 (combined developmental disorder) used the following ICF-CY codes to describe the situation".

Within the aforementioned evaluation process, there remains the issue of matching the WHO qualifier with existing test standards when well-established assessment instruments or tests are used. The term "moderate difficulty" might have different meanings for different members of a team, including the parents. Furthermore, test scores will have to be represented by a WHO qualifier. This represents a methodological challenge, which is not yet solved. In this context, some professionals question why they should use WHO qualifiers if (empirically) well-established assessment instruments in their field of work are already available.

As Pretis could show (2015b), the use of electronic tools can also generate statistical data that are able to discriminate differences: the ICF-CY was able to differentiate different groups of children with the same disability and their different needs for support. The ICF itself highlights this possibility of using the classification as an epidemiological tool. Abstract ICF-CY codes might be used in future scenarios to better match the needs of the children and families with service provision, to compare services (e.g. concerning the needs of the target groups or regarding effectiveness/efficiency). The latter might be seen as a big advantage for financing bodies; however, service providers might also see certain dangers of using the ICF-CY as a cost-cutting tool.

Furthermore, the issue of full participation of everybody involved (parents, children and professionals) has to be highlighted: the philosophy of the ICF-CY focuses on a common language between teams and not on reducing families to narrow professional perspectives. The electronic version facilitates access for parents (e.g. access to child or process related documents).

However, for some parents the technical skills or linguistic requirements for using the ICF-CY can be a challenge. Therefore, current initiatives also focus on the linguistic transfer of the ICF-CY coding system into parent- and youth-friendly versions. It can be hypothesised that parents will only see the benefits of using the ICF-CY if they a) understand the philosophy behind it and b) are able to fully participate in its usage.

The situation in Swiss schools is different

Concerning the implementation of the ICF-CY in the area of special needs of schoolchildren in Switzerland, the situation is different. The ICF-CY was introduced into the Swiss school system by means of a top-down-strategy. The school administration required teachers to use the ICF-CY related description tools (see Figure 10.2) to describe and plan educational processes for school-children with special needs.

By means of a "standardized assessment procedure" (SAV; Hollenweger & Lienhard, 2011) for children with complex and profound learning needs and the "structured school talks" (*Schulstandortgespräche*) for children with minor learning difficulties, the special needs of children in schools are addressed and described using ICF-CY item-lists (assessed as relevant for the school and pre-school context). Subsequent educational goals can then be set and an assessment made regarding service delivery. Additionally, facilitating and hindering contextual factors is also included and should be addressed, particularly when working with toddlers (Hollenweger & Lienhard, 2011).

A third stage to the process addresses the service needs of a child. Using the earlier analysis, necessary services and educational resources (e.g. application of a specific curriculum, assistant teacher, counselling or therapeutic services such as physiotherapy etc.) are defined for each child. The significant difference of this approach is that it is a top-down strategy, whereas in the other German-speaking areas (Germany, Austria, German-speaking community of Belgium) service providers still deal with bottom-up processes and therefore still remain in the aforementioned "wait and see" position, as the challenges of the ICF-CY (complexity, time-consumption, practicability) seem to outweigh the advantages (common language, transparency and abstract comparability).

Highlights from this chapter

The ICF-CY towards a problem-solving tool for the "team around the child": what are the strengths and opportunities for future usage of the ICF-CY and where might be the stumbling blocks?

- The ICF-CY can be used as a common language if we succeed in making it accessible to all people involved in the "team around the child". Children and families are seen through a holistic approach: integrating their unique personality, their body functions and structures and their participation in concrete environments. In this sense, the usage of the ICF-CY can help to move away from persisting deficit-oriented views on a child and family. However, it will be necessary to make this complex and abstract list of items accessible (in terms of reduced complexity) and understandable (mainly for parents and children/young people).

- The ICF-CY can describe the situation of a child through a more resourceful and strength-oriented approach than the ICD-10 or the DSM-V narratives, for example. Using the ICF-CY also provides a picture of what the child is able to do and which facilitating factors might be available. The ICF-CY can also suggest evaluations – based on WHO qualifiers, if the terms and qualifiers used are well defined or matched with evidence-based assessments.

- The ICF-CY is a descriptive tool, not a diagnostic assessment tool. Therefore, it cannot assess the degree of disability or provide easy answers to issues of eligibility (of services or financial allowances). The definition, when a person is disabled and for which services/ allowances he or she is eligible cannot be directly answered by the ICF-CY; however, assessment procedures (and therefore defined cut-off scores) can be transferred secondarily into WHO qualifiers.

- The ICF-CY will only be used in the field of preventive services if professionals and parents perceive concrete (positive) impacts: be it that they find it easier to obtain services, that the team around the child can make decisions more easily, that planning and documentation processes are quicker or that financing bodies perceive the potential to increase the efficiency of services.

- An electronic version might help to increase the use of the ICF-CY if data or results can easily be linked to existing clinical documentation systems and if data protection issues are addressed.

To ensure the practical use of ICF-CY, future implementation research will primarily have to focus on the "added value" of using a common language between professionals themselves and for parents and adolescents with disability to participate fully. The ICF-CY may not need more information campaigns or basic training materials, but there is a need to develop transfer strategies to highlight greater efficiency of services, intensified communication within the team around the child and therefore an improved match between the needs of vulnerable children or their parents and service provision.

References

Amorosa, H., & Keller, P. (2012). ICF-Checklisten für das Kinder- und Jugendalter. Präsentation zur Multiplikatorenfortbildung. Retrieved May 19, 2016, from www.fruehfoerderung-viff. de/neue-seite-3/neue-seite-5/neue-seite/SearchForm?Search=checklist&action_results=L

Bering, R. (2013). Implementierung der Internationalen Klassifikation der Funktions-fähigkeit, Behinderung und Gesundheit (ICF) zur Klassifizierung von psychischen

Beeinträchtigungen. Ausschuss "Psychische Behinderungen" der DVfR. Retrieved May 19, 2016, from www.dvfr.de/fileadmin/download/Stellungnahmen/ICF_Papier_%C3%BCberarbeitet_23_8_13.pdf

Castro, S., & Pretis, M. (2016). Die Anwendung des ICF-CY Core-Sets in der Frühförderung bei Kleinkindern mit Autismus-Spektrum-Störungen. *Frühförderung Interdisziplinär, 35*(5), 146–154.

Deutscher Bundestag. (2014). *Antrag zum Bundesteilhabegesetz.* Berlin: Drucksache 18/1949. Retrieved June 2, 2017, from http://dip21.bundestag.de/dip21/btd/18/019/1801949.pdf

Espei, A. (2014). *Hilfsmittelversorgung und die RehaKind-Bögen. Workshop at the 2nd ICF-CY Anwenderkonferenz,* Hamburg, Germany.

European Commission. (2010). European disability strategy 2010–2020: A renewed commitment to a barrier-free Europe. Retrieved from http://eur-lex.europa.eu/legal-content/EN/TXT/PDF/?uri=CELEX:52010DC0636&from=EN

Francescutti, C., Martinuzzi, A., Leonardi, M., & Kostanjek, NFI. (2009). Eight years of ICF in Italy: Principles, results and future perspectives. *Disability and Rehabilitation, 31*(S1), 4–7.

Gemeinsamer Bundesaussschuss. (2004). *Richtlinie Rehabilitation.* Berlin: Bundesanzeiger Banz.

Hollenweger, J., & Lienhard, P. (2011). *Dossier zum standardisierten Abklärungsverfahren zur Ermittlung des individuellen Bedarfs (SAV).* Presentation at the Schweizerische Konferenz der Kantonalen Erziehungsdirektoren, Switzerland.

ICF-Train. Retrieved July 5, 2016, from www.icf-training.eu.

ICF- MedUse. Retrieved July 5, 2016, from www.icfcy-MedUse.eu.

Kraus de Camargo, O. (2007). Die ICF-CY als Checkliste und Dokumentationsraster in der Praxis der Frühförderung. *Frühförderung Interdisziplinär, 4,* 158–166.

Kraus de Camargo, O., & Hollenweger, J. (2011). *ICF-CY: Internationale Klassifikation der Funktionsfähigkeit.* Behinderung und Gesundheit bei Kindern und Jugendlichen.

Kraus de Camargo, O., & Simon, L. (2015). *Die ICF-CY in der Praxis.* Bern: Huber.

Pechstädt, K., & Svaton, V. (2016). ICF-Train in der praktischen Umsetzung im Heilpädagogischen Kindergarten und der Integrativen Zusatzbetreuung Scheifling. *Frühförderung Interdisziplinär, 35*(5), 161–164.

Pletschko, T., Gmoser, S., Leeb, L., Schwarzinger, A., Slavc, I., & Leiss, U., (2013). Advantages of ICF-based approach in school reintegration of pediatric brain tumor patients: The School Participation Scale (S-PS-24/7). *Journal of Cancer Therapy, 4,* 825–834.

Pretis, M. (2014). *Der Einsatz der ICF-CY in der elektronischen Version in Frühförderung und I-Kitas.* Presentation at University Passau, Passau.

Pretis, M. (2015a). *. . . Und was sagen die Daten . . .* Presentation at 3rd ICF-CY Anwenderkonferenz, München.

Pretis, M. (2015b). Erlebte Fördereffekt und Familienorientierung in der Frühförderung. *Frühförderung interdisziplinär, 1*(34), 19–31

Pretis, M. (2016). *ICF-basiertes Arbeiten in der Frühförderung.* München: Reinhardt.

Pretis, M., & Stadler, W. (2016). Neues EU-Projekt zur ICF-CY im Bereich Frühförderung und Sozialpädiatrie: Icfcy-MedUse. *Frühförderung Interdisziplinär, 35*(5), 165–168.

Reutlinger, C., Isermann, J., & Niebuhr, U. (2016). *Ziel- und Ressourcenorientierte Rehabilitation mit Hilfe einer elektronischen Version der ICF-CY.* Paper presented at the 4th ICF-CY Anwenderkonferenz, Zürich.

Sanches-Ferreira, M., Silveira-Maia, M., & Alves, S. (2014). The use of the International Classification of Functioning, Disability and Health, version for Children and Youth (ICF-CY), in Portuguese special education assessment and eligibility procedures: The professionals' perceptions. *European Journal of Special Needs Education, 29*(3), 327–343.

Simon, L., Kindervater, A., & Irmler, M. (2016). *Mapping der ICF-CY Verwendung in Deutschland. Workshop im Rahmen der 4.* ICF-CY Anwenderkonferenz, Zürich.

Wolf, H-G., Berger, R., & Allwang, N. (2016). Der Charme der ICF-CY für die interdisziplinäre Frühförderung. *Frühförderung Interdisziplinär, 35*(5), 127–137.

Chapter 11

ICF applications in health care for children with cancer in Sweden

Laura Darcy, Maria Björk, Mats Granlund and Karin Enskär

The International Classification of Functioning, Disability and Health (ICF) and its version for children and youth, the ICF-CY, can contribute to the present knowledge on the lives of young children with cancer, with an international and interdisciplinary language. In this context, the term health can be seen as a multidimensional concept in which both illness and non-illness/well-being are dimensions that can be present at the same time, rather than two opposite concepts. Health is the result of a continuous process rather than something that one individual has; it is a resource for everyday life rather than the objective of living (WHO, 1986). The ICF was developed to classify different dimensions on individuals' health as a unified standardised common language and framework, to be used across disciplines (WHO, 2007). It acknowledges that health and illness are complex concepts and promotes a biopsychosocial model of health, in which the context is as important as the individual and his/her needs. The view of health as functioning in everyday life can be operationalised using the ICF model of body structure, body function, activities and participation and environmental factors (Rosenbaum & Gorter, 2012)

The ICF-CY version (children and youth) relates more to child development and its environment, allowing a more precise classification of factors of importance for children's health (Simeonsson et al., 2003; Simeonsson, Scarborough, & Hebbeler, 2006). It provides a classification as a hierarchical system by organising information on health into four interacting components designated by letters: body structure (s), body function (b), activities and participation (d) and environmental factors (e). The components body structure and body function cover all body systems and functions, activities and participation cover all life areas from basic learning to social skills and environment factors include physical, social and attitudinal aspects of support. Personal factors such as age, gender and race provide social and cultural background but are not as yet included in the ICF-CY classification system due to the large social and cultural variance associated with them. The qualifiers denote the grade of difficulty in a particular dimension and are generally used to describe the magnitude of a problem from the person's point of view and as impairment in body structure, limitation in body function, restriction of activities and participation or barriers in the environment (WHO, 2007). Therefore, the ICF-CY classification system can be very useful to describe the everyday functioning of children with cancer.

Childhood cancer impacts on functioning and relationships between children and the various contexts of their lives: family, hospital, preschool and the larger community (Labay, Mayans, & Harris, 2004). In previous research and clinical work around childhood cancer, the focus has been on the illness and its treatment rather than on the everyday functioning of the children during their illness trajectory. Children must be seen within a context and a biopsychosocial model, such as the ICF/ICF-CY, makes it simpler to understand how the child is influenced by other and how she influences them. Using a biopsychosocial model, a comprehensive view of the child can be developed based on body functions, activity performance, participation and the environment where the child lives her life. The original ICF-CY classification consists of over 1500 codes describing characteristics of an individual's body, his/her activities and participation and the environment. For practical reasons, shorter sets of codes have been developed to guide delivery of care for some illnesses but few of these are for children and none for childhood cancer (Simeonsson, 2009).

Constructing a code set for childhood cancer

A set of ICF-CY codes (code set) was developed to provide insight on the impact that childhood cancer has on functioning and relationships, throughout the cancer trajectory. Questionnaires and interviews from a longitudinal study of children's functioning trajectories while having cancer were used. The main study included questionnaire and interview data from 13 children and their parents connected to a paediatric oncology centre in the West of Sweden. Data were gathered at six different time points over a three-year period from 2011 to 2013. Information on the study was given to children and their parents by the oncology centre's outreach nurses and families who were interested in participating were contacted by the researcher; contacts were made by phone. By then, more information on the study was given and arrangements were made for the data to be collected. The children, nine girls and four boys, were aged 1 to 5 years at the start of the study. Nine children were diagnosed with leukaemia and four children with brain or solid tumours. Ethical approval for the study had been obtained before the study began. The interviews lasted between 77 and 100 minutes and were audio-recorded and transcribed in full. The majority of the interviews took place in the child's home, at the request of the family, although some were conducted at the hospital. Verbal and written informed consent was obtained from parents and consent from children over 3 years of age was also obtained. The quality and degree of the children's participation in the interviews and questionnaires varied, but became more apparent over time, as the children matured. Mothers and fathers were also interviewed but with focus on the child's experiences of life with cancer. The data derived from the interviews and questionnaires revealed information on the child's body functions and body structures, their daily activities and participation and on the environmental factors influencing their participation, over a three-year period from diagnosis.

Step I: linking interview data to ICF-CY codes

As a first step, an ICF-CY set of codes describing the everyday life situations of the young child with cancer, was developed. A purposeful sample of 12 rich transcripts of interviews with children and parents were selected; interviews were conducted at 3–9 weeks, 6, 12 and 18 months post-diagnosis. The 12 transcripts were read through and meaning units described as words or sentences that revealed information about difficulties with the child's body structures, functioning in everyday life, activities, participation or environment, were picked out from the text (Graneheim & Lundman, 2004). One or more labels describing meaningful concepts were identified from the meaning units and linked to ICF-CY codes, using a modified version of Cieza's rules for linking text to ICF-CY codes (Cieza et al., 2002; Cieza and Stucki, 2005). Each ICF-CY component can be categorised to four levels of details. The linking process focused on the first three of these levels of detail – for example, "*You can't take the last lot of medicine in the naso-gastric tube, you see (5-year-old girl)*" was linked to **e1101** (products or substances for personal consumption) and to **e1151** (assistive products and technology for personal use in daily living), which are environmental factors.

To ensure validity and reliability in the process of coding meaning units in the texts using the ICF-CY codes, every tenth meaning unit was coded independently by a second person. The coders were both trained in the ICF-CY. Coding disagreements led to discussion with an expert in ICF-CY until agreement was reached. This process revealed a congruence of 74%, which is an acceptable level of validity and reliability (Polit & Beck, 2008).

Over 3,000 meaning units were extracted from the interview transcripts and coded. The five most commonly used ICF-CY codes were identified amongst these to encourage the development of a set of codes that is as descriptive as possible. This resulted in a comprehensive code set of 60 ICF-CY dimensions describing everyday health and functioning of young children with cancer. These can be found in Table 11.1.

Step 2: identifying codes in a data set

As a second step, the 60 previously identified ICF-CY codes were then identified data collected from children and parents in the form of questionnaire or interview at all six data collection time points throughout the study. The identification of codes in questionnaire and interview data allowed us to identify issues that are relevant for young children's health and functioning in everyday life, throughout their cancer trajectory, using a common language, the one of

Table 11.1 Comprehensive set of ICF-CY codes (n = 60)

Codes describing Body Functions

Chapter b1 mental functions
b114 orientation functions
b125 dispositions and intra-personal functions
b1252 dispositions and intra-personal functions, activity level
b1253 dispositions and intra-personal functions, predictability
b126 temperament and personality functions
b1264 temperament and personality functions, openness to experience
b1265 temperament and personality functions, optimism
b1266 temperament and personality functions, confidence
b130 energy and drive functions
b1302 energy and drive functions, appetite
b134 sleep functions
b152 emotional functions
b180 experience of self and time functions
Chapter b2 sensory functions and pain
b280 sensation of pain
Chapter b5 functions of the digestive, metabolic and endocrine systems
b510 ingestion functions
b5106 vomiting
b530 weight maintenance
b525 defecation
Chapter b7 neuromusculoskeletal and movement-related functions
b730 muscle power
Chapter b8 functions of the skin and related structures
b810 protective functions of the skin

Codes describing Activities and Participation

Chapter d2 general tasks and demands
d210 undertaking a single task
d230 undertaking multiple tasks
d250 managing one's own behaviour
Chapter d4 mobility
d450 walking
d455 moving around
Chapter d5 self-care
d530 toileting
d540 dressing
d550 eating
d560 drinking
Chapter d7 interpersonal interactions and relationships
d710 basic interpersonal interactions
d720 complex interpersonal interactions
d740 formal relationships
d7504 informal relationships with peers
d760 family relationships
d7602 siblings relationships
d7603 extended family relationships
Chapter d8 major life areas
d815 preschool education
d880 engagement in play
d8800 solitary play

(Continued)

Table 11.1 (Continued)

---

d8803 shared cooperative play
Chapter d9 community, social and civic life
d920 recreation and leisure
d9202 arts and culture

Codes describing Environmental Factors

Chapter e1 products and technology
e1100 products or substances for personal consumption, food
e1101 products or substances for personal consumption, drugs
e115 products and technology for personal use in daily living
e1151 assistive products and technology for personal use in daily living
e120 products and technology for personal indoor and outdoor mobility and
   transportation
Chapter e3 support and relationships
e310 immediate family
e315 extended family
e320 friends
e325 acquaintances, peers, colleagues, neighbours and community members
e355 health professionals
Chapter e4 attitudes
E4 attitudes
e420 individual attitudes of friends
e425 individual attitudes of acquaintances, peers, colleagues, neighbours and
   community members
Chapter e5 services, systems and policies
e5800 health services
e5801 health systems

Codes describing Body Structures

Chapter s3 structures involved in voice and speech
s320 structure of the mouth
Chapter s8 skin and related structures
s840 structure of the hair

---

the ICF-CY. Mothers' responses were used first, as it was primarily mothers who filled in the questionnaires. If the mother's response was missing, then responses from fathers were used and if these were not available, then responses from children were used.

Step 3: dichotomizing responses to facilitate interpretation

As a third step, the 30 ICF-CY codes identified in questionnaire items and interview responses were then dichotomised as "no difficulty" for the child or "difficulty for the child". Furthermore, the ICF-CY codes from interviews were also dichotomised to being a difficulty for the child or no difficulty for the child: codes describing impairment in everyday body function (b codes) were dichotomised as "no impairment" (0) or "impairment" (1), codes describing limitations in everyday life caused by body structure (s codes) were dichotomised to "no limitation" (0) or "limitation" (1), codes describing restricted activities and participation in everyday life (d codes) were dichotomised to "no restriction" (0) or "restriction" (1), codes describing barriers to the child's everyday life in the form of physical, social and attitudinal factors in the environment (e codes) were dichotomised to "no barrier" (0) or "barrier" (1). Both questionnaire and interview data responses (dichotomised) were then fed into IBM SPSS data program version 21 for Windows for descriptive analysis. This resulted in the possibility to follow changes, in everyday health and functioning of this group of young children, as the data collected is of longitudinal nature. The results revealed patterns of difficulties in the children's health and functioning in everyday life at group level and differences at individual level, over the course of three years.

Results

At the beginning of the cancer trajectory, health and functioning in everyday life had changed substantially for all children and difficulties were at their peak. Physical difficulties were the most highlighted immediately after diagnosis and the beginning of treatment. Specifically, the greatest difficulties the child experienced immediately after diagnosis and start of treatment were limitations in body functioning related to pain and difficulties in eating and defecating. These were followed by self-care issues such as difficulty with mobility, feeding oneself and going to the toilet. They missed their friends and preschool a lot "*I'm never allowed to go, I just have fever all the time*" (3-year-old, six months after diagnosis). Children were upset with having to go to the hospital and described difficulties in communication with health care services. Difficulties affecting health and functioning in everyday life declined and changed from 6 months to 18 months after diagnosis. The children described themselves in terms of feeling human again: "*I'm almost like a real child again – almost like myself*" (four year old, 1 year after cancer diagnosis). Difficulties related with temperament and personality, such as self-confidence, and difficulties eating due to lack of energy, were experienced by the children during this period. Body impairments had minimal impact but those mentioned during this time were issues in the mouth and mucous membranes. The need for structured psychosocial support was an area that came to the fore 6 to 12 months after diagnosis. Relationships with and support from the immediate family, including access to parents and siblings were highlighted, alongside difficulties related to communication with and support from health services.

Although an overall decrease in all areas of difficulties was seen during the cancer trajectory, from two years after diagnosis onwards an increase in difficulties with personal interactions with others, inappropriate social skills and access to and support from healthcare professionals was described. Two years after diagnosis, an increase in difficulties with activity and participation was seen for all children. The difficulties described at this time related to the treatment's negative effect on everyday activities such as feeling left out from the peer group. Difficulties with emotional functioning, such as socially inappropriate behaviour, were apparent three years after diagnosis. Difficulties with personal interactions with family, peers, health care and preschool personnel were highlighted, during this time. Difficulties with the child's access to, support from and communication with health care services increased again in the post-treatment period. At this time, the difficulties described were related to the child's and family's needs of where to turn to for information on starting school, concern about long-term effects of treatment and support for parents and siblings.

Individual variances in patterns of experienced difficulties were seen for each child, over time. The linking of information to ICF-CY codes allowed a comparison of difficulties within body, activity and participation thereby providing biopsychosocial patterns of functioning. The amount of difficulties experienced was partially related to the type of diagnosis and type of treatment but also partially related to the time of data collection in the cancer trajectory. For children with leukaemia, physical difficulties started to reduce immediately after treatment (Darcy, Björk, Knutsson, Granlund, & Enskär, 2015). Physical difficulties for the children with brain or solid tumours rose immediately after diagnosis, when they underwent surgery and received chemotherapy and / or radiation treatment. Towards the end of the trajectory, similar patterns of social and emotional difficulties in transitioning back to a "normal life" are described for all children, regardless of cancer diagnosis. Overall, difficulties in the area of emotions were low and steady throughout all children's trajectories but changed from the child feeling sad and having low energy levels, to being aware of side effects of treatment and body changes (Darcy et al., 2015). The process of developing and identifying the codes from the ICF-CY code set in interviews and questionnaires over the study's three years, revealed pattern changes in the everyday life of young children with cancer that could otherwise have remained unidentified.

Conclusion

The ICF-CY provided a valid way to follow health and functioning in the everyday lives of young children with cancer. The structure of the ICF-CY, in body structures and functions, activities and participation and environmental factors, allowed for coverage of important aspects of living a life with cancer. Gathering longitudinal data from a child and her family's perspective over three years of life with cancer provided a new perspective on changes that occur over time. Additionally, the results show that the ICF-CY can be used to support the collection of this data of functioning nature, throughout the cancer trajectory, adding unique knowledge to current available evidence on the everyday life of young children with cancer.

The ICF-CY codes identified in this study could be used to develop a clinical assessment tool for those caring for young children. Such a tool, based on the ICF common language, could be used to support the delivery of care for children living an everyday life with a long-term illness, by informing service provision with functioning-based assessment data.

Highlights from this chapter

- The experiences of young children with cancer change over time and reflect different dimensions of functioning, in different time points throughout the cancer trajectory.
- The ICF-CY provides a valid tool to support information gathering about health and functioning in the everyday lives of young children with cancer.
- This functioning-based information can provide data for the development of more in-depth assessment tools that can better inform the provision of care for children with long-term illnesses.

References

Cieza, A., Brockow, T., Ewert, T., Amman, E., Kollerits, B., Chatterji, S., & Stucki, G. (2002). Linking health-status measurements to the international classification of functioning, disability and health. *Journal of Rehabilitation Medicine, 34*(5), 205–210.

Cieza, A., & Stucki, G. (2005). ICF linking rules: An update based on lessons learned. *Journal of Rehabilitation Medicine, 37*, 212–218.

Darcy, L., Björk, M., Knutsson, S., Granlund, M., & Enskär, K. (2015). Following young children's health and functioning in everyday life through their cancer trajectory. *Journal of Pediatric Oncology Nursing, 33*(3), 173–189.

Eriksson, U., & Sellström, E. (2010). School demands and subjective health complaints among Swedish schoolchildren: A multilevel study. *Scandinavian Journal of Public Health, 38*(4), 344–350.

Graneheim, U. H., & Lundman, B. (2004). Qualitative content analysis in nursing research: Concepts, procedures and measures to achieve trustworthiness. *Nurse Education Today, 24*(2), 105–112.

Labay, L. E., Mayans, S., & Harris, M. B. (2004). Integrating the child into home and community following the completion of cancer treatment. *Journal of Pediatric Oncology Nursing, 21*(3), 165–169.

Polit, D. F., & Beck, C. T. (2008). *Nursing research: Generating and assessing evidence for nursing practice.* Philadelphia: Lippincott Williams & Wilkins.

Rosenbaum, P., & Gorter, J. W. (2011). The 'F-words' in childhood disability: I swear this is how we should think! *Child: Care, Health and Development, 38*(4), 457–463.

Simeonsson, R. J., Leonardi, M., Lollar, D., Bjorck-Akesson, E., Hollenweger, J., & Martinuzzi, A. (2003). Applying the International Classification of Functioning, Disability and Health (ICF) to measure childhood disability. *Disability and Rehabilitation, 25*(11–12), 602–610.

Simeonsson, R. J., Scarborough, A. A., & Hebbeler, K. M. (2006). ICF and ICD codes provide a standard language of disability in young children. *Journal of Clinical Epidemiology, 59*(4), 365–373.

Simeonsson, R. J. (2009). ICF-CY: A universal tool for documentation of disability. *Journal of Policy and Practice in Intellectual Disabilities*, 6(2), 70–72.

World Health Organisation (1986). *First International Conference on Health Promotion*. Ottawa: WHO.

World Health Organization (WHO). (2007). *International classification of functioning, disability and health – version for children and youth*. Geneva: WHO Library.

Chapter 12

The ICF-CY in habilitation services for children

Margareta Adolfsson

Habilitation services is the name for interdisciplinary health care organisations in Sweden serving children and young people aged 0 to17 years with a wide range of disabilities categorised as mobility, behavioural, intellectual and multiple disabilities, their families and other networks. The construct of *habilitation* is used in childhood since it focuses on acquiring skills, whereas *rehabilitation* focuses on regaining lost skills. Despite this difference, the objective of services is consistent and the WHO definition of rehabilitation can apply to both: "A process aimed at enabling people with disabilities to reach and maintain their optimal physical, sensory, intellectual, psychological and social functional levels. Rehabilitation provides disabled people with the tools they need to attain independence and self-determination" (WHO, 2016). Habilitation teams include social, psychological, pedagogical and medical competencies with a marked preponderance of the latter (Figure 12.1).

The interdisciplinary approach enables a broad focus on children's needs (Kessel, Rosenfield, & Anderson, 2008). As an example, this means that if a child has difficulties playing with other children, the problem can be viewed from several perspectives and interventions discussed across disciplines. The physician worries about the impact of the epilepsy, the physiotherapist might suggest treatment focusing on muscle strength and running skills whereas the occupational therapist talks about hand and arm functions to obtain the ability to catch and throw a ball. The psychologist might raise the need of making the child aware of his/her own behaviour and relations to others, such as following rules, and the social worker adds to the discussion thoughts about requirements within the family and other interactions. Because the proposal on too many interventions at the same time would lead to nothing being done, priorities must be agreed together with the family.

A family-centred approach involves both parents and children in the intervention planning and addresses also the needs of families due to the importance of families for children's development and well-being. The collaboration is fundamental because the perspectives of professional team members and family members usually differ (Stenhammar, 2010; Thomas-Stonell, Oddson, Robertson, & Rosenbaum, 2009). For example, while a child wants to be active, parents might be more concerned about the child's general development and

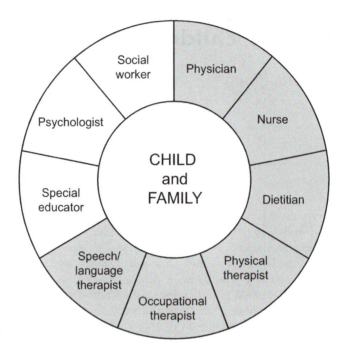

Figure 12.1 Disciplines in Swedish habilitation teams. Grey marked disciplines belong to the medical competence. Modified from Adolfsson (2011)

functioning in everyday life situations, and professionals might focus on more specific functions and abilities.

Based on evidence and first hand experiences from Sweden, this chapter provides suggestions of how the ICF-CY can be used in various services for children and youth with disability. Initially, two short sections intend to frame the practical examples that come later. The examples are first related to intervention planning, including the advantages of the ICF-CY model as a structure to organise information, to identify functional problems or to be used as a common language during collaborative problem solving. The possibility that the use of the model can contribute to increased motivation of the child is also highlighted. Secondly, the ICF-CY classification is recognised as a means to identify what is measured in the assessment of a child's functioning by allowing the identification of content in specific measures. Thirdly, the chapter describes reduced sets of ICF-CY codes with the purpose of limiting the exhaustiveness of the classification. Core and code sets developed internationally by the selection of appropriate categories for specific purposes are presented with complete information on availability. With the hope to further provide suggestions for practical use, a manual for the completion of ICF-CY based certificates for eligibility for services is presented. At last, the implementation of the ICF-CY into services, such as habilitation ones, is discussed.

The ICF-CY in interdisciplinary work

Consistent with an interdisciplinary approach for clinical practices, the ICF–CY reflects a systems-theory perspective due to its focus on how child factors interact with environmental factors (Granlund et al., 2012). In the ICF-CY multidimensional model, participation is the key construct and preferably the goal for interventions but activity can be seen as a linking construct (Figure 12.2). When a child has activity limitations, it is likely that there are also problems with the body functions and in addition, it is necessary to assess what kind of problem the child has with participation. Objectively, participation can be assessed as a child's attendance in different everyday life situations. However, as a social construct, participation is about motivation and involvement, which might require a subjective view (Granlund, 2013; WHO, 2007). This adds information about a child's own feeling of belonging and engagement in the everyday life situation at hand.

Engagement – and participation – requires the ability to act autonomously within a social context, however not necessarily without support from others (Perenboom & Chorus, 2003). Personal support is invaluable in compensating for impaired physical abilities for children who have attained independence and self-determination as illustrated by this example: a child with severe physical disability decided, during a craft class, to create an animal from wood. He could not handle tools by himself but asked the personal assistant to get a piece of wood and begin sawing. During this procedure, the child leaned against the assistant and seemed engaged to a high extent while the piece was created. This child was encouraged to make own choices and could keep the control over the situation, but it is not necessary that children are surrounded by this kind of understanding from their networks. The ICF-CY is a framework that helps habilitation teams to describe and explain how different networks can support a child's participation and by doing that, promote his/her well-being. Preferable, the support also includes a future focus, i.e. to prepare the children for adult lives where they can act autonomously and perceive life satisfaction (Ben-Arieh & Frønes, 2011; UNESCO, 2003). This long-term focus includes not only the aspect of well-being "here-and-now" but also an aspect of well becoming in adulthood.

ICF-CY – a model and a classification for daily work

For different purposes in daily work, the ICF-CY provides an overall model but also a detailed classification (Figure 12.2). The multidimensional model reminds professionals of the different aspects of a child's everyday functioning to be included in discussions before decisions are taken. Keeping the model in mind makes professionals not only consider bodily functions and abilities but it enhances their focus on participation and the impact of the environment (Adolfsson, Granlund, Björck-Åkesson, Ibragimova, & Pless, 2010; Jelsma & Scott,

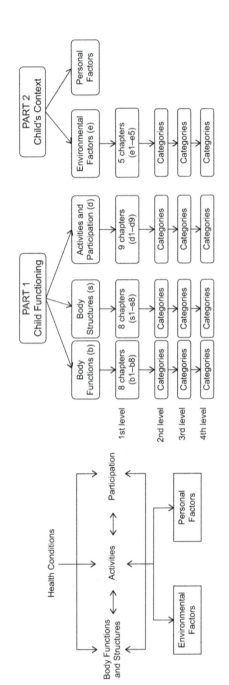

Figure 12.2 ICF-CY is both a multidimensional model and a hierarchical structured classification (WHO, 2007)

2011). The ICF-CY has been reported to help them raise their eyes and see what is most important for each individual child.

The ICF-CY hierarchical structured classification can be seen as a comprehensive dictionary of 1685 categories relevant for describing functioning (Simeonsson, Sauer-Lee, Granlund, & Björck-Åkesson, 2010). The classification reflects an ongoing influence of factors at different levels in an interactive and hierarchical system. Among the hierarchical listed categories, the ones on the second level are most suitable for collaborative team discussions whereas the more detailed categories on third and fourth levels can support discipline-specific assessment (WHO, 2007). As an example, a child's engagement in play (second level) constitutes a common concern during a meeting, following the assessment of the child's play by the special educator in terms of solitary, onlooker, parallel or shared cooperative play (third-level categories).

ICF-CY in intervention planning

Structure to organise information

The ICF-CY multidimensional model provides a structure to organise the information about functioning that is collected during an intervention planning meeting, which is in line with the ethical guidelines for clinical use of the ICF-CY (WHO, 2007). Table 12.1 provides an example related to Peter who is

Table 12.1 Example of multidimensional information about a child's communication

Information	ICF-CY Dimension and Content	
Peter's speech is not mature	Body functions	To perceive and produce words or signs related to mental functions
He cannot pronounce the word correctly		Forming the sound, articulate
Peter learns matching words and pictures for some objects	Activities and participation	Acquiring words, phrases and sentences related to activity
He started talking spontaneously at home about school without leading questions		Perceiving or producing words/signs related to activity
The family uses pictures sometimes to prepare Peter for coming activities	Environmental factors	Personal support and assistive technology

a child with communication difficulties. The information from the parents and the professionals was clarified by the structure of the ICF-CY and contributed to a common understanding of Peter's strengths and weaknesses in a holistic manner. Using a functional approach, all components are taken into account, which was confirmed during a follow-up of an in-service training on the ICF-CY. The professionals reported how they listened to descriptions of a child's functioning and participation in a context and to the family's needs more carefully (Adolfsson et al., 2010). They asked more, broader and deeper questions and considered the family's wishes and priorities of child participation to a higher extent before they went further in the planning procedure and decided on interventions. The ICF-CY model reminded them to reflect on how different dimensions affect each other and, as said earlier, the model helped them to see what was most important for the child at that moment.

Identification of functional problems

Another area of utility is the identification of functional problems with multidimensional explanations that can serve as a basis for decisions on goals and interventions. Quite often, a problem is given a solution-related formulation without telling what it means for the child's functioning. As an example, the problem reported by parents is that a washbasin is too high for a girl using a wheel chair. A functional problem would rather be that she couldn't independently wash her hands. Of course, one solution could be to lower the washbasin but it might provide negative consequences for the rest of the family. Further analysis of the problem and taking into account the goal that she should be able to wash her hands without assistance, alternative solutions could be discussed. Suggestions would be to change the taps so she can reach them better from the chair, remove a sink cabinet to let her come closer or add a handle so she can be standing for a short while.

Collaborative problem solving

The ICF-CY model may also support collaborative problem solving processes. The example in Table 12.2 displays the first steps in such a process conducted at a team meeting in a preschool for children with disability. During the meeting, supervised by a professional knowledgeable in the ICF-CY, the nurse, special educator, child manager and physiotherapist reported about discipline-specific problems without a main focus on Lisa's participation in the group activity. At first hand, they provided information about Lisa's impairments (body) and how she behaved in the preschool (activities and participation). The discussions were perceived interesting and highlighted that Lisa did follow instructions from some of the therapists, which made them understand that they used different approaches. However, it was long before anyone paid attention to "the empty box Environment" that included their own interaction with the girl and organisation of the activities. When understanding their own importance

Table 12.2 The first steps in a collaborative problem solving process with the problem formulated as a participation restriction

Problem	Problem Explanation
Lisa does not participate in group activities. • She does not come when teachers call. • She does not stay. • She does not show interest.	ACTIVITIES AND PARTICIPATION • Does not follow instructions, are not used to demands • Limited communicative ability • Uses schedule pictogram for play ENVIRONMENTAL FACTORS • Professionals do not act consistently • Group activities just before lunch • Content is not adapted to Lisa • Professionals have not tried and evaluated different communication methods (pictogram, other pictures, symbols) BODY FUNCTIONS AND STRUCTURES • Lisa gets easily tired • Motor and cognitive severities • Problems with stomach, epilepsy, sleep

as environmental factors, they could see Lisa's functioning in a context, formulate a problem that better described her participation in the activity at hand and found plausible environmental-based explanations that could be positively influenced with simple interventions. At the end of the meeting, all members perceived that it was helpful to have access to the ICF-CY model during the discussions; it clarified Lisa's functioning but also supported the team discussion.

This model for collaborative problem solving could also serve as a support base for discussions with parents. It would help professionals and parents identify the child's needs and those areas where the goals should be targeted. The matrix seen in Table 12.2 intends to guide professionals to formulate a functional problem, which then should be followed by a goal at the level of participation. This visual support directs the initial discussion to activities and participation, avoiding an overriding focus on body functions, i.e. medical perspectives. Unfortunately, usually goals do not reflect very well the child's functional needs and problems (Jeglinsky, Brogren Carlberg, & Autti-Rämö, 2014). Although in-service training of interdisciplinary teams can lead to an effect on the clarity of individual plans with enhanced readability and clarity, significant changes in the distribution of information among ICF-CY dimensions cannot be assumed (Adolfsson et al., 2010; Klang Ibragimova, Pless, Adolfsson, Granlund, & Björck-Åkesson, 2011).

Children's motivation

Children themselves can play an active role in problem solving. They can identify challenges such as barriers in the environment that affect their impairment and decrease their abilities to do the things they want to do (Kramer & Hammel, 2011). An important issue, therefore, is to listen to and find the child's motivation for interventions and even if the adults keep a strict child perspective, it is not always consistent with the child's perspective (Nilsson et al., 2015). As suggested by Rosenbaum and Gorter (2012), a populated version of the ICF-CY model can include five F-words: fitness, function, friendship, family and fun. To motivate children for interventions, they would be encouraged to tell about their interests, i.e. what they perceive as Fun and professionals should discuss with the family ways to develop and maintain friendship. Most likely, this will make the children more alert and motivated for actions related to health, i.e. interventions, which can be integrated in everyday life situations. By socialising, the children's functions, such as skills and abilities, will be used and, as a consequence, the fitness (body functions) will improve. One example is a teenage boy with CP hanging around with friends on their mopeds. The friends questioned in a mean way why he was going to a physiotherapist but got the prompt answer that he just went there to stretch his muscles when he could not get his leg over the saddle. So he was quite motivated for the intervention and went to the physiotherapist to be able to go on with their friendship.

Identification of content in measures

The ICF-CY classification has been used as a mean to identify and compare content in commonly used measures. By linking assessed variables with the ICF-CY language, the framework can serve an organising tool to document the content included in existing tools. Besides, it can identify variables as part of the development of assessment measurements for children (Simeonsson et al., 2003). Castro and colleagues (2013) have studies the number of variables in three of those measurement tools that are widely used as diagnostic tools for children with ASDs in preschool (ages 2–6 years). The linking process that was conducted aimed to identify functional aspects that might improve the documentation of children's functioning and complement diagnostic with the aim to inform teachers and support interventions in preschools. Results from their study suggest that mental functions are covered to a high extent as well as their communication and learning skills. On the other hand, the measures do not focus much on how the environment might affect the children's functioning or how they participate in household chores (ICF-CY Chapter d6) or social life and leisure activities (ICF-CY Chapter d9). Also, the measures do not focus on fine- or gross motor functioning (ICF-CY Chapter d4). By providing this kind of information, professionals can decide on the measure that is most appropriate for a specific purpose but also what needs to be discussed in addition to traditional assessment during, for example, planning meetings to get the holistic picture of a child's functioning.

Despite the benefits of the ICF-CY, the classification with its many categories can be a practical challenge. The classification needs to be comprehensive to cover the broad spectrum of categories necessary for descriptions of child functioning; however, less complicated and user-friendlier tools have been requested.

Reduced sets of ICF-CY codes

With the purpose to improve the utility of the ICF–CY for clinical use and make the classification more user-friendly, reduced sets of categories, so called core or code sets, have continuously been developed (Adolfsson et al., 2010; Bickenbach, Cieza, Rauch, & Stucki, 2012; Wiegand, Belting, Fekete, Gutenbrunner, & Reinhardt, 2012). The core/code sets constitute general agreed-on lists of essential ICF–CY categories and are clinically applicable to identify the needs for interventions. They consider all dimensions in the ICF–CY model and can be applied in clinical practice, research, teaching and administration. In clinical practice, they can for example be used as checklists by interdisciplinary habilitation teams aiming at directing what needs and problems of children should be discussed with the parents but also to know *what* to measure (however not *how* to measure). It means that the information provided from the core/code sets guides the professionals to know who will at first hand meet with and assess the child in more detail. As the ICF–CY terminology can be hard to understand as it is formulated in the classification, users are advised to adapt the categories to simple questions, maybe including examples, before they are used together with families.

The code sets can focus on universal issues but they can also focus on specific issues such as everyday life situations, health conditions or type of functional needs. Some examples relevant for children with disability and available for use are presented next.

Universal developmental code sets

Today, four universal developmental code sets that reflect functioning for children in different developmental stages are available for clinical practice. The 40–60 categories included are intended to serve as a universal reference for the least amount of information that is necessary to use when screening child functioning of children with or without disability (Ellingsen, 2011). These code sets are published at (www.icfcydevelopmentalcodesets.com).

Code sets for everyday life situations

Code sets were developed for three everyday life situations that are mentioned by habilitation professionals as common problems for young children and their families: sleeping, mealtimes and play. As an example, the 14 categories applicable for sleeping are displayed in Table 12.3 but the content in all three code sets can be found in the article by Adolfsson and colleagues (2013). The categories

Table 12.3 Content in autism measures for preschool children linked to chapters in the ICF-CY (Castro et al., 2013)

	BADOSOLD	ADI-R	CARS
Activities and participation			
d1 Learning and applying knowledge	3	4	3
d2 General tasks and demands	3	1	2
d3 Communication	5	6	3
d4 Mobility	0	0	0
d5 Self-care	2	1	1
d6 Domestic life	0	0	0
d7 Interpersonal interactions	3	2	1
d8 Major life areas	1	1	0
d9 Community, social and civic life	0	0	0
Body functions			
b1 Mental functions	9	8	9
Environmental functions			
e3 Support and relationships	0	0	0
e4 Attitudes	2	0	0

ADOS – Autism Diagnostic Observation Schedule; ADI-R – Autism Diagnostic Interview Revised; CARS – Childhood Autism Rating Scale

are intended to serve as checklists for problem solving processes. During the developmental procedure, which finally identified a total of 14, 21 and 30 categories, respectively, it became obvious that parents and professionals have different opinions on what needs to be discussed, i.e. what categories should be included in such a checklist. Discrepancies concerned for example how the environment might affect a child's functioning, which shows the importance of dialogues before decisions on interventions. The two categories appropriate for all three code sets concerned the support and individual attitudes of the immediate family, which confirms the parents' importance for a child's functioning and development and reflects the importance for habilitation professionals to consider the everyday functioning of families.

Health conditions in childhood

The ICF Research Branch has developed a rigorous scientific process resulting in a substantial number of core sets for different conditions and settings (Bickenbach et al., 2012). They are all available at www.icf-research-branch.org, but these are usually not specific for children. However, three age-specific core sets for CP have recently been developed (Schiariti, Selb, Cieza, & O'Donnell, 2015) and core sets for autism and ADHD are under development (Bölte, de Schipper, Holtmann et al., 2014; Bölte, de Schipper, Robison et al., 2014). Through similar processes, work to identify core functioning features applicable to other health conditions is continuous and widespread. For example, core categories for young children with ASDs for the age groups 0–2 and 3–6 years are published by Portuguese researchers (Castro & Pinto, 2013), an EDD code set for infants below 3 years of age with early delay and disabilities was developed in Taiwan (Pan, Hwang, Simeonsson, Lu, & Liao, 2015), and a code set for children with severe disabilities is under development in Denmark (Melchiorsen & Östergaard, 2010). This continuous work around the world raises hopes for an improved clinical utility of the ICF-CY in the future.

Functional needs in childhood

Another available code set (The Communication Supports Inventory: Children & Youth, CSI-CY) is a free tool providing content and guidance to the assessment of students with complex communication needs, including those who use Alternative and Augmentative Communication. The assessment tool has child participation in focus and the procedure starts from the question "how well can the child participate in activities". It is intended to support the development of individual educational plans that are comprehensive enough to capture the children's strengths as well as weaknesses (Rowland et al., 2012). The code set is available at www.icfcy.org/aac/, where it is presented as a means to go beyond the mere assessment of skills, such as understanding language or having the ability to spell. Instead, the CSI-CY includes how children act in a daily environment and how they play with other children or take part in conversations, while all the time looking at functions and what an individual child can do rather than focusing on diagnosis.

The CSI-CY describes the developmental skills for both AAC and typical language development and tells what level the children have and what they need to work on. It illustrates that children can communicate even without speech. As it is completed by both parents and teachers, the information is based on what everyone sees under a variety of circumstances, making it possible to talk about different aspects of a child's functioning and participation.

Utility of core or code sets in habilitation services

Using core or code sets as checklists in dialogues with parents intends to clarify an individual child's needs and problems and to put them into a social context. It can most likely support common decisions on goals, preferable focusing on participation and everyday functioning, not exclusively on body functions and abilities.

To enhance knowledge on the aspects that are usually discussed to decide on goals, individual educational plans for students with complex communication needs were analysed (Klang et al., 2016). The plans were documented by educators and school-based speech and language therapists before the CSI-CY was developed. Findings showed an uneven distribution of goals across the ICF-CY chapters with most of them relating to activities and only one-third to participation dimensions. Hopefully, an evaluation of the use of the CSI-CY will prove that a change has happened and that the goals focus on the children's functioning in social contexts to a greater extent. Overall, evaluations of the effects of the ICF-CY are lacking (Jelsma, 2009; Wiegand et al., 2012). Nevertheless, an enhanced awareness of the value of the ICF-CY as a framework for practical work seems to encourage clinical reasoning and improve a holistic approach when identifying and describing children's everyday functioning.

ICF-CY based certificates for eligibility

Certificates proving eligibility are often required in contacts with authorities. One example concerns families applying for disability allowance from social security services. For this purpose, a functional certificate based on the ICF-CY has been developed and proven successful to complement the doctor's statement about diagnosis and to contribute to an increased understanding from the administrators about the needs of a child and his/her family (Enström Öst, Agdalen, Aydin, Josephson, & Mirjam, 2013). The certificate includes brief information about health and body functions, the child's social context and the family's everyday functioning. The main part of the certificate includes functional information related to the nine life areas in the ICF-CY component activities and participation. On the parents request or the authority, the certificate can be completed by anybody in an interdisciplinary service team, based on a variety of data such as own professional knowledge, information from parents or notes in patient records.

For completion of the certificate, a manual to guide holistic descriptions of the child's functioning with focus on participation in everyday life situations is followed. The manual provides suggestions about what to consider for each life area, with brief information about the content, which is structured according to the chapter blocks (Table 12.4). It states that not all areas need to be

Table 12.4 Content in the code set for young children's (0–6 years) sleeping

Activities and Participation	Environmental Factors	Body Functions
Carrying out daily routines. For example, getting ready for sleep, getting up in the morning, budgeting time, adapting to time demands and managing changes in daily routine.	Drugs – e.g. type of drug and amount for medical purposes. Products and technology for use in daily living. For example, furniture such as bed, personal care equipment, adapted or specially designed devices and orthopaedic devices.	Sleep functions – i.e. mental functions needed to get enough sleep, going from wakefulness to sleep, sustaining the state of being asleep and getting optimal rest and relaxation. Emotional functions – i.e. appropriateness, regulation and range of emotion such as love, hate, anxiety, tension, sorrow, joy, fear or anger.

Activities and Participation	Environmental Factors	Body Functions
Changing basic body position – for example, rolling over in bed.	Climate – e.g. temperature, humidity, atmospheric pressure. Light – e.g. light intensity such as sun light, light quality such as colour contrasts or shadows. Sound – e.g. sound volume, quality, acoustics, background noise. Support from or individual attitudes of immediate family such as parents, siblings, grandparents, foster parents.	Sensations associated with cardiovascular and respiratory functions, such as feelings of irregular beat, tightness of chest, dyspnoea, air hunger. Defecation functions – e.g. frequency of defecation, faecal consistency, air or gases from the intestines, faecal continence. Muscle tone functions – i.e. decreased or increased tension or spasticity in isolated muscles or parts of the body. Spontaneous movements, such as infant general movements or repertoire of specific movements such as hands toward midline.

described in detail but emphasis should be placed on areas where limitations and restrictions are apparent. The manual can be used for various purposes – informal or formal – as long as functional descriptions are requested and both professionals and parents are encouraged to use it as needed.

Implementation of the ICF-CY into habilitation services

As indicated throughout this chapter, an implementation of the ICF-CY into habilitation services would most likely provide the interdisciplinary team with advantage in the form of a common language and a conceptual framework to improve communication. The implementation process, though, has proved time consuming; it requires motivation of the professionals and carefully planned preparation of the leaders (Adolfsson et al., 2010; Pless, Ibragimova, Adolfsson, Björck-Åkesson, & Granlund, 2009; Rentsch et al., 2003; Wiegand et al., 2012). According to a diffusion of innovation theory, professionals need time to communicate the idea of using the ICF-CY in daily work and decide on adoption or rejection of the actions that its implementation would be imply (Rogers, 2003). There have been indications that the implementation process can be going on for as long as two and a half years (Adolfsson et al., 2010) and during that time, a good deal of effort is used for adaptation of materials, of patient records and strategies for habilitation planning and knowledge transfer. Parts of this work could be done before implementation and a well-planned process would probably help to accelerate the process. However, when professionals attempt to apply the ICF-CY to their daily work, they might realise shortcomings in the organisation of their own professional actions and the need to revise routines to fit with the ICF-CY model, which cannot be seen as only a bad thing.

Training of professionals on the use of the ICF-CY cannot stop only on introducing the model. To obtain sustainable effects, it has to be contrasted to the perspectives of the organisation at stake and by that be framed within a context (Pless & Granlund, 2012). The goal of using the classification as an innovation must be clarified by the leaders so that the professionals know well which routines will be changed. In addition, as many adaptations as possible should be prepared before training occurs so they can begin to be used immediately.

Changes in the routines take place through social networks within a professional group. As the professionals have different backgrounds and various motives to learn about the classification, the training should preferably be flexible (Pless & Granlund, 2012; Pless et al., 2009). The ones who have demonstrated a positive attitude prior to the training will benefit most from it and become ready to apply it directly to everyday work (Rogers, 2003). It is a good idea to engage these individuals in the implementation process. To stimulate the adoption, it is essential that the ICF-CY is perceived consistent with the values of the professional group, that the training makes it understandable and usable, and that the benefits are presented as easily visible. If good examples are presented, it stimulates the participants to try to use the classification and explore ways to modify it to suit own needs.

At last, for habilitation services as for other organisations, a final statement can be taken from Wiegand et al. (2012): to make the ICF-CY "real", it has to be used in practice.

Highlights from this chapter

- The ICF-CY enhances a professional focus on participation and on the impact of the environment on children's functioning.
- Categories on the second ICF-CY level are suitable for collaborative team discussions.
- The ICF-CY provides a structure to organise information about a child's everyday functioning, contributing to a common understanding of strengths and weaknesses.

- The ICF-CY model supports collaborative problem solving processes with families.
- Children become motivated when intervention planning starts from their interests and preferences about participation.
- Using the ICF-CY to identify and compare content in measures supports decisions on what to use for a specific intervention purpose.
- Code sets including a reduced number of ICF-CY categories are useful in dialogues with families about a child's needs.
- A functional certificate based on the ICF-CY contributes to increased understanding about the needs of the child and family.
- An implementation of the ICF-CY is time-consuming and requires carefully planned preparation of adapted routines.
- Training of professionals in the use of the ICF-CY should be put into context.

References

Adolfsson, M. (2011). *Applying the ICF-CY to identify everyday life situations of children and youth with disabilities.* Doctoral thesis, Jönköping University, Jönköping.

Adolfsson, M., Björck-Åkesson, E., & Lim, C.-I. (2013). Code sets for everyday life situations of children aged 0–6: Sleeping, mealtimes, and play. A study based on the International Classification of Functioning, Disability and Health for Children and Youth. *British Journal of Occupational Therapy*, *76*(3), 127–136. doi:10.4276/030802213X13627524435144

Adolfsson, M., Granlund, M., Björck-Åkesson, E., Ibragimova, N., & Pless, M. (2010). Exploring changes over time in habilitation professionals' perceptions and applications of the International Classification of Functioning, Disability and Health, version for Children and Youth (ICF-CY). *Journal of Rehabilitation Medicine*, *42*(7), 670–678. doi:10.2340/16501977-0586

Ben-Arieh, A., & Frønes, I. (2011). Taxonomy for child well-being indicators: A framework for the analysis of the well-being of children. *Childhood*, *18*(4), 460–476.

Bickenbach, J. E., Cieza, A., Rauch, A., & Stucki, G. (2012). *ICF core sets: Manual for clinical practice.* Göttingen, Germany: Hogrefe.

Bölte, S., de Schipper, E., Holtmann, M., Karande, S., de Vries, P., Selb, M., & Tannock, R. (2014). Development of ICF core sets to standardize assessment of functioning and impairment in ADHD: The path ahead. *European Child & Adolescent Psychiatr*, *23*(12), 1139–1148. doi:10.1007/s00787-013-0496-5

Bölte, S., de Schipper, E., Robison, J., Wong, V., Selb, M., Singhal, N., . . . Zwaigenbaum, L. (2014). Classification of functioning and impairment: The development of ICF core sets for autism spectrum disorder. *Autism Research*, *7*(1), 167–172. doi:10.1002/aur.1335

Castro, S., Ferreira, T., Dababnah, S., & Pinto, A. I. (2013). Linking autism measures with the ICF-CY: Functionality beyond the borders of diagnosis and interrater agreement issues. *Developmental Neurorehabilitation*, *16*(5), 321–331. doi:10.3109/17518423.2012.733438

Castro, S., & Pinto, A. I. (2013). Identification of core functioning features for assessment and intervention in autism spectrum disorders. *Disability and Rehabilitation*, *35*(2), 125–133. doi: 10.3109/09638288.2012.690494

Ellingsen, K. M. (2011). *Deriving developmental code sets from the International Classification of Functioning, Disability and Health – for Children and Youth (ICF-CY)*. PhD thesis, University of North Carolina at Chapel Hill, Chapel Hill.

Enström Öst, C., Agdalen, T., Aydin, E., Josephson, M., & Mirjam, W. (2013). *Att tala samma språk. Gemensam struktur vid bedömning av vårdbidrag [Speaking the same language. Common structure in assessing the care allowance].* Stockholm: Inspektionen för Socialförsäkring. Rapport 2013: 12.

Granlund, M. (2013). Participation – challenges in conceptualization, measurement and intervention. *Child: Care, Health and Development, 39*(4), 470–473. doi:10.1111/cch.12080

Granlund, M., Nilsson, S., Maxwell, G., Carlstein, S., Wright, C., Hargrave, J., . . . Castro, S. (2012). *Swedish disability research concerning children and youth in need of additional support: A systematic review.* Retrieved from Jönköping.

Jeglinsky, I., Brogren Carlberg, E., & Autti-Rämö, I. (2014). How are actual needs recognized in the content and goals of written rehabilitation plans? *Disability and Rehabilitation, 36*(6), 441–451. doi:10.3109/09638288.2013.797511

Jelsma, J. (2009). Use of the international classification of functioning, disabilty and health: A literature survey. *Journal of Rehabilitation Medicine, 41*, 1–12.

Jelsma, J., & Scott, D. (2011). Impact of using the ICF framework as an assessment tool for students in paediatric physiotherapy: A preliminary study. *Physiotherapy, 97*(1), 47–54. doi:10.1016/j.physio.2010.09.004

Kessel, F., Rosenfield, P. L., & Anderson, N. B. (Eds.). (2008). *Interdisciplinary research: Case studies from health and social science.* Oxford: University Press.

Klang Ibragimova, N., Pless, M., Adolfsson, M., Granlund, M., & Björck-Åkesson, E. (2011). Using content analysis to link texts on assessment and intervention to the International Classification of Functioning, Disability and Health – version for Children and Youth (ICF-CY). *Journal of Rehabilitation Medicine, 43*(8), 728–733. doi:10.2340/16501977-0831

Klang, N., Rowland, C., Fried-Oken, M., Steiner, S., Granlund, M., & Adolfsson, M. (2016). The content of goals in individual educational programs for students with complex communication needs. *Augmentative and Alternative Communication, 32*(1), 41–48. doi:10.3109/07434618.2015.1134654

Kramer, J. M., & Hammel, J. (2011). "I do lots of things": Children with cerebral palsy's competence for everyday activities. *International Journal of Disability, Development and Education, 58*(2), 121–136. doi:10.1080/1034912x.2011.570496

Melchiorsen, H., & Östergaard, H. (2010). *Udarbejdelse af ICF-CY core set til börn med svare handicaps [Development of ICF-CY core set for children with severe disabilities].* Paper presented at the ICF-CY conference, Marselisborgscentret, Aarhus, Denmark.

Nilsson, S., Björkman, B., Almqvist, A.-L., Almqvist, L., Björk-Willén, P., Donohue, D., . . . Hvit, S. (2015). Children's voices – differentiating a child perspective from a child's perspective. *Developmental Neurorehabilitation, 18*(3), 162–168. doi:10.3109/17518423.2013.801529

Pan, Y.-L., Hwang, A.-W., Simeonsson, R. J., Lu, L., & Liao, H.-F. (2015). ICF-CY code set for infants with early delay and disabilities (EDD Code Set) for interdisciplinary assessment: A global experts survey. *Disability and Rehabilitation, 37*(12), 1044–1054. doi:10.3109/09638288.2014.952454

Perenboom, R. J. M., & Chorus, A. M. J. (2003). Measuring participation according to the International Classification of Functioning, Disability and Health (ICF). *Disability and Rehabilitation, 25*(11–12), 577–587.

Pless, M., & Granlund, M. (2012). Implementation of the International Classification of Functioning, Disability and Health (ICF) and the ICF Children and Youth Version (ICF-CY) within the context of augmentative and alternative communication. *Augmentative and Alternative Communication, 28*(1), 11–20. doi:10.3109/07434618.2011.654263

Pless, M., Ibragimova, N., Adolfsson, M., Björck-Åkesson, E., & Granlund, M. (2009). Evaluation of in-service training in using the ICF and ICF version for children and youth. *Journal of Rehabilitation Medicine, 41*(6), 451–458. doi:10.2340/16501977-0359

Rentsch, H. P., Bucher, P., Dommen Nyffeler, I., Wolf, C., Hefti, H., Fluri, E., . . . Boyer, I. (2003). The implementation of the 'International Classification of Functioning, Disability and Health' (ICF) in daily practice of neurorehabilitation: An interdisciplinary project at the Kantonsspital of Lucerne, Switzerland. *Disability and Rehabilitation, 25*(8), 411.

Rogers, E. M. (2003). *Diffusion of innovations* (5th ed.). New York: Free Press.

Rosenbaum, P., & Gorter, J. W. (2012). The 'F-words' in childhood disability: I swear this is how we should think! *Child: Care, Health and Development, 38*(4), 457–463. doi:10.1111/j.1365-2214.2011.01338.x

Rowland, C., Fried-Oken, M., Steiner, S. A. M., Lollar, D., Phelps, R., Simeonsson, R. J., & Granlund, M. (2012). Developing the ICF-CY for AAC profile and code set for children who rely on AAC. *Augmentative and Alternative Communication, 28*(1), 21–32. doi:10.3109/07434618.2012.654510

Schiariti, V., Selb, M., Cieza, A., & O'Donnell, M. (2015). International Classification of Functioning, Disability and Health Core Sets for children and youth with cerebral palsy: A consensus meeting. *Developmental Medicine & Child Neurology, 57*(2), 149–158. doi:10.1111/dmcn.12551

Simeonsson, R. J., Leonardi, M., Lollar, D., Björck-Åkesson, E., Hollenweger, J., & Martinuzzi, A. (2003). Applying the International Classification of Functioning, Disability and Health (ICF) to measure childhood disability. *Disability and Rehabilitation, 25*(11/12), 602.

Simeonsson, R. J., Sauer-Lee, A., Granlund, M., & Björck-Åkesson, E. (2010). Developmental and health assessment in rehabilitation with the ICF for Children and Youth. In E. Mpofu & T. Oakland (Eds.), *Rehabilitation and health assessment: Applying ICF guidelines* (pp. 27–46). New York: Springer.

Stenhammar, A.-M. (2010). *Lyssna på mig! Barn & ungdomar med funktionsnedsättningar vill vara delaktiga i möten med samhällets stödsystem En systematisk kunskapsöversikt [Listen to me! Children & young people with disabilities want to be involved in meetings with community support systems. A systematic review].* Master's thesis, Halmstad University, Halmstad.

Thomas-Stonell, N., Oddson, B., Robertson, B., & Rosenbaum, P. (2009). Predicted and observed outcomes in preschool children following speech and language treatment: Parent and clinician perspectives. *Journal of Communication Disorders, 42*(1), 29–42.

UNESCO. (2003). *Open file on inclusive education: Support materials for managers and administrator.* Paris: UNESCO.

WHO. (2007). *International Classification of Functioning, Disability and Health for Children and Youth (ICF-CY).* Geneva: World Health Organization.

WHO. (2016). *Rehabilitation.* Retrieved from www.who.int/topics/rehabilitation/en/

Wiegand, N. M., Belting, J., Fekete, C., Gutenbrunner, C., & Reinhardt, J. D. (2012). All talk, no action? The global diffusion and clinical implementation of the International Classification of Functioning, Disability, and Health. *American Journal of Physical Medicine & Rehabilitation, 91*(7), 550–560. 510.1097/PHM.1090b1013e31825597e31825595.

Implementation of the International Classification of Functioning, Disability and Health (ICF) in the Turkish education system

Mehmet Yanardağ and İbrahim H. Diken

Introduction

The concept of disability has been transformed as a consequence of the introduction of the ICF in 2001. This conceptual change aligns with the United Nations CRPD, which states that "disability results from the interaction between persons with impairments and attitudinal and environmental barriers that hinder their full and effective participation in society on an equal basis with others" (WHO, 2011, p. 4). It is impossible to grade the physiological conditions, physical-environmental context and psychosocial functions of an individual with SENs without considering a multidimensional approach in terms of an educational and rehabilitative intervention process. Often, individuals miss the opportunity to take part on special education interventions and therapies that would be good for them; for this reason, a new classification system is needed that accounts for multi-dimensionality when planning and delivering interventions. In this context, the idea of implementing the ICF in the field of SEN in Turkey emerged. This chapter aims to provide evidence on the demographics of SEN in Turkey. Furthermore, the authors aim to share the conclusions of ICF-based studies in Turkey in terms of how the model can has been integrated into the current education and rehabilitation system for individuals with special needs.

System for individuals with special educational needs in Turkey

Although health care and medical technology standards in Turkey have been improving, the proportion of individuals with SEN is still high at 12.29%, (TÜİK, 2009). Within this group, 2.58% have orthopaedic disabilities (e.g. CP, poliomyelitis, other congenital malformations, etc.), sight, hearing or speech disabilities and intellectual disabilities. The remaining 9.70% have chronic illness. When the proportion of these people is examined across age groups, it is seen that there is an increase in SEN at older ages owing to better identification and aging process. This is especially observed in individuals with chronic ill-nesses. The proportion of children with SEN with orthopaedic, sight, hearing, speech and intellectual disability is 1.54% in the 0- to 9-year-old group. On the other hand, the proportion of children with SEN and chronic illnesses in the same age group is higher, at 2.60% (TÜİK, 2009). The increasing proportions demonstrate the need to provide services such as medical intervention, special education, language-speech therapy, physiotherapy, occupational therapy, social services, psychological counselling and guidance, etc. for these individuals in Turkey. At the same time, the laws and regulations for these services should be based on relevant international standards. Several international organisa-tions such as the United Nations (UN), UNICEF, the WHO and the European Union (EU) have undertaken concerted efforts to enact policy documents that regulate international legal arrangements for service provision for individuals with SEN and these arrangements have influenced the policy and legal regula-tions at a national level in Turkey.

The advancement of these international regulations over time has led to an improvement in some national policies for individuals with SEN in this country. In Turkey, the "Law No. 5378" was introduced in 2005 as a new leg-islation to ensure all preventive measures aimed at reducing the occurrence of impairments or limiting disabilities, and providing services for health, educa-tion, rehabilitation, care and employment. According to this new legislation in Turkey, these issues are to be dealt with through the social security system and through the coordination of different ministries, including the Ministry of Health (medical care and rehabilitation), the Ministry of Education (special education and rehabilitation) and the Ministry of Family and Social Policies (residential care and rehabilitation) (Official Legal Gazette of Turkey, 2005). In addition, the legislation has effects on improvements to basic issues such as accessibility, employment, safety and social life participation for individuals with SEN (Engelsiz Türkiye İçin: Yolun Neresindeyiz Mevcut Durum ve Öneriler, 2013). Until 2006, education and rehabilitation services for individuals with SEN were provided by Social Services and by the Child Protection Agency, which is affiliated to the Ministry of Family and Social Policies. The legislation of SEN services changed in May 2006, with a new regulation involving items from Law No. 5378 in 2005 and Law No. 573 in 1997, (Official Gazette No 26184). For the readers of this book, these legislative regulations for individuals with SEN in Turkey are summarised in Table 13.1.

According to the legislation approved in 2006, the Ministry of Education provides the education and rehabilitation services. The basic principles behind the 2006 legislation are that individuals with SEN should benefit from special education services. They should have access to education in the early years of life. Additionally, special education services should be provided in natural envi-ronments. Special education services should be provided based on IEP. Parents of individuals with SEN should be actively involved in each aspect of the special education provision. Special education services are designed based on principles

Table 13.1 Legislative regulations for individuals with SENs

Year	Law No/Official Gazette No.	Aim
1997	573/23011	To describe the diagnosis, evaluation and placement process and procedures for individuals with SENs in Turkey.
2005	5378/25868	To ensure the all preventive measures aimed at reducing impairments or limiting disability and, provide services for health, education, rehabilitation and care, as well as to co-ordinate ministries that deliver various services to the individuals with SENs in Turkey.
2006	26184	To transfer the responsibilities for special education and rehabilitation services from the Ministry of Family and Social Policies to the Ministry of Education.
2006	26230	To introduce and disseminate the ICF for disability into the Turkish system.
2012	28360	To improve educational standards and resolve issues related to maintaining educational opportunities for individuals with SENs in Turkey.
2013	28603	To emphasise and disseminate the utility of the ICF model in the provision of education, rehabilitation and other services for individuals with SENs in Turkey.
2014	6518/28918	To emphasise the need to follow the international classification and descriptions to determine the requirements of individuals with SENs who live in residential care and rehabilitation centres in Turkey.

of social integration and mutual harmony with society (Official Legal Gazette of Turkey, 2006a, 2012). In addition to the educational regulations for individuals with SEN, the same law (No. 5378) includes several arrangements that are based on the international human rights treaty (Article 26) of the UN, about health and rehabilitation services for these individuals as preventive measures, the importance of early intervention, maintenance of treatment and the same access to medical services as their peers (Official Newspaper of the Turkey Law, 2005; UN, 2006).

Individuals with SEN, who are not cared for by their families at home, receive residential care and rehabilitation services under the Ministry of Family and Social Policies in Turkey. Legislation for these care services is regulated by "Law No. 6518", published in 2014 (Gazette no. 28918). All these regulations are based on the CRPD of the UN (Article 25) in order to provide quality services via different kinds of care models such as: home care, rehabilitation

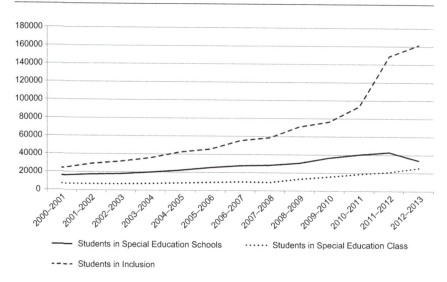

Figure 13.1 Number of students in inclusive and special education between 2000 and 2013 in Turkey

Source: http://sgb.meb.gov.tr/www/milli-egitim-istatistikleri-orgun-egitim-2012-2013/icerik/79

shelters, living centres, privately rented flats, family counselling and rehabilitation centres and private care centres (Official Legal Gazette of Turkey, 2014; UN, 2006).

After various policy changes for the provision of education, health, social care and rehabilitation for individuals with SEN, quantitative improvements have been observed since 2002 in some aspects of these services such as: an increase in the number of students with special educational needs in mainstream and special education schools (Figure 13.1), an increase in the number of kindergartens within special education schools, primary and secondary schools for all kinds of special needs, primary and secondary schools for inclusive education, SEN vocational schools and special education in a vocational training centre, as well as improvements in the gross schooling ratio, research centres for counselling and private centres for special education and rehabilitation. Before 2000, there was not as much provision for inclusive education for children with SEN in mainstream schools in Turkey as there is today, due to a lack of regulations, failure of human resources and quality issues of the educational process (Eğitim Reformu Girişimi, 2014).

Limitations of the provision for individuals with special educational needs

In Turkey, medical staff are the only accountable professionals who are able to provide a traditional medical diagnosis which can be converted into an educational category (e.g. intellectual disability, physical disability) for eligibility to specialised service provision. However, merely checking the condition is insufficient to determine the service requirements for children with SEN and to access education and rehabilitation services, children with SEN have to be diagnosed and receive a health report, as these services are funded by the social security system. Otherwise, they cannot access the system and benefit from these interventions and services.

Although the introduction of legislations and quantitative improvements in education, health, care and rehabilitation services for individuals with SEN has been observed in Turkey, as noted earlier, several limitations are still seen in the services, especially in the provision of good practices. Several reasons may account for these limitations: inadequate standards and policies for managing the services, negative attitudes toward individuals with SEN, insufficient services for individuals with SEN, lack of adequate funding for meeting the requirements, lack of accessibility to participation in social life and inequity with peers in benefiting from resources such as educational and medical services.

Currently, there is a call for collaboration among the Ministry of Education, the Ministry of Health and the Ministry of Family and Social Policies based on an interdisciplinary approach to perform educational planning during infancy and childhood. Although the legislation concerning services state that "an educational evaluation for an individual with special needs is conducted with the assessment of all developmental features, ability of academic skills, and educational necessity of that person" (Official Gazette no. 26184, item 7), these individuals with SEN are assessed only through psychological measurement tools in research centres for counselling before initiating educational interventions (Engelsiz Türkiye İçin: Yolun Neresindeyiz Mevcut Durum ve Öneriler, 2013, p. 181).

As stated in the legislative regulation for educational evaluation, an interdisciplinary team should focus on body function and structures (i.e. mental, sensory, speech, neuromuscular, etc.) of the individuals with SEN. In addition, activity level and participation should be measured in order to understand the individual's ability in regards to executive functions and to apply knowledge to general life tasks. Moreover, the environmental conditions of the individual should be evaluated in terms of the ability to use technology and products, level of support and relationships, attitudes and knowledge, services and his or her rights (WHO, 2001, 2007). This aligns with the classification model of the ICF.

The limited value of psychometric assessment should be highlighted. In order to use an assessment tool with an individual with SEN, that tool has to have acceptable psychometric properties such as validity and reliability, and be appropriately standardised for that population. For example, in Turkey cognitive function has traditionally been evaluated with the old version of the Stanford-Binet Intelligence Scales and Wechsler Intelligence Scale for Children. However, there are a limited number of professionals who are able to manage the educational evaluation, which is undertaken in the research centres for counselling and special education and rehabilitation centres; these are child-development specialists, occupational therapists and physiotherapists. All these issues also affect the planning and practice phases of the educational intervention process for children with SENs. Specifically, preparing an IEP is a main cause for concern in terms of determining short and long-term goals. Kargın, Acarlar and Sucuoğlu (2005) determined that 77.1% of all teachers were not able to design IEPs for their students with SEN in their class and 70.9% were not able to follow the education program defined for their students with special education needs.

Another big issue is that the educational evaluations for children with SENs, and the IEPs design are prepared by the same specialist. After the process, these IEPs are given to the special education and rehabilitation centres that deliver special education services and other interventions for children with SEN. These IEPs have to be considered and followed by the special education teachers and other staff in the special education and rehabilitation centres. These teachers and staff do not describe any new targets or add targets to the IEPs. However, it wouldn't be surprising if some targets for a particular child were not described her in sufficient detail as the experience of others involved in the education of the child was not considered. As such, wrong or inappropriate targets in the IEPs can result in an ineffective intervention, wasted expenditure and time and staff burnout. Therefore, both specialists in research centres for counselling and the staff in special education and rehabilitation centres in Turkey should have the ability to prepare an IEP successfully and efficiently.

It is expected that there will be increasing numbers of infants and children with SEN participating in ECI programs, and this will expose some limitations of these services. The limitations could be summarised as the following: there is no interdisciplinary monitoring system for children who are likely to be in an at-risk group, there is no system for transferring information about these children among the intervention centres, and there is no model for developmental evaluation of the children with SENs in the primary health care system (system of family general practitioners) (Research Report and Analysis for Equity and Academic Achievement in Turkish Education System, 2014).

As stated earlier, there is room for improvement of services in Turkey, especially in terms of quality and sustainability of provision for individuals with SEN. Although there are policy regulations, there are considerable limitations in relation to implementation. At this point, the classification system, ICF, developed by the WHO could provide the necessary framework to support service provision for individuals with SEN in Turkey. In the next section of this chapter, the ICF model is discussed in relation to these barriers in SENs provision in Turkey.

How the ICF has been used to address these limitations

The ICF is a classification system developed by the WHO to define the functioning of an individual in his/her natural environment, without traditional disability categories or diagnoses. It is based on a biopsychosocial model covering all aspects of functioning from the individual to the societal level (WHO, 2001). A child and youth version of the ICF was published to focus on defining functional characteristic of developing children (ICF-CY; WHO, 2007). The ICF-CY has been used in various sectors and across disciplines, such as education (Hollenweger, 2011; Hollenweger & Moretti, 2012; Maxwell, Koutsogerogou, 2012; Moretti, Alves, & Maxwell, 2012), medical (Ta Chiu et al., 2013) and rehabilitation fields (Maini, Nocentini, Prevedini, Giardini, & Muscolo, 2008; Pless & Granlund, 2012). From the literature about the ICF-CY, it can be seen that it has been used in three main ways: as a tool for research, a tool for educational process and a theoretical framework. According to a recent review, although the ICF/ICF-CY is not being used frequently in education, it is helpful in providing a common language among professionals, and it has the potential to be implemented in the education system for evaluation purposes, educational planning, interdisciplinary team work, eligibility identification and resource allocation (Moretti et al., 2012).

The recommended standards for measuring function and disability should be taken into consideration when attempting to describe procedures and practices at a national level. The WHO (2007) proposed the ICF/ICF-CY as a framework and classification system to help in the evaluation and intervention processes in SEN provision. According to the model, special needs are not seen as being within the child, but are viewed as the result of child-environment interaction, covering a detailed classification of body functions and structures, activities, participation and environmental factors. For this reason, the ICF-CY can be helpful in the definition of the child's educational requirements when preparing IEPs (Castro, Pinto, & Simeonsson, 2014).

In 2011, the WHO published the World Report on Disability, according to which each nation should provide a data collection process for individuals with SEN, and this process needs to be standardised and internationally comparable for reference and monitoring progress on disability policy (WHO, 2011). It is suggested that standardised descriptions of disability should be delivered based on the ICF, which can enable international comparisons of data. After several international regulations and publishing reports about the ICF/ICF-CY by the WHO, Turkey has endorsed these international regulations for SEN provision. The first time that the ICF was seen in the legislation was in "Law No. 5378" in 2005. One year later, in 2006, a new legislation was published, titled "Regulations About Disability Criteria, Classification, and Health Report for Disabled Persons" (Official Gazette no 26230). The purpose behind the 2006 legislation was to use an international classification and criteria for domains of health, education and rehabilitation for individuals with SEN, with reference to the ICF. The second section of the legislation covers two items. The first states that categorisation of individuals with SEN in Turkey should derive from the ICF. The second item states that education, teaching, practice and dissemination activities, should be conducted by state-based organisations, civil organisations and universities, using the ICF to describe functioning of individuals with SENs, to collect, record and compare data from several disciplines and monitor services.

In addition to the 2006 legislation, a new regulation about disability criteria, classification and health reports for individuals with SEN, was published in 2013 (Official Gazette no 28603). The aim of the legislation was to implement an evaluation process for health reports. Moreover, the new legislation was published to provide dissemination for using the ICF and related criteria, to develop a common application in SEN provision (Official Legal Gazette of Turkey, 2013).

Although Turkey was one of the first countries, together with Italy and Switzerland, to endorse the ICF by law, there are several limitations with regard to its implementation. There are inconsistencies between the ICF regulations at policy level and its application in service provision. Despite the regulations aiming to introduce the ICF in the Turkish education, health, rehabilitation and other services, the same regulations adopt medical-based approaches for the identification of an individual with SEN and referral to services, which is incompatible with the ICF model. The same legislation includes the ICF as a theoretical novelty and the medical model of ICD-10, (The 10th Review of International Statistical Rating on Health Problems and Illness) for practical daily use (Official Legal Gazette of Turkey, 2006b, 2013). It seems that although these laws in Turkey have endorsed the ICF model, the medical model has been maintained as a way of identifying individual who need special education or other services. In fact, in order to refer these individuals for the appropriate services (e.g. special education, speech and language therapy, physiotherapy, occupational therapy, psychological counselling, etc.), not only body function and structure factors must be evaluated and described but also, and especially, activities and forms of participation, and contextual factors (such as technology, support level, relationships, attitudes). Based on a purely medical model, an individual who needs educational and other interventions sees the extent of his/her requirements described using a grade system. This medically based grade system is calculated as a result of several assessment procedures in the authorised hospitals in Turkey. Based on this medical model approach other necessary services may be identified, such as social and financial needs of individuals with SEN. However, the medical model creates inequality between individuals with SEN in relation to the services they benefit from. This is partially due to the fact that only medical doctors are regularly monitoring the child's needs. Other professionals should be included in the evaluation team, i.e. special education teacher, child-development specialist, social worker, psychological counselling, psychology, physiotherapist, who, together, can undertake a holistic assessment of the child. There is a clear need to integrate medical and educational evaluation and monitoring; the strengths of individuals with SEN should also be highlighted in addition to the health weaknesses, which are more aligned with the ICF model. Some projects related to ICF applications in SEN provision have been carried out in Turkey, in order to support the integration of the ICF model. The following section introduces two of these projects.

Good practice in the use of the ICF in Turkey

A recent project, ICF-Train, completed in 2015, was a Lifelong Learning Project funded by the EU and carried out by 6 European countries and 12 partners. Turkey was one of the countries and the official partner from Turkey was Anadolu University. The main groups within the project were specialists, professionals and clients in service provision and training in the ECI field. The target content of the project was the development of a combined web 2.0 online team assessment tool and real-time online training tool to use the ICF-CY. The tool encourages the use of the ICF-CY system by professionals and clients in ECI services. In the scope of this project, ICF-CY mainstream training courses for specialists working in ECI were developed and delivered. The project also aimed to improve the quality of professional communication based on information technology expert training. Parents were regarded as part of the teams of expert in early intervention services and had access to the web-based tool and its outcomes. Moreover, the ICF-Train enabled comparability of quality of services across users. The web tools included various information sections about the child with SEN and his/her parents, and an evaluation-intervention-monitoring process which was multidisciplinary. The tool provides a match between the observation resources of each child's strengths and barriers and the ICF-CY codes, resulting in a graphic representation of the child's functioning. An individual education plan is prepared based on this graphic representation and assessment. The project also facilitates self-development of the experts involved, as it includes an online library and e-learning platform. In addition, the tool stimulates communication and the sharing of knowledge regarding the condition of the child with special needs among the team members when they provide and embed new information into the ICF-CY training tool. The project results and tangible outcomes have facilitated the use of the ICF-CY for both research and practice in Turkey.

Another project titled "European Competence Initiative-Early Childhood Intervention" (ECI 2.0) was completed in 2013 and was also funded by the EU. It involved five European countries and nine partners. The project aimed to improve the skills of professionals working in early childhood intervention, by preparing specific materials which included ECI training modules, an open collection of training materials that can be shared among all professionals ("Resource Pool") and a self-assessment instrument for ECI professionals. Social networks and the use of a web-based pool of resources have the advantage to decrease the isolation of professionals, especially in remote ECI centres in Turkey. The online training assessment tool allows not only for monitoring of the staff training process on ECI, but it also enables comparability of staff knowledge over time. The ECI 2.0 project provided parent oriented materials ("modules") involving several tasks and skills to reach developmental milestones, which are linked to the ICF-CY domains for the ages of 0–36 months.

To prevent further impairments and facilitate activity level and participation, these materials could be applied to the children with SENs or who are in an at-risk group. The modules included five submodules based on developmental areas: self-care, social-emotional development, cognitive development, motor development and expressive and receptive language. All tasks and skills in the submodules are organised chronologically. Several purposeful activities and play can be found in each developmental area and they are all linked to ICF-CY codes, enabling monitoring of interventions following a biopsychosocial approach (covering body function and structure, activity and participation and environmental context).

Conclusion

Although the ICF-CY is accepted and is mentioned in the Turkish law, the educational evaluation of individuals with SEN still follows a medical model approach and the ICD-10 is still the gold standard classification. Therefore, there is a conflict in the Turkish policy between the willingness to use the ICF, and its practical implementation, which is limited by the very much present medical model. There are other reasons that should be pointed out that might explain the difficulty in implementing the ICF-CY in practice: the need for training on the ICF, the requirement for the measurement tools that are compatible with the ICF classification system and the need for guidance on how to transfer health information into ICF-CY based information, avoiding "labelling" and potential stigmatisation. Further research evidence is needed to determine attitudes, the training needs of service providers and the effectiveness of the ICF-based evaluation and intervention process for individuals with SEN in Turkey so that the effectiveness of its application into early intervention services can be appreciated in full.

Highlights from this chapter

- There have been a limited number of research projects and studies about ICF and ICF-CY in Turkey, even though the classification system has been introduced by law.
- Two European funded projects have provided some materials to help professionals and parents to achieve effective intervention using an ICF-based approach.
- More evidence is required regarding the effectiveness of the ICF-based approach, which should include an interdisciplinary team model, preparation of individualised education programs, monitoring and placement in the Turkish educational system and support services.

> • Providing training on ICF for professionals and developing new measurement tools to be linked to the ICF components will facilitate more intensive use in the education system in Turkey.

References

Castro, S., Pinto, A., & Simeonsson, R. J. (2014). Content analysis of Portuguese individualized education programmes for young children with autism using the ICF-CY framework. *European Early Childhood Education Research Journal, 22*(1), 91–104.

Eğitim Reformu Girişimi. (2014). *Türkiye Eğitim Sisteminde Eşitlik ve Akademik Başarı Araştırma Raporu ve Analizi [Research Report and Analysis for Equity and Academic Achievement in Turkish Education System].* İstanbul: Sabancı Üniversitesi.

Engelsiz Türkiye İçin: Yolun Neresindeyiz? Mevcut Durum ve Öneriler. (2013). *Sabancı Üniversitesi Yayınları.* İstanbul: İmak Ofset.

Hollenweger, J. (2011). Development of an ICF-based eligibility procedure for education in Switzerland. *BMC Public Health, 11*(Suppl 4), 1–8.

Hollenweger, J., & Moretti, M. (2012). Using the international classification of functioning, disability, and health children and youth version in education systems: A new approach to eligibility. *American Journal of Physical Medicine & Rehabilitation, 91*(13), S97–S102.

Kargın, T., Acarlar, F., & Sucuoğlu, B. (2005). Öğretmen, yönetici ve anne-babaların kaynaştırma uygulamalarına ilişkin görüşlerinin belirlenmesi. *Özel Eğitim Dergisi, 3*(2), 27–39.

Maini, M., Nocentini, U., Prevedini, A., Giardini, A., & Muscolo, E. (2008). An Italian experience in the ICF implementation in rehabilitation: Preliminary theoretical and practical considerations. *Disability and Rehabilitation, 30*(15), 1146–1152.

Maxwell, G., & Koutsogerogou, E. (2012). Using social capital to construct a conceptual international classification of functioning, disability, and health children and youth version-based framework for stronger inclusive education policies in Europe. *American Journal of Physical Medicine & Rehabilitation, 91*(13), S118–S123.

Moretti, M., Alves, I., & Maxwell, G. (2012). A systematic literature review of the situation of the international classification of functioning, disability, and health and the international classification of functioning, disability, and health-children and youth version in education. A useful tool or a flight of fancy? *American Journal of Physical Medicine & Rehabilitation, 91*(13), S103–S117.

Official Newspaper of the Turkey Law (Resmi Gazete). (1997). Law No. 573, Publishing No. 23011.

Official Newspaper of the Turkey Law (Resmi Gazete). (2005). Law No. 5378. Publishing No. 25868.

Official Newspaper of the Turkey Law (Resmi Gazete). (2006a). Publishing No. 26184.

Official Newspaper of the Turkey Law (Resmi Gazete). (2006b). Publishing No. 26230.

Official Newspaper of the Turkey Law (Resmi Gazete). (2012). Publishing No. 28360.

Official Newspaper of the Turkey Law (Resmi Gazete). (2013). Publishing No. 28603.

Official Newspaper of the Turkey Law (Resmi Gazete). (2014). Law No. 6518. Publishing No. 28918.

Pless, M., & Granlund, M. (2012). Implementation of the international classification of functioning, disability and health (ICF) and the ICF children and youth version (ICF-CY) within the context of augmentative and alternative communication. *Augmentative and Alternative Communication, 28*(1), 11–20.

Ta Chiu, W., Feng Yen, C., Wen Teng, S., Fang Liao, H., Hwa Chang, K., Chou Chi, W., Ho Wang, Y., Hon, & Liou, T. (2013). Implementing disability evaluation and welfare services based on the framework of the international classification of functioning, disability and health: Experiences in Taiwan. *BMC Health Services Research, 13*, 416–425.

Türkiye İstatistik Kurumu. (2009). *Türkiye Özürlüler Araştırması 2002* (2. Basım). Ankara: Devlet İstatistik Enstitüsü Matbası.

United Nations. (2006). *Final report of the Ad Hoc Committee on a comprehensive and integral international convention on the protection and promotion of the rights and dignity of persons with disabilities.*

World Health Organization. (2001). *International Classification of Functioning, Disability and Health* (ICF). Geneva: World Health Organization.

World Health Organization. (2007). *International Classification of Functioning, Disability and Health for Children and Youth (ICF-CY).* Geneva: World Health Organization.

World Health Organization. (2011). *World report on disability.* Malta: WHO Press.

Chapter 14

Human rights of children with disability

Exploring the role of the ICF-CY

Juan Bornman

Introduction

Human rights refer to those rights that are considered universal to humanity, regardless of ethnicity, gender, ability or any other consideration. They empower the most vulnerable members of society, such as children with disability, and create opportunities for them to thrive by providing them with voice and choice. Children with disability and their primary caregivers face significant threats to their human rights all over the world. Governing bodies such as the UN and the WHO have advocated for universal human rights through the CRC, the CRPD and the ICF-CY.

This chapter describes a large study that investigated the human rights of children with mild to moderate intellectual disabilities in South Africa, using the CRC and the ICF-CY as the guiding frameworks. The environmental factors defined in the ICF-CY (namely, the physical, social and attitudinal environments in which children live) were used to provide evidence for their right to protection, care and access – thereby making it a suitable framework for this study.

International human rights conventions

Two United Nation Conventions are particularly important when looking at the human rights of children with disability – namely, the Convention on the Rights of the Child (UN, 1989) and the more recent CRPD (UN, 2006) of which Article 7 in particular focuses on children. Both conventions are based on the principles of equality and non-discrimination, regarding what is best for the child and respecting the view and opinion of the child. The rights in these documents can be divided into three broad categories – namely, ***provision rights***, which refer to necessary services and goods, such as the right to access medical services, to be taken care of, to an education and to a safe home; ***protection rights***, such as the right to be protected from abuse and the right to safety; and ***participation rights***, which refer to the right to be respected and to be an active participant in family, school and community life by providing these children with some action, such as the right to be heard and the right to play (Alderson, 2000).

ICF framework

The ICF (WHO, 2001) has been praised for its vast utility, providing a common language that can be used across disciplinary boundaries (conceptualising and classifying disability within a holistic framework of human health and functioning, rather than on the basis of pathology) and describing the functioning of individuals with disability across settings and disciplines (Adolfsson, 2013; Simeonsson et al., 2014). The ICF and its extension for children and youth, the ICF-CY (WHO, 2007), marked a shift in attitudes and approaches concerning children with disability away from viewing them as objects of charity, health care and social protection, towards viewing them as individuals with rights. As such, the ICF-CY and the United Nation's human rights conventions pertaining to children with disability (i.e. the CRC and CRPD) complement one another. The ICF-CY describes children in the context of environmental and personal factors (which can act as barriers or facilitators), thereby providing a framework for documenting both the deprivation of rights and the conditions under which those rights can be realised (Simeonsson, 2006). In other words, the more an environment accommodates the needs of children, the fewer barriers to development and learning exist, thus resulting in a greater possibility of fulfilling the child's human rights. In doing so, the ICF-CY can provide evidence for the rights to protection, care and access (Simeonsson, 2009).

Link between needs and rights

More than 20 years ago, Woodhouse (1994) already stated that children's rights flow from their needs. Therefore, by listening to children's voices and experiences, evidence of their needs can be found. Maslow's Hierarchy of Needs (Maslow, 1970) was thus used to inform the CRC (van Bueren, 1998).

Listening to children's own voices regarding their human rights

While children with disability have the right to express their views, their voices are often not heard, even in developed countries that actively advocate for the rights of individuals with disability (Mitchell, 2014). Eliciting their views in research is also difficult, as research methodologies are often inappropriate for them (Jorgenson & Sullivan, 2009); significant research time is required when conducting research with children with disability (Connors & Stalker, 2007); many ethical issues such as assent and power relations have to be considered (Ajodhia-Andrews, 2016), and researchers should not only recognise that these children have a voice, but they should actively work towards eliciting this voice.

Despite these challenges, which are further confounded by the multifaceted and messy nature of research within childhood disability, the voices of children with disability should be prioritised.

Through capturing the unique personal experiences of children with disability, they are positioned as active contributors to research agendas that might have an impact on policy and legislation (Watson, 2012). They are thus not seen as objects of study but rather as active agents whose needs, priorities and aspirations are important. The fact that they are right bearers is highlighted by amplifying their voices and their differing needs and experiences in their respective environments. The approach followed in the six studies included in this chapter is thus firmly intertwined with the constructs of participation and rights.

Research evidence: a case of six studies

Main aim

The study aimed to investigate the human rights of South African children with mild to moderate intellectual disabilities between 8 and 14 years old from both a parental and child perspective. Due to progressive realisation and economic constraints in a low- and middle-income country such as South Africa, human rights may be unmet for some children, particularly those in high-risk environments and those with disability (Berry, 2007; Cherney, Greteman & Travers; Ward & Stewart, 2008).

This main aim was realised by means of six different sub-aims, published as separate studies, each with a different aim – namely,

i   to conduct a needs analysis through a systematic review of the needs of children with disabilities in low- and middle-income countries (2001–2011) (Lygnegård, Donohue, Bornman, Granlund, & Huus, 2013);

ii   to describe the perceptions of Afrikaans-speaking parents regarding the human rights of their children with mild to moderate intellectual disability according to ICF-CY environmental codes (Erasmus, Bornman, & Dada, 2015);

iii to examine how socio-economic and other risk factors are associated with positive human rights from the children's perspectives (Donohue, Bornman, & Granlund, 2014);

iv   to determine if caregiver age, caregiver education, household size and family income increased the odds of children with intellectual disabilities to also have a co-occurring motor delay and/or unintelligible speech (Donohue, Bornman, & Granlund, 2015);

v   to obtain a broader understanding of how children with intellectual disability rate their human rights (self-rated needs) compared with ratings made by their primary caregivers (proxy-rated needs) (Huus, Granlund, Bornman, & Lygnegård, 2015); and

vi   to explore and compare the awareness of primary caregivers from urban and rural areas of the human rights of their children with intellectual disabilities (Huus, Dada, Bornman, & Lygnegård, 2016).

Participants

A multiphase sampling procedure (province, school and children) was used. Per capita income was used to purposively select three of South Africa's nine provinces. Gauteng has the highest average annual income (approx. US $9,6681), while KwaZulu-Natal and Limpopo have the lowest (approx. US $4,767 and $4,259, respectively). Permission was obtained from the appropriate Provincial Departments of Education.

School districts with government-funded special schools for children with intellectual disability were identified using the National List of Special Schools (RSA, 2010) and resulted in singling out 13 districts in Gauteng, 12 districts in KwaZulu-Natal and five in Limpopo. The Gauteng districts were all urban, whilst the KwaZulu-Natal and Limpopo districts were rural. To maintain comparable ratios between districts in provinces, two districts in Gauteng, two in KwaZulu-Natal and one in Limpopo were randomly selected for inclusion. Seven of the potential nine school principals in Gauteng consented (two schools used English as the medium of instruction and five used Afrikaans), three of the potential five principals in KwaZulu-Natal consented (all used isiZulu) and one of the potential two principals in Limpopo (where Xitsonga was used) consented.

Teachers at the identified schools received a standard set of instructions to identify children between 8 and 14 years old with intellectual disability and no co-morbid sensory disability. Informed consent letters were sent home, with 234 children receiving consent, although two children themselves declined to participate. In order to ensure that the children could respond appropriately to the task, they were provided with three training items as well as three trial items (Donohue et al., 2014). If the children provided inappropriate answers to two of the three items, they were excluded. Twelve children failed the trial items, resulting in 220 participants.

The participants thus comprised 220 8- to 14-year-old children with mild to moderate intellectual disabilities, spread over four language groups: Afrikaans (n = 55), English (n = 51), isiZulu (n = 64) and Xitsonga (50). The 220 primary caregivers' relationship to these children comprised 59.9% mothers, 17.5% fathers and 22.6% others (e.g. grandmothers or siblings).

Materials

A custom-designed questionnaire with three sections was developed for the primary caregivers and used in all six studies. Section 1 focused on biographical factors such as caregiver age, education, household size and family income.

Section 2 was related to child factors and based on the Ten Question Questionnaire (TQQ), the most widely used standardised, rapid, low-cost screening measure that has shown high reliability in low- and middle-income countries across different languages where professional resources were extremely scarce (Lorencz & Boivin, 2013). The TQQ's ten items consist of five questions related to cognitive development, two related to motor development and one question each related to vision, hearing and seizures. Each item is a yes/no question – e.g. *Does the child have difficulty in walking or moving his/her arms or does he/she have weakness and/or stiffness in the arms or legs?*

Section 3 focused on the questions related to Article 23 of the CRC (i.e. children with disability should have a decent life, access to needed resources, health care, education and rehabilitation services) (UN, 1989). A four-point rating scale with two positive options (3 = Sometimes; 4 = Always) and two negative options (1 = Never; 2 = Seldom) was used – e.g. *Does your child have clean water to drink at home?* This questionnaire was designed in English and then translated into Afrikaans, isiZulu and Xitsonga, using a blind-back translation procedure (Bornman, Sevcik, Romski, & Pae, 2010).

All questions in Section 3 were also correlated with ICF environmental codes and included physical, social and attitudinal factors grouped into the five potential domains – namely, products and technology (e1), natural environment and human changes to the environment (e2), support and relationships (e3), attitudes (e4) and services, systems and policies (e5).

Two different expert panels of professionals with experience in the field were asked to comment on all items in the questionnaire. Revisions were made based on their suggestions (Erasmus, 2014). Two pilot studies were subsequently conducted to further refine the questionnaire and the methods for data collection. The first was with five typically developing children between 7 and 9 years old who attended a regular government-funded primary school in Gauteng. Results showed that the Likert scale options had to be repeated for the children with every item. A scripted routine was also suggested for data collection with the children in order to heighten procedural integrity. The second pilot study included ten children with intellectual disability between 9 and 13 years old, at a government-funded special school in Gauteng (similar to the ones included in the main study) but who had not been included in the main study. No further alterations were requested.

To decrease the potential confounding effects of receptive language (understanding) and expressive language (production) commonly associated with intellectual disabilities, children completed the questions of Section 2 and 3 of the questionnaire using the Talking Mats Visual Framework (Murphy & Boa, 2012). An A3 hard fibre mat with four images along the top representing the four-point response category based on the Likert scale discussed earlier was used. *Never* was depicted by a basket empty of apples, *Seldom* by a few apples, *Sometimes* by more apples and *Always* by a basket full of apples, as shown in Figure 14.1.

Figure 14.1 Example of a completed talking mat

Each questionnaire item was represented by a laminated card (10cm x 10cm) depicting a key word and an associated visual image. For example, the graphic Picture Communication Symbol (PCS) for "toys" depicted generic toys that children were familiar with, such as a ball, a car and a doll. In some cases – e.g. for "food" – the symbols were adapted to represent the staple foods that South African children would be familiar with. Each item on the questionnaire was read aloud and the matched PCS symbol was shown one by one to each participant, asking them to place the matching PCS symbol under the relevant response category on the mat. A series of three training items was developed to ensure that participants understood the instructions and were able to complete the required task. Thereafter they were presented with three trial items with an expected response – e.g. *How often do you play with live snakes?* With each item, children were asked to first consider it as a yes/no question and then, depending on their answer, to refine it as *Yes, always*; or *Yes, sometimes*; or *No, never*; or *No, seldom*.

Procedures

After ethics approval had been obtained from the relevant authorities, informed consent was requested from primary caregivers via the classroom teachers. Children for whom consent was obtained were individually brought to a quiet room at the school. The scripted routine was followed, commencing with obtaining assent from the children. Interviewers were all fluent in the language of instruction at the school and explained to the children that everything they said would be confidential, they could choose whether they wanted to participate and that they could stop at any point without any negative consequences.

It was stressed that there were no right or wrong answers. Each individual session lasted approximately 20 to 25 minutes.

Data analysis

Data was analysed with SPSS Version 2.0. First, reliability measures were computed, followed by descriptive statistics (means, standard deviations and frequencies). Next, inferential statistics were performed, depending on the specific focus of the study. A complete description of this aspect is beyond the scope of this chapter, but is included in the respective published studies.

Results discussion

A total of 11 papers were included in Study 1, the systematic review that focused on the needs of children with disability in poverty settings (Lygnegård et al., 2013). Only two studies focused on generic needs (the needs of all children), while all 11 studies focused on special needs (needs specific to children with disability – e.g. assistive devices, wheelchairs and hearing aids). This underscores the fact that this group of children is still seen as having "different" needs, thereby heightening their exclusion from broader society. Furthermore, three studies focused on their needs from the service provider's perspective, five from the primary caregiver's perspective, two from the perspective of both service provider and primary caregiver, while only one focused on the children themselves – albeit from the service provider's perspective. Most of the studies focused on lower-order needs (physiological needs) without addressing higher-order needs related to safety, love and belonging, self-esteem and self-actualisation. Results also showed that the rights of children with disability are threatened by intolerant attitudes in the broader society, increasing their risk of being shamed and bullied.

In Study 2, the focus fell on the perceptions of one of the subgroups of primary caregivers – namely, Afrikaans-speaking parents. These parents mostly felt that their children had rights (90.7%) and that their basic rights (water and food) were *always* met. While the majority of parents stated that their children *always* had toys to play with at home (91.84%), only slightly more than half (53.06%) reported that their child always had friends to play with at home. The specific rights mentioned by the parents were linked to environmental factors of the ICF-CY (part of Part 2 of the ICF-CY [contextual factors]), using the rules suggested by Cieza et al. (2005). This resulted in 916 ICF-CY linkages to 36 second-level codes (Erasmus et al., 2015). Four of the potential five environmental codes were represented, of which *attitudes* (e4) was mentioned most frequently (40%). In the ICF-CY, attitudes are about the attitudes that are the observable consequences of customs, practices, ideologies, values, norms and beliefs that influence individual behaviour and social life at all levels. The fact that attitude was mentioned most frequently in this study highlights the importance of addressing attitudes as part of human rights, as well as the fact that the ICF-CY is effective in capturing this aspect. Parents stated that they wanted their immediate families to show love, respect and acceptance of their child with intellectual disability. *Support and relationships* (e3) was mentioned in the second place (28% of the time) and refers to the people who provide practical, physical or emotional support and who nurture, protect and assist them, as well as relationships to other persons, in their homes, school, during play or in other aspects of daily life. Parents in the study stated that they found it difficult to ask family and friends to help in taking care of their child with disability. This was mostly related to the fact that their child needed special care and support. *Services, systems and policies* (e5) was mentioned in the third place (22%). In the ICF-CY, services may be general or specially designed, public or private, and provided at local, community, national or international level by individuals, associations, organisations or governments. Systems refer to the administrative control of these services, while policies are constituted by rules, regulations, convention and standards. The parents who took part in the study were of the opinion that their children with mild to moderate intellectual disabilities were entitled to services in schools and therefore any discrimination against them would be unacceptable. Parents wanted to be proactive and hence took the necessary steps to ensure that their children received appropriate services at school. Although *products and technology* (e1) was mentioned, this was only done 10% of the time. In the ICF-CY, products and technology are defined as any product, instrument or technology that is either adapted or specifically designed to improve the functioning of persons with disability. Thus, few mentions might possibly be ascribed to the fact that the children in this study had neither physical disabilities (in which case physical accessibility would have been important) nor primary sensory disabilities (in which case technology such as hearing aids would have been important). *Natural environments and human-made changes to the environment* (e2) (in other words animate and inanimate elements of the natural and or physical environment that have been modified by people) was not mentioned at all and this may possibly be due to the fact that the participants in the study did not have primary physical disabilities. The results showed that different rights can be grouped and linked to ICF-CY environmental codes, which contributed to parents' perceptions of the needs and rights of their children. Parents also consider some rights as more important than others. Thus, the results from Study 2 seem to support the findings of Simeonsson (2006) who suggested that the ICF-CY can document barriers in the child's environment.

Study 3 examined how risk factors were associated with positive human rights from the perspective of the children themselves. Results showed that child participants generally reported high degrees of access to basic resources (access to food, clean water and somebody to care for and protect them), with little variability in their responses (Donohue et al., 2014). They reported the lowest degree of access to things with which to play. The risk index (which comprised four socio-economic risk factors – namely, income, education, household size and relationship status) showed that for each point increase on the risk index, children were 1.64 times more likely to report low scores for access to food. This means that for every additional socio-economic risk experienced, children were one and a half times more likely to report that they do not always have food. Many South African families live in poverty and have reported that the only nutritious meals their children receive is at school (Dei, 2014). The same negative effect was also noted for having their own bed to sleep in. While co-sleeping is not unusual in some cultures (Owens, 2004), results from this study indicated that children in higher-risk conditions were significantly more likely to report that they did not have their own bed, suggesting a financial explanation rather than a cultural one. A positive effect of risk was found with relation to having somebody available to explain confusing concepts to them. For every point increase on the risk index, children were 1.44 times more likely to report that they had somebody available to them to help explain to them confusing things. This may possibly be related to the fact that some of these children were living in large households with several older adults at home to assist these children and/or to the fact that these children's caregivers may have been more likely to be unemployed, at home and more available to talk to the children. In conclusion, Study 3 suggested that provision rights (e.g. food and housing) of children in high-risk environments should be monitored in order to ensure that their basic needs are met.

Study 4 explored whether socio-economic risk factors were related to the presence of motor delays or unintelligible speech in this cohort of children (Donohue et al., 2015). A test of the full model with four predictors (namely, caregiver age, caregiver education, family income and household size) against a constant-only model was run. For motor delay it was not significant ($p = 0.33$) and not for intelligible speech ($p = 0.27$). However, household size was found to be negatively related to whether children had intelligible speech, where each increase in household size made it 1.25 times less likely that the child would have intelligible speech. This is in line with earlier research that found that families in crowded homes tend to speak less and use less complex language with children, resulting in smaller vocabularies and lower IQs (Evans, Maxwell, & Hart, 1999). Impoverished living conditions (such as overcrowding) are stressful and can hinder optimal parenting as well as expose children to more environmental toxins, thereby having a negative effect on these children's rights and creating environmental barriers.

Article 12 of the CRC states that children should have the right to form their own views and express them freely in accordance with their maturity and age (UN, 1989). Therefore the focus of Study 5 was to compare the own rating (self-rating) by children with intellectual disability of six human rights aspects to the responses of their primary caregivers (as proxy ratings). The six aspects that were compared were i) clean water to drink at home, ii) food to eat at home, iii) things to play with at home, iv) own bed to sleep in at home, v) someone to care for the child and protect the child at home and vi) friends to play with at home. Results showed that for more complex needs (i.e. higher needs on Maslow's hierarchy) and thus more complex rights (e.g. the right to having somebody to play with as mentioned in Article 31 of the CRC), inter-rater agreement between the children's self-rating with the proxy rating was lower. The results furthermore showed that for basic needs (such as water and food) the use of proxy ratings can indeed be used. They also showed that socio-economic variables affected whether the self-raters and proxy raters answered similarly – higher socio-economic status (in other words fewer risk factors) was related to higher agreement, irrespective of whether basic needs or higher-order needs were rated. The results from Study 5 (Huus et al., 2015) therefore highlighted the importance of promoting children's rights to express themselves by considering both the child's own voice (as self-raters) and that of their primary caregiver (as proxy raters).

Finally, in Study 6, the primary caregivers were divided into two cohorts – those living in urban and those living in rural areas. They were asked two questions: firstly, whether they thought their child with intellectual disability actually had rights and, if yes, to list and prioritise the rights they could think of (Huus et al., 2016). An expert panel linked the participant responses to the CRC articles by means of a deductive content analysis. Results showed that 85.8% of primary caregivers thought that their children had rights, with a statistically significant difference between the urban and rural primary caregivers ($p \leq 0.001$). More urban primary caregivers believed that their children had rights compared to their counterparts from the rural areas. Furthermore, primary caregivers from the urban areas could also list more rights (average of 3.3 rights) than caregivers from the rural context (average of 2.2 rights). In total, 22 rights mentioned in the CRC were addressed, and they were grouped according to protection, provision or participation rights. Provision rights were mentioned most frequently (377 times), followed by protection rights (172 times) and participation rights (only 17 times). In both urban and rural contexts, primary caregivers mentioned the right to education (a provision right) most frequently. Education of children with disability is a pertinent contemporary issue in South Africa as it was estimated that approximately 480 036 children with disability – almost half a million children – are currently out of school (Department of Education, 2014). Furthermore, there is no reliable system in place to track these children, but it appears as if poverty continues to be a driver of educational exclusion in South African schools. Although this study showed that primary caregivers from both rural and urban contexts were aware of their children's rights, those from the urban areas were more aware that different possibilities exist. Hence they are perhaps better equipped to provide opportunities for their children to exercise their rights than their counterparts from rural areas.

Conclusion

Despite international recognition of the importance of the human rights of children with disability – and the ratification of the CRC and CRPD by more than 85 countries – the reality is that many of these children, particularly those

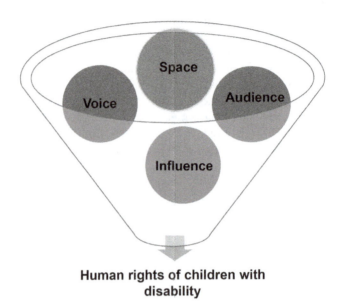

Human rights of children with disability

Figure 14.2 Four constructs required in addressing the human rights of children with disability

who require more support, are marginalised. The ICF-CY was used effectively to document a diverse collection of environmental factors such as poverty, the extent to which needs are met, as well as context (rural and urban). This chapter demonstrated the effect of environmental factors, as captured by the ICF-CY, on the human rights of children with disability through six related studies. By including the constructs of space, voice, audience and influence (Lundy, 2007), the human rights of children with disability may be a step closer to realisation – as shown in Figure 14.2. In this chapter *space* was included by providing children the opportunity to express their opinion (e.g. through the use of alternative methods such as Talking Mats), *voice* by providing them with the appropriate means to express themselves (e.g. through PCSs), *audience* (by engaging with the children in a one-on-one situation and listening to their opinions without judgement) and *influence* (by acting upon the children's opinions through information dissemination). It is hoped that future research will continue to unpack the relationship between human rights and the environment.

Acknowledgement

I am grateful to each of the authors who participated in the six different studies. I would also like to recognise the contribution of the staff members and postgraduate students from the Centre for Augmentative and Alternative

Communication at the University of Pretoria, particularly with data collection, and Mrs Liza Rossetti-Siefe, who provided technical support. This work was supported by the National Research Foundation in South Africa and the Swedish International Developmental Cooperation Agency Grant UID #70883.

Highlights from this chapter

- In low- and middle-income countries, lower-order needs were more frequently described, and there is a scarcity of studies on higher-order needs in which children's own voices are heard.
- When linking the rights mentioned by Afrikaans-speaking parents of children with intellectual disability to ICF-CY codes, attitudes (i.e. showing low acceptance of and respect for children with disability) were mentioned most frequently.
- For children with mild to moderate intellectual impairment, socio-economic risk factors were negatively related to some human rights (e.g. access to food) and positively related to others (e.g. having someone available to care for and protect the child).
- Children living in large households were less likely to have understandable speech.
- Primary caregivers (as proxy raters) and children with intellectual disability (as self-raters), provided similar answers in respect of lower-order needs (e.g. access to food and water), but larger differences were found in respect of higher-order needs (e.g. having friends to play with and access to toys). Socio-economic variables affected the degree of agreement between self-raters and proxy raters.
- Primary caregivers in both rural and urban areas were aware of the rights of their children with intellectual disability, although there were significant differences between them. For both groups though, education (a provision right) was mentioned most frequently.

References

Adolfsson, M. (2013). Applying the ICF-CY to identify children's everyday life situations: A step towards participation-focused code sets. *International Journal of Social Welfare, 22,* 195–206.

Ajodhia-Andrews, A. (2016). Reflexively conducting research with ethnically diverse children with disabilities. *The Qualitative Report, 21*(2), 252–287. Retrieved from http://nsu-works.nova.edu/tqr/vol21/iss2/6

Alderson, P. (2000). *Young children's rights: Exploring beliefs, principles and practices.* London: Jessica Kingsley.

Berry, L. (2007). Protecting South Africa's children: What differences will the new Children's Bill make? *Continuing Medical Education, 25*(4), 168–171.

Bornman, J., Sevcik, R. A., Romski, M. A., & Pae, H. K. (2010). Successfully translating language and culture when adapting assessment measures. *Journal of Policy and Practice in Intellectual Disabilities, 7*, 118–118. doi:10.1111/j.1741-1130.2010.00254.x

Cieza, A., Geyh, S., Chatterji, S., Konstamjsek, N., Üstün, B., & Stucki, G. (2005). ICF linking rules: An update based on lessons learned. *Journal of Rehabilitation Medicine, 37*(4), 212–218.

Connors, C., & Stalker, K. (2007). Children's experiences of disability: Pointers to a social model of childhood disability. *Disability & Society, 22*(1), 19–33.

Dei, F. A. (2014). *An evaluation of the school feeding programme: A case study of Magog primary school.* Unpublished master's thesis, University of South Africa, Pretoria, South Africa. Retrieved from http://uir.unisa.ac.za/bitstream/handle/10500/18779/dissertation_dei_fa.pdf?sequence=1

Department of Basic Education. (2014). Annual report 2013/2014. Retrieved from www.govza/sites/www.gov.za/files/DBE_Annual_Report_2013-14_a.pdf

Donohue, D. K., Bornman, J., & Granlund, M. (2014). Examining the rights of children with intellectual disability in South Africa: Children's perspectives. *Journal of Intellectual and Developmental Disability, 39*(1), 55–64. doi:10.3109/13668250.2013.857769

Donohue, D. K., Bornman, J., & Granlund, M. (2015). Household size is associated with unintelligible speech in children who have intellectual disabilities: A South African study. *Developmental Neurorehabilitation, 18*(6), 402–406. doi:10.3109/17518423.2014.890256

Erasmus, A. (2014). *An investigation into the realization of children's rights in South Africa: Perceptions of Afrikaans-speaking primary caregivers of children with intellectual disabilities.* Unpublished master's thesis, University of Pretoria, Pretoria, South Africa. Retrieved from www.repository.up.ac.za/handle/2263/25680

Erasmus, A., Bornman, J., & Dada, S. (2015). Afrikaans-speaking parents' perceptions of the rights of their children who have mild to moderate intellectual disabilities: A descriptive investigation. *Journal of Child Health Care, 20*(2), 234–242. doi:0.1177/1367493515569326

Evans, G. W., Maxwell, L., & Hart, B. (1999). Parental language and verbal responsiveness to children in crowded homes. *Developmental Psychology, 35*, 1020–1023.

Huus, K., Dada, S., Bornman, J., & Lygnegård, F. (2016). The awareness of primary caregivers in South Africa of the human rights of their children with intellectual disabilities. *CHILD: Care, Health and Development, 42*(6), 863–870.

Huus, K., Granlund, M., Bornman, J., & Lygnegård, F. (2015). Human rights of children with intellectual disabilities: Comparing self-ratings and proxy ratings. *CHILD: Care, Health and Development, 41*(6), 1010–1017. doi:10.1111/cch.12244

Jorgenson, J., & Sullivan, T. (2009). Accessing children's perspectives through participatory photo interviews. *Forum: Qualitative Sozialforschung/Forum: Qualitative Social Research, 11*(1), Art. 8. Retrieved from http://nbn-resolving.de/urn:nbn:de:0114-fqs100189.

Lorencz, E. E., & Boivin, M. J. (2013). Screening for neurodisability in low-resource settings using the ten questions questionnaire. In M. J. Boivin & B. G. Giordani (Eds.), *Neuropsychology of children in Africa: Perspectives on risk and resilience.* New York: Springer.

Lundy, L. (2007). 'Voice' is not enough: conceptualising Article 12 of the United Nations Convention on the Rights of the Child. *British Educational Research Journal, 33*(6), 927–942.

Lygnegård, F., Donohue, D. K., Bornman, J., Granlund, M., & Huus, K. (2013). A systematic review of generic and special needs of children with disabilities living in poverty settings in low- and middle-income countries. *Journal of Policy Practice, 12*, 296–315. doi:10.1080/15588742.2013.827141

Maslow, A. (1970). *Maslow's hierarchy of needs: Motivation and personality* (2nd ed.). New York: Harper & Row.

Mitchell, M. (2014). *Ever seen or heard? The voice of children in family law.* Australian Human Rights Commission. Retrieved from www.humanrights.gov.au/news/speeches/ever-seen-or-heard-voice-children-family-law-0

Murphy, J., & Boa, S. (2012). Using the WHO-ICF with talking mats as a goal-setting tool. *Augmentative and Alternative Communication, 28*(1), 52–60.

Owens, J. A. (2004). Sleep in children: Cross-cultural perspectives. *Sleep and Biological Rhythms, 2,* 165–173. doi:10.1111/j.1479-8425.2004.00147.x

Republic of South Africa (RSA). (2010). National list of special schools. Retrieved from www.thuthong.doe.gov.za/ResoirceDownload.aspx?id=40391

Simeonsson, R. J. (2006). *Classification of communication disabilities in children: Contribution of the International Classification of Functioning, Disability and Health.* Geneva, Switzerland: WHO.

Simeonsson, R. J. (2009). The ICF-CY: A universal tool for documentation of disability. *Journal of Policy and Practice in Intellectual Disabilities, 6*(2), 70–72.

Simeonsson, R. J., Lollar, D., Björck-Åkesson, E., Granlund, M., Brown, S. C., Zhuoying, Q., Gray, D., & Pan, Y. (2014). ICF and ICF-CY lessons learned: Pandora's box of personal factors. *Disability and Rehabilitation, 36*(25), 2187–2194. doi:10.3109/9638288.2014.892638

United Nations (UN). (1989). *United Nations Convention on the Rights of the Child (CRC).* Geneva, Switzerland: Author.

United Nations (UN). (2006). *United Nations Convention on the Rights of Persons with Disabilities (CRPD).* Geneva, Switzerland: Author. Retrieved from www.ohchr.org?EN/HRBodies

Van Bueren, G. (1998). *The international law on the rights of the child.* The Hague: Kluwer Law International.

Ward, T., & Stewart, C. J. (2008). Putting human rights into practice with people with an intellectual disability. *Journal of Developmental Physical Disabilities, 20*(3), 297–311.

Watson, N. (2012). Theorising the lives of disabled children: How can disability theory help? *Children & Society, 26,* 192–202.

Woodhouse, B. B. (1994). Out of children's needs, children's rights. The child's voice in defining the family. *Journal of Public Law, 8,* 321–341.

World Health Organization (WHO) (2001). *International Classification of Functioning, Disability and Health (ICF).* Geneva, Switzerland: Author.

World Health Organization (WHO) (2007). *International Classification of Functioning, Disability and Health for Children and Youth (ICF-CY).* Geneva, Switzerland: Author.

A compendium of worldwide applications of the ICF

Susana Castro and Olympia Palikara

Since 2007, with the publication of the International Classification of Functioning, Disability and Health for Children and Youth (ICF-CY), a considerable amount of research has been developed on applications of this new classification system. Ultimately, research on ICF-CY applications has aimed to improve the lives of children, young people and their families, as well as to facilitate the work of the professionals dealing with childhood intervention, education and care. However, this widespread research has not been lacking in controversy. Mentioned as a tool for research, as a tool for supporting education and childhood interventions and as a tool to improve communication between professionals of different backgrounds and/or countries and/or disciplines, the ICF-CY has received considerable criticism alongside substantial praise for its new perspective on disability and development. Regardless of the amount of praise and controversy it has received, there is something we can agree upon: the publication of the ICF-CY has made educators, academics, researchers and rehabilitation professionals question our own approaches to children's education and care; once one gets familiarised with the ICF-CY model and system, one has necessarily to question how much we see each child as a unique whole – a biopsychosocial being.

The present book is the very illustration of that controversy versus praise alongside the change in perspective about disability and development that the ICF-CY model triggered in policy and practice in various countries. The book combines in one international compendium, examples of good practice in using the ICF/ICF-CY and examples of criticisms, highlighting areas for further development. For instance, we commend the ICF-CY applications at policy level in Taiwan, Portugal and Japan, in ECI programmes in Portugal, Sweden and Turkey, in the study of children's human rights in South Africa, in understanding cancer trajectories and habilitation processes in Sweden and in general education and care as mentioned by our American contributors, but we also praise the mention to areas of concern that have been hindering successful applications of the ICF-CY. For example, the indispensable need for extensive training on its usage, which has been highlighted by our contributors from Portugal, Switzerland, Turkey and Sweden, as well the general criticism that perhaps the ICF-CY model is still very much detached from the education field, as suggested by our contributor from Switzerland, country in which adaptations to the model were made for a more coherent application in the education system. In England, we hope that potential future applications of the model benefit from the research evidence that has been built up in this country (as presented in Chapter 3) but also from lessons learned at the international level. We hope that this book may trigger the debate around the usefulness of the ICF/ICF-CY in the current context of special education needs provision in England, which has not happened so far, at least not at the policy level.

At the international level we hope that this first collection of applications of the ICF-CY in various contexts of education and care is followed by future compilations of research evidence addressing the criticisms to the ICF that were pointed out at this stage.

Recently, the WHO has issued a communication that the two versions of the classification (adult and children and youth version) should merge forming one single ICF manual. This decision has, itself, been source of lively debate on whether this will continue to work on the best interest of children. In this book, our contributors used the ICF or the ICF-CY term depending on the version that was used in their studies and depending on what they believe is the best classification system for young people. Our conclusion does not provide a straightforward answer to this debate, but we are pleased to be able to combine all different views into one single publication and highlight research evidence supporting a multidimensional approach for thinking about development and disability, the one that is operationalised by both the ICF and the ICF-CY. Despite the recognition that ICF is the official acronym in use, we believe that the contributions in this book (using both ICF and ICF-CY) enrich the body of evidence that has surrounded the historical evolution of the classification.

We conclude with the expectation that this publication feeds on to the debate about ways of using the ICF model and classification, keeping the best interest of all children and young people at the heart of all research, professional and individual initiatives.

Index

Made in the USA
Monee, IL
27 May 2022

97088344R00142